# IMPERIAL GINA

THE STRICTLY
UNAUTHORIZED BIOGRAPHY
OF GINA LOLLOBRIGIDA
By

# Luis Canales

BRANDEN PUBLISHING COMPANY, Inc.
Brookline Village, Boston

**Library of Congress Cataloging in Publication Data**
Canales, Luis, 1943-
    Imperial Gina : the strictly unauthorized biography of
    Gina Lollobrigida / by Luis Canales. -- 1st ed.
        p. cm.
    Includes bibliographical references.
    ISBN 0-8283-1932-4 Casebound
    ISBN 0-8283-2150-7 Paperback

    1. Lollobrigida, Gina, 1928-    . 2. Motion picture actors and
    actresses--Italy--Biography.  3. Photographers--Italy--Biography.
    I. Title.
    PN2688.L6C37  1990
    791.43'028'092--dc20
    [B]                                                          90-32867
                                                                  CIP

BRANDEN

**BRANDEN PUBLISHING COMPANY**
17 Station Street
Box 843 Brookline Village
Boston,  MA USA

For my mother Santa Canales

and my aunt Cachita Canales

who also were actresses

## ALSO BY LUIS CANALES

*Japan: Bewitching and Alienating*

*Contos Tristes*

*Mishima by Canales*

# PICTURE CREDITS
# ILLUSTRATION CREDITS

Reproduction of most photographs appearing in this work was made possible through the permission of the following individuals and corporations:

Columbia Pictures; Metro-Goldwyn-Mayer Inc. and Arcola Corporation; Cantery Productions, Inc. and Lowe's Incorporated; Universal Pictures: Turner Entertainment co.; Ames Adamson (Orion Press, New York); *Manchete*; Leo Fuchs/Orion Press; Sipa/Orion Press; Perlugi/Orion Press; Angeli/Orion Press; Sipa Press; Orion Press (Tokyo); Ron Galella, Ltd.; *Paris-Match*; *Ciné-Revue*; *Time*; *Mainichi Shimbun*; Nobuyoshi Yamada (Foreign Correspondents Club of Japan); Films Ariane; SCOOP - Service De Diffusion D'Articles; Arnoldo Mondadori Editore, Studio Patellani and *Il Messaggero*.

While every effort has been made to contact the copyright holders of all the illustrations, the author was unable to receive replies and/or locate them all. Where possible, the author will, in future editions of the book, acknowledge those who have not been mentioned.

# CONTENTS

# ACKNOWLEDGMENTS

Research material on an international film actress like Gina Lollobrigida requires a true scavenger hunt, and I am very thankful to all those who assisted me from different corners of the world. Likewise, I wish to express my thanks to those who shared their time with me discussing the Italian actress.

Signora Evelina Luzzi, director of the Istituto Italiano Di Cultura (Kyoto), was most helpful providing me with Gina Lollobrigida's filmography and her address in Rome. I also extend my thanks to Dr. Giorgio De Marchis (Istituto Italiano Di Cultura, Tokyo) for supplying me with additional information concerning signora Lollobrigida's career.

The author also wishes to say "grazie" to Anna Lenzuni (Biblioteca Centrale, Florence) for providing me with a microfilm containing a 1971 significant piece on the actress. Signor Dino Satriani (*Oggi*) and the Editors of *Epoca* assisted me concerning former issues of the respective magazines featuring articles on Gina Lollobrigida.

Still on the Italian front, Dr. Paolo Mecci (Mayor of Subiaco, Gina's hometown) gave me much help by sending me important clippings related to Gina and her people. "Grazie" also goes to signorina Maria Rosaria Zaccaria of the Biblioteca Comunale in Subiaco and signor Emilio Ciolli (school teacher) for doing their best to contribute to my research during my visit there. Signor Ricci Gregorio, a friend of the actress' father, was most kind narrating episodes of the Lollobrigidas during Gina's childhood.

My chief helpers in Subiaco were former Mayor Giuseppe Cicolini and signora Rosa Antonucci (director of the Scuola Elementare Statale). Signor Cicolini's explanations about the Lollobrigidas during World War II and subsequent stories related to the actress were most appreciated. Gina's childhood friend, signora Antonucci, kindly shared reminiscences of her lasting friendship with the Italian star. "Grazie" also to the unknown ladies of Subiaco who eagerly chatted with me about Gina Lollobrigida. To the actress' gardener and to her secretary, who had much patience with me at the gate of Gina's Roman villa: I express my thanks.

Signor Francesco Lepri and signor Antonio Capri of *Il Messaggero* (Rome) assisted me considerably going through archives to produce material for my project. My Italian friends Marina Maiocco (Sauze d'Oulx) and Walter Baccon (Milan) deserve a special note of thanks for constantly mailing me clippings on signora Lollobrigida's present day activities in Italy.

In France, my "merci beaucoup" goes to avant-garde novelist Hervé Guibert, Jackie Fixot and Colette Guerineau (*Paris-Match*), Christian Batifoulier (*Le Monde*), Janine Rualt (Films Ariane), Ute Mundt (*Vogue*) and the celebrated movie director Christian-Jaque.

Still in European territory, "merci beaucoup" to Gérard Neves (*Ciné-Revue*, Brussels) and "muchas gracias" to Juán Antonio P. Millán and M.D. Devessa (Filmoteca Española, Madrid) for assisting me with material on Lollobrigida's films made in spain. To my dear friend, Fernanda Manso (Lisbon), "muito obrigado" for preparing the way for my visit to the Cinemateca de Lisboa where I also found gems of information for my research.

Peter Todd (British film Institute) supplied me with indispensable literature on Gina's film career; Martin Humphries (The Cinema Museum, London) and ron Rönnqvist (Helsinki), also contributed to the project.

In the United States I am very thankful to: Val Almendarez, Jeffrey S. Mintz and Kristine Krueger of the National Film Information Service (Margaret Herrick Library - Academy of Motion Picture Arts and Sciences), Audrey Weinstein (*Star Magazine*), Mary J. Frere (Time-Life Books, Inc.), Iain W. Calder (*National Enquirer*), Jerry Ohlinger's Movie Material Store Inc. (New York), and Bruce York (Memory Shop West, San Francisco). I am also thankful to Eleanor R. Panossian (New York), who joined me in the hunt for a publisher.

To Dário M. de Castro Alves (Brazilian Mission to the Organization of American States, Washington D.C.) and the late John Huston my sincere thanks. Former Brazilian Ambassador to Italy, Portugal and several other counties, my friend Dário offered me much support throughout the writing of this book; a few weeks before he passed away, John Huston was most generous sending me an autographed copy of his autobiography *An Open Book* to help me clarify doubts I had concerning his controversial film *Beat the Devil* which Gina did for him in 1953.

My next debt is to publishers who granted me permission to quote passages from their works: The Curtis Publishing Company (*The Saturday Evening Post*), *Saga of a Siren*, Aug. 13, 1960; Doubleday & Company, Inc., *Errol Flynn - The Untold Story* by Charles Higham; St. Martin's Press Incorporated, *Hollywood's Most Enduring Star: Burt*

# 9--Imperial Gina

*Lancaster* by Robert Windeler; W.H. Allen Publishers, *Sean Connery - His Life and Films* by Michael Feeny Callan; William Morrow & Company, Inc., *Sophia: Living and Loving* by A. E. Hotchner, and *The Secret Lives of Tyrone Power* by Arce Hector; Martin Secker & Warburg Limited, *French Cinema* by Roy Armes; Citadel Press, Inc. *The Films of Anthony Quinn* by Alvin H. Marrill, and Princeton University Press, *Italian Film In The Light of Neorealism* by Millicent Marcus. I am most debted to actress Janet Leigh, who signed - and granted permission to quote from her autobiography *There Really Was a Hollywood* Doubleday & Company.

South of the border, I was assisted by Marta Godeas (Buenos Aires) and my cousin Claudia Mazza, who raided old bookstores in São Paulo hunting for magazines of the Fifties and Sixties featuring Gina Lollobrigida. In Rio I am most thankful to senhor Roberto Muggiati for providing me with *Manchete* photo covers displaying the actress and for numerous Gina photographs printed in the referred magazine during the 1967 Rio Carnival.

I bow my head and say "arigato" to Orion Press President, Jintaro Takano and Junichi Nakamura (Manager) in Tokyo for their assistance; Orion Press' stock of Lollobrigida photographs and related materials was of immense help.

In Japan I also wish to say "arigato" to Shigeo Shimada (*The Japan Times*), the *Mainich Shimbun* and the *Yomiuri Shimbun* for furnishing me with literature concerning Gina Lollobrigida's two visits to Japan. I am also obliged to Sumiko Nakagawa, Masaaki Tokuchi and Goro Nishimura, who were most helpful in the search of Lollobrigida films released on video. I was also assisted in various ways by Masao Johma, Hirofumi Shibadaira, Shinichi Mine, Chiaki Takeuchi, Masahiko Okazaki, Fusae Kishida and the librarians Hitomi Takemoto and Junji Sumie (Kyoto University of Foreign Studies). Kiyoko Watanabe was a chief collaborator in Kyoto locating references to Gina Lollobrigida in the Spanish weeklies *Semana* and *Hola!* Also, thanks to Miss Watanabe's close assistance I learned how to operate a Japanese Word Processor, on which I recorded the final copy of the manuscript.

During the five years that I worked with this book I was also supported by international friends and colleagues residing in Japan. British poet and writer James Kirkup deserves a special thanks for his collaboration through the actual writing of the manuscript. The poet and colleague was most generous writing to friends of friends - from

Kyoto to New York, from Paris to London - who actually presented relevant information on Gina. Vincent T. Buck (Shiomi & Yamamoto Law Office) was most considerate in reading the complete manuscript to certify that nothing in it invited a lawsuit from signora Lollobrigida. *The Japan Times'* columnist and friend Stephanie L. Cook dedicated almost as much care to the manuscript as I did. Her extensive revisions of my writing to clarify the language are highly appreciated; without Miss cook's cooperation my work would have been twice as hard.

Freelance writer and English teacher, Bernard Farrell (Kobe). Italian Professor Giorgio Amitrano and Portuguese Professor Marco Guerra (Osaka University of foreign Studies), Ivo Meenen (German Consulate, Kobe), Professor and Publisher John Terry (Kyoto University of Foreign Studies and Dawn Press), Portuguese Professor Jorge Dias, and French Associate Professor Jacque Pernot (Kyoto University of foreign Studies), British freelance photographer Frank Leather (Kyoto), Graham Lower (Ashiya), Araceli Corral (Kyoto) and Monsieur Divyam (Kyoto) in one way or another also contributed to my work and they deserve a word of thanks.

The author is deeply grateful to Branden Publishing Company, Inc., and its president, Adolpho Caso, for making this book a reality. I am also very thankful to my mother for her support and for her having taken me to see my first Lollobrigida film back in the Fifties.

To actress Gina Lollobrigida, for her brilliant careers, and for the thrill she has brought into my life, "grazie mille".

**Miss Italy Contest at Stresa (1947)**

From left to right: Lucia Bosè (1st place--unfortunately her figure is cut in the photo), unidentified contestant, Gianna Maria Canale (2nd place), Gina Lollobrigida (3rd place), Bianca Reina, Leonessa Landini, Liliana Sansoni, Titti Torre, Eleonora Rossi Drago. Photo Patellani.

As Nedda in Mario Costa's *I pagliacci* (1948).
Author's collection

# INTRODUCTION

Show business has always fascinated me. In my youth I used to devour movie magazines and I never let a weekend go by without seeing a picture in one of the many São Paulo cinemas; Westerns, musicals, Italian comedies, historical films, I loved them all. The dream of my life then was to visit Hollywood. In my naivete I thought that as I strolled along the main boulevards in the Land of Make Believe I'd spot movie stars from left to right.

In early 1965 at the age of 21, the dream became reality but, alas, the only stars I saw in Tinseltown were those embedded in the sidewalk of Hollywood Boulevard, each containing the name of a celebrity. The Grauman's Chinese Theater displayed movie idols' foot and hand prints engraved in its entrance sidewalk, but not a shadow of a star walked by me. I did, nevertheless, see some of their gorgeous houses (only from the outside, of course) in Beverly Hills. I particularly remember a pink one that resembled a small castle; I was told it belonged to Jayne Mansfield. Some two or three years later while I was attending Brigham Young University in Provo, I got a janitorial job and found myself one day cleaning an actor's bungalow in Provo Canyon where Robert Redford's "Sundance" now stands; according to the crew who worked with me the bungalow we cleaned was Redford's.

My favorite idols fell into two groups: Americans and Europeans. Names such as Marilyn Monroe, Janet Leigh, Kim Novak, Carroll Baker, Anthony Perkins, Kirk Douglas, and Elvis Presley, among others, belonged to my constellation of American luminaries while Brigitte Bardot, Sophia Loren, Sarita Montiel, Marcello Mastroianni, Alberto Sordi and Louis Jourdan made the European cast. (With the passing of years I gradually lost interest in Marilyn, Elvis and Brigitte.) Gina Lollobrigida rose above both groups for I always thought of her as the queen of the international cinema.

By the spring of 1984, 19 years after my Hollywood experience, I had finished reading biographies of about 50 movie stars: Tyrone Power, Errol Flynn, Lauren Bacall, Joan Crawford, Simone Signoret,

Sophia Loren, Frances Farmer, Elizabeth Taylor and Katharine Hepburn - just to name a few - when I realized that a biography of Gina Lollobrigida had not yet been written. I knew that there was an Italian publication about Gina and her films, but not a biography per se. "Why don't I write it?" The thought popped into my mind as I sat in my Kyoto apartment one night reading Susan Hayward's story.

Would I be capable of capturing on paper the life of this woman of so many talents who had made movies in Europe and the United States and then had proceeded to travel around the globe as a professional photographer? Most of all, how would Gina feel if she knew that a Brazilian in Japan was writing about her life? Knowing that Gina has always been a very private person, I hated to think of myself as an intruder. Could I write about her life, or part of it, without acting like a Hedda Hopper or a Louella Parsons?

Even as I wrestled with my own personal doubts, I knew nothing could keep me from writing the book; the opportunity was too precious to lose. I began my research in the spring of 1984 when I finished reading the last pages of Susan Hayward's biography. The first source of information was my memory. It wasn't difficult to go back in time and list the Gina films I had seen in the Fifties and Sixties. I was amazed at how much I had retained about her pictures: titles, co-stars, plots, etc. A brief visit to the Italian Cultural Institute (Kyoto) provided me with her complete filmography plus the star's address in Rome.

My next step was to write to Gina informing her of my desire to record her life story and ask for her cooperation. Because I am an unknown freelance writer I didn't expect an immediate reply. On top of that, since I couldn't compete with experienced authors who have written for years on show business, I expected to be discredited by the actress. Nevertheless, my admiration for her convinced me that I was the person for the job.

Once I had exhausted the major Tokyo, Kyoto, and Osaka bookstores hunting for foreign cinema literature that might possibly contain information on Gina, my next stop was the main office of Orion Press (Tokyo). There I pored over a large variety of European magazines and Lollobrigida photographs.

Taking into consideration that I live in Japan - not the best place for this kind of work - I was very satisfied with the results of my domestic search. Even though Lollobrigida is famous in this country,

# 15--Imperial Gina

movie references to her in a Western language aren't easily available, so I was delighted to have found as much as I did.

In April of 1985, exactly a year after I had started working on the project, I struck gold with the Academy of Motion Picture Arts and Sciences. I was offered a large file on the actress for $300. I bought it on the spot. When the thick folder arrived from Beverly Hills I savored it during the hours when I wasn't lecturing on campus. The material covered Gina's career from the early Fifties to the mid-Eighties.

My first year of research hadn't been a disappointing one. Throughout those twelve months I had secured constant support from friends in different parts of the world who were hunting for information on Lollobrigida and mailing their findings to me in Japan. Still, even though I had been successful with my "Lollobrigidienne" studies, I had not yet heard from the actress; a year had elapsed since I had written my first (followed by several subsequent) letters to her.

One day, I received a letter from New York with a return address unknown to me. Something in my heart told me it was from someone related to the star or from Gina herself, since I knew that she was in Manhattan at the time. My curiosity was overwhelming but at the same time I hesitated to open the envelope. Still, good news or bad, I had to read the letter, so I opened it. "We are the attorneys for Ms. Lollobrigida," announced the senders in the very first line. The letter went on to state that Gina wasn't interested in a biography and opposed my writing it. I was disheartened.

Twenty-four hours later, after I had pulled myself together, I realized that Lollobrigida's reaction was natural. Hadn't I read in Peter O'Toole's biography and in several others how reluctant the stars were to agree to an interview with an author who had committed years of research to write a book entirely on them?

Finally, I concluded that against my will I was forced to write an unauthorized biography leaning more towards her careers: a combination of biography and tribute.

Once, Academy Awards winner Ingrid Bergman asked the Italian actress when she was going to write her own story before someone else wrote it with damaging misinformation. I guess I must be that "someone," but I have no intention of showering readers with inaccuracies.

In the summer of 1985 I left for Europe to expand my research on Lollobrigida. The pilgrimage took me to Paris, Madrid, Lisbon, Rome, and Gina's hometown, Subiaco. (My bank account couldn't offer me more than that.)

Subiaco was the highlight of my trip for I longed to see the town where Gina was born and lived until the Lollobrigidas moved to Rome in 1945. The visit was very successful, for I had the opportunity and the privilege of visiting the town's former Mayor, signor Giuseppe Cicolini, and signora Rosina Antonucci, Gina's childhood friend. Both of these people kindly shared with me their thoughts about Gina. Walking through medieval Subiaco and talking to old folks who have known the star since she was born was my most memorable experience in that part of Italy.

Rome. One hot August morning as my Lollobrigida research was approaching its end in that part of the world, I left my hotel near Stazione Termini and took a bus as far as the Colosseum. There I transferred to another that took me to the ancient road where the Caesars trod, Via Appia Antica. My destination: number 223, the villa of Gina Lollobrigida.

The ride was a new experience and I felt stimulated to be in an area with an absorbing historical past. There was so much to see and to learn from the ancient ruins, the sentinels of time. At a certain point, after passing the Catacombs, the driver indicated that from there on the bus would take another route and that I had to get off and walk to number 223.

As I continued along the seemingly endless road that runs all the way to Naples, I felt the perspiration saturating my suit. I saw tree after tree and scattered ruins, but no number 223.

"Luis, you're out of your mind. Who in the world do you think you are to march up and ring the bell at Gina Lollobrigida's villa? Are you being realistic?" Well, realistic or not, I was there and I wouldn't turn around. After all, I wasn't just another fan pleading for an autograph; I had come with a real purpose. I knew Gina had dined with V.I.P.s and that most of her acquaintances and friends were international movie directors, stars, sovereigns and presidents, and that it would be practically impossible for me to see her without proper connections. Nevertheless, there still remained one key fact that I considered very important. Gina is a human being and she probably wouldn't turn me away if she were at home. I recalled reading somewhere in an article that the actress "had a gold heart in a tigress' body." But despite my Quixotic spirit I have to confess that I was apprehensive as I searched for that number.

# 17--Imperial Gina

"Scusi signore, but would you happen to know where number 223 is?" I asked a gentleman in a car parked under a tree.

"Oh,sí," he replied politely, indicating a desire to help. "It's almost at the end of the next block before you arrive at a small fountain. You'll see a green gate at your left. That's number 223. Buona fortuna."

More trees. More ruins. The burning sun. Then I saw the small fountain ahead of me and the green gate on the left. A sign on the large portal read: "Attenti al cani" (beware of dogs). I didn't have to ring the bell for the gate was open and an old gentleman, the gardener, I believe, was sweeping the path. I approached and addressed him in what I thought was Italian, but what was closer to a hodgepodge of Spanish and Portuguese with a few Italian words.

"Scusi signore, I've come from Japan exclusively to see signora Lollobrigida, I'm writing a book about her and I'd like very much to talk with her if it's possible. Is she at home now?"

"La signora Lollobrigida left about 9:30 this morning." (It was around 11 a.m. when I arrived there.)

"Do you know when she'll be back?"

"No signore. La signora Lollobrigida may come back late or not even be here for a few days. She might have left on a trip, who knows?"

Since I'm stubborn I stated again the purpose of my visit and once more asked if she was perhaps after all at home. The gardener gave me his word she wasn't.

"I can't return to Japan without seeing signora Lollobrigida," I insisted. (Still a tiny part of me felt relieved; at least I'd have a good excuse to say that I hadn't met the actress because she had left before my arrival.)

Then I asked the patient man if I could just walk into the garden to take a quick look or a photo of the grounds.

"No signore. I can't let you do that."

I didn't want him to think of me as one of the paparazzi, so I changed the topic.

"I wish I could make an appointment to see signora Lollobrigida. I telephoned her from Kyoto a couple of times and nobody answered. (Probably the number had been changed.) It's important that I see her before returning to Japan."

"Sí, signore. I understand your situation but unfortunately there's nothing that I can do for you. Come back tomorrow. Who knows - she may be here."

I thought of the long bus ride, the lengthy walk and the hot sun. I'd be glad to do it all over again a hundred times if I only knew she'd be there. Anyway, I told the gardener that I'd come again the following morning, and turned to leave. He advised me of an easier and faster route via the subway connecting with a bus that would leave me just a block from the villa. The news heartened me and I handed him my visiting card with a copy of a *The Japan Times* article I had written about Gina, asking him to pass them on to her. Then he indicated he had to close the gate.

"Grazie signore, grazie. Arrivederci."

I stood there by the gate trying to decide what to do next. I wasn't sure whether I should stay there waiting for Gina or go back to my hotel. I was determined to see signora Lollobrigida and my final judgment was that it wouldn't hurt to wait for a while just in case she returned.

I tried to look over the gate but it was taller than I. Jumping up with my neck craned didn't help either. The trees and the shrubs that surround the whole villa blocked any attempt at a peeck. I paced back and forth and took some photographs of the gate, the road, and a few ruins. Meanwhile a tourist bus parked a few meters from where I was standing. I wonder what the casual vacationers thought of me wearing a three-piece blue suit with the "Ricoh" dangling from my neck on a hot summer day. The bus drove off and I was left alone again to meditate. Finally I decided I'd better leave.

The next day, with or without the help of the Roman deities, I stood there again facing the tall green gate. However, I was just as uncertain as I had been 24 hours before. The gate was locked. I rang the bell near the intercom and a polite female voice - the secretary, I suppose - answered. I repeated my self-introduction.

"I'm sorry," she responded, "la signora Lollobrigida hasn't returned. She isn't in Rome."

"Would you happen to know when she'll be back?"

"That I don't know. I'm very sorry," she answered.

I bombarded her with questions, insisting on the purpose of my visit. But she already knew all about it and I was getting nowhere with the conversation. Both the gardener and the secretary had been

# 19--Imperial Gina

paragons of patience and I really didn't want them to have the wrong image of me.

I thanked her and left. However, after I had walked for a few yards I thought that I shouldn't give up so easily. After all, I had flown thousands of miles to see Gina Lollobrigida and since I was right there facing her villa I should be a little bit more persuasive.

With that thought in mind my stubbornness forced me to ring the bell again. The lady didn't refuse to answer my questions, although the give-and-take sounded like a recording of our previous conversation. However this time, I added that if she could make an appointment for me with signora Lollobrigida, I'd postpone my return to Japan.

"That's not possible," she told me. "I don't know when she'll return to Rome and I can't schedule a visit for you without talking with her first."

I saw no use in continuing to push her. I thanked the lady, apologized for being so persistent and said "arrivederci."

I sat on a rock under a tree. "Some Roman centurion or peasant probably sat here to relax on a hot summer day like this centuries ago," I thought. An hour later I was still there hoping that Gina would return. I looked at some ruins across the road from the villa and reflected on my quixotic Roman adventure. Would I ever meet my Dulcinea?

Gina in *Bread, Love and Jealousy* 1954, *Fast and Sexy* 1958, *The Wayward Wife* (1953). Photos by Frank Leather (author's collection).

As Leila in René Clair's *Beauties of the Night* (1952)
Author's collection

Gina on cover of *Time*, 1954 By Boris Chaliapin.   Courtesy of *Time* (Magazine cover photographed by Frank Leather).

*Beautiful But Dangerous* (1955). The Lollobrigida film that bewitched me. In the photo la Cavalieri (Gina) duels with her rival Manoita (Tamara Lees). Behind the two ladies is actor Marco Tulli as the judge of the duel. Twentieth Century-Fox (Author's collection).

# Chapter 1

## Infatuation of a Fifteen-Year-Old Boy

I remember the first time I saw Gina Lollobrigida; the place, a theater in São Paolo either in 1957 or 1958; the movie, *La donna più bella del mondo* (Beautiful But Dangerous, 1955), released in Brazil as *The World's Most Beautiful Woman*, a precise translation of the original Italian.

When I left the theater I couldn't get Lollobrigida out of my mind. She was incredibly beautiful. She was "simpatica" and exuded life as she victoriously faced her rival, Manolita (Tamara Lees), in a fencing duel at the Bois de Boulogne.

Some time later I saw her again in a revival of *Pane , amore e fantasia* (Bread, Love and Dreams, 1953), one of her several successful films of the Fifties, co-starring the celebrated Vittorio De Sica.

The effect of my second encounter with Gina was again sheer magic. Captivating and natural as the unforgettable Bersagliera, a poor but volcanic peasant girl, Gina was quite a contrast in *Beautiful But Dangerous* playing the role of the opera singer Lina Cavalieri who had enjoyed enormous success in Paris at the turn of the century. The result of seeing these two Lollobrigida performances was a lasting dedication to "the world's most popular actress."

Thinking back, I realize that it wasn't just Gina's beauty that bewitched me; it was her power to communicate with the audience. Gina is aware of this. Once when Hedda Hopper asked the actress why her popularity was far larger than her compatriot movie stars', she answered "the public can love a person without thinking of the talent. It is something like sympathy, a fluid that comes through the screen to the people."

It was exactly that "sympathy" along with her beauty and that "peculiar fluid" that made me adore her. I was so enchanted with Gina that I had to see more of her for she had become my favorite actress and goddess.

It was a platonic love and I adored her on the screen, which by then had become something of an altar. My devotion to her at that period of my adolescence could have very well turned into a screen-play, the story of the infatuation of a 15-year-old boy for a remarkably beautiful woman. Ironic as it may appear, later in her brilliant career Gina played the part of an older woman in *Un bellissimo novembre* (That Splendid November, 1968) where a youth of 17 is in love with his gorgeous aunt.

In my fantasy world I thought of Gina in real life as I had seen her on the screen. I believe this happens with most teen-agers who fall in love with their idols - from movie stars to soccer and baseball players. Naturally, as I grew older, I understood that the parts she portrayed on the celluloid were separate from her personality in daily life. Nevertheless, her role in *Bread, Love and Dreams* does reveal much of the real Gina: "impulsive, enthusiastic, stubborn," a fighter and a woman of flawless beauty.

"The fluid that comes through the screen to the people" had penetrated my veins and flowed into my heart; whenever I left a movie theater after seeing another of her films, I felt I had interacted with her personally. But to see Gina on the screen wasn't enough. I had to have her in sight continuously, night and day. So I began to use her photographs as bookmarks and I covered my textbooks with pictures of her that I found in Brazilian and foreign publications.

Once, I remember, a Brazilian magazine carried a full size Gina Lollobrigida pin-up wearing a pink dress tight from the waist up and with an almost full-length skirt. She was wearing short hair. Very carefully, not to damage the picture, I took off the staples from the center of the magazine, removed the double central page with the large Gina pin-up and had it framed.

Until I turned 20 my brother and I shared a bedroom, so it was impossible to have all the walls to myself. Since we have always been opposites in everything, while I had Gina for my goddess he idolized

# 25--Imperial Gina

soccer players; the wall next to his bed was plastered with photos of his favorite soccer stars, quite a contrast with the soft Gina pictures over on my wall.

In 1955 Gina starred in a film that increased my love for her: *Trapeze*. For a boy born and raised under the big top, as I had been, circus films had always been a delight for me, and for all the Canales clan as well. *Trapeze* was a very special treat, for it brought me happy memories of my childhood and offered me the opportunity to see Gina acting in an environment familiar and dear to me. As a child I had lived among fire-eaters, clowns, aerialists, trained dogs and international acrobats. A trapeze for me was a very familiar object, but a flying one carrying Gina was an image that I could never forget.

When Joan Crawford was at her apogee as a box-office attraction, her admirers ran to see her films and couldn't have cared less how the gossip columns praised or criticized her pictures. It was a Joan Crawford film and that was all that counted; the public had paid to see her. Such was my attitude towards a Lollobrigida picture. Regardless of whether the reviews were favorable or ill-disposed, I appeared at the theater to see my favorite star.

When *Go Naked in the World* (1960) was released in São Paolo, I was probably 17. The first day the film was shown, I found myself at the theater half an hour before the first session. Because it was a weekday the audience was sparse, and I felt as though Gina was performing for me alone.

Sometime in 1984 while reading Carroll Baker's autobiography (*Baby Doll*) I came across a paragraph describing the star's immeasurable infatuation with Elizabeth Taylor while both worked on *Giant*(1956). Miss Baker "loved," "adored," and "worshipped" la Taylor, considering her the "pinnacle of what being a star meant." She wanted to be close to her idol on and off the set to admire her violet eyes. She was so infatuated that she gave the cold shoulder to co-star James Dean to devote all her time to the actress. Thus, while Carroll Baker adored Liz Taylor in front and behind the camera, I had to content myself with worshipping Gina on screen.

My devotion to the Italian actress had been steady since my initiation in the late Fifties. Gina did 28 pictures during that decade, and I wish I had seen them all. Unfortunately, I was still a child when she did her earlier films and I wasn't aware then of the existence of the movie star who would whisk a world of fantasy into my life.

Nor could I have anticipated that the infatuated youth would turn, as years went by, into a lasting admirer of Gina's many talents.

Three decades have passed since the 15-year-old boy saw Gina Lollobrigida for the first time. I can't say that he has left me completely, or I wouldn't have written this book. Dedicating from the mid to late Eighties to produce this biography of the actress was a marvelous and rewarding experience that brought back loving memories of times when life for me consisted of "movies, schoolwork and Lollobrigida." Has anything really changed?

At the Cannes Film Festival in 1961 (*Paris-Match* Gragnon - author's collection).

# 27--Imperial Gina

The green gate of Gina's vilage on the Appia Antica. I was here twice hoping to meet the actress (photo by the author).

Via Appia Antica (Rome); the ancient road where the Caesars trod (photo by the author).

Palazzo Romano on Via Papa Braschi II (Subiaco), the building where Gina was born in 1927.

The bed in which Gina was born. (Photo by former Mayor Giuseppe Cicolini's son, 1986).

Gina's hometown, Subiaco. I took this photo during my visit there in the summer of 1985.

# Chapter 2

## The Beginning

It was in the uplands of the Apennines in central Italy that the tale of the Sabine women took place approximately in the year 290 A.D. The subjects of Romulus, founder of Rome, kidnapped the wives and daughters of the Sabines and when the defeated husbands were about to attack the enemy, the brave women, holding their offspring in their arms, intervened between the conquerors and the defeated. From the violent union of these two ancient tribes, as the story goes, emerged the people of Rome.

Three hundred years after the episode known as *The Rape of the Sabines* the young Italian monk Benedict of Norcia chose the Sabine village of Subiaco as his retreat at the end of the 5th century A.D. He shut himself away in a cave in Mount Taleo and, after many years spent in prayer, founded his first monastery not far from Nero's villa. By 1872 Subiaco had become the center of the Order of the Benedictines.

Taking the provincial road from Subiaco one reaches The Holy Cave of St. Benedict (Monastery of St. Benedict) and Santa Scolastica, the larger of Subiaco's monasteries, two of the most treasured tourist attractions of the historical town. The composition of Santa Scolastica is exceptionally interesting for its Romanesque campanile which dates back to the 11th century, the Gothic, Cosmatesque and Renaissance cloisters, and the beautiful neo-classical church by the Italian architect Giacomo Guarenghi.

Subiaco (population 9,000) is located 50 miles east of Rome in the midst of beautiful hills and valleys. I marvelled at medieval Subiaco with its alleyways, Roman arches, and splendid views that suddenly emerged as I turned unfamiliar corners in its winding ancient streets. Before my trip I hadn't been aware of the importance of Subiaco in Roman history. It was the birthplace of Lucrezia Borgia, boasted Italy's first printing press in 1464, and saw a period of much prosperity in the epoch of the Great Roman Empire. Nero had a magnificent villa built there with several artificial lakes. Unfortunately, everything was completely destroyed when the dam across the river broke.

It was a cloudy morning when I left Rome for Subiaco. Three roads connect the town with the Roman capital but the difference in mileage is minimal. The bus took the shortest route through Via Tiburtina-Valeria, passing by Tivoli, famous for its Roman gardens, the temples of Vesta and Sibila, and the villas of the poets Horace, Catulle and Mècenè. I was travelling through historical places to visit the hometown of a modern Roman goddess.

The Lollobrigidas were not rich, but they weren't poor either. Signor Giovanni Mercuri Lollobrigida owned a small furniture factory employing some fifteen workmen and also rented out a few houses. Signora Giuseppina Mercuri Lollobrigida was a housewife. Their income was enough to decently support four daughters: Giuliana, Luigia (Gina), Maria and Fernanda. Luigia didn't know that she had been born on a very important date for Americans, the fourth of July. (Most movie references to the actress have 1927 for her birth date. A few entries quote 1928, and one or two 1929. Gina turned sixty in 1987, therefore 1927 is the correct date.)

"This one will be heard of," said the midwife when the healthy Luigia was born. At seven months she was strong and vivacious with black hair and large, exquisite dark eyes. Who would have guessed then that the baby Luigia would grow up to be what Italians would one day call "Gina nazionale" (national Gina), "the pride of Italy." The French would affectionately dub her Lollo and at the pinnacle of her career, she'd be recognized as the world's most beautiful woman. For the Italian public Gina came to represent the personification of feminine beauty.

Ginetta, as her friends and classmates used to call her, grew up as an active and intelligent girl revealing special talent in art. In her childhood she preferred to spend hours alone sketching rather than playing with her dolls. Papà Lollobrigida, noticing his daughter's natural aptitude for drawing, later hired a tutor from Rome to teach little Ginetta to paint. After the Lollobrigidas moved to the capital in 1945, Ginetta enrolled at the Academy of Fine Arts where she received a scholarship; painting, sculpting and singing kept her busy.

Talking with her long standing friend Rosina was one of Ginetta's favorite pastimes until the Lollobrigidas left Subiaco. The two girls played together and shared their thoughts about the future. Once Ginetta told Rosina that her dream was to play *Madame Butterfly* and Mimi of *Bohème*. She cherished a desire to become a soprano lirico until movies came to take her away, even though she wasn't interested in making films as a career. Ginetta loved to go to the movies, but that was the extent of her interest.

On her seventh birthday, she sang in a local recital and afterwards went to the town's theater to see a Clark Gable movie. It was then, claims a columnist, that the girl decided to become a movie star. The source is misleading. Gina has consistently maintained throughout the years that her first love was singing.

Ginetta's debut on the stage was in 1935 playing the role of a sailor with an amateur theatrical group at age seven or eight. In that same year, she also played a glowworm in a school pageant. It was during this representation that Ginetta had her first crush - on a nine-year-old elf! Mother Lollobrigida wasn't worried; she wisely knew that puppy love wouldn't hurt her daughter. Years later, however, she chased away a businessman from Bologna who was flirting with her Ginetta. She was determined that the girl should marry a doctor. Signora Lollobrigida's dream came true when on January 14, 1949, Gina married the Yugoslavian physician Doctor Milko Skofic.

As a child (against her father's approval) Ginetta liked to visit Subiaco's theater. When doing so, she had to hide under a chair or behind a curtain during the intermission because papà would some- times make spot checks on her. When found, she was scolded and sent home immediately. But the danger of being caught didn't prevent the spirited child from sneaking off to the movies. The Lollobrigidas had very strait-laced convictions of what was proper for their daugh- ters. Thus, the girls were forbidden to go to the cinema, but if there was a Shirley Temple movie in town, Ginetta would go without fear of incurring her father's anger.

At age 12, Ginetta showed more interest in movies, mainly kissing scenes. After each show she'd see the projectionist and talk him into snipping off for her the footage of some love scenes she had enjoyed seeing. It was difficult to resist the request of the captivating girl, and the picture was ruined to make her happy. She particularly relished Gary Cooper's love scenes and she had a collection of them. Ginetta must have been one of those very charming girls who always get what they want, for the projectionist would not only damage the picture to please her but also splice all of the love scenes together into a moving romantic collage. Ginetta would invite her girlfriends and together enjoy a delicious session of cinematic kisses.

Ginetta's destiny for a love affair with the screen would one day become a reality she didn't expect. Meanwhile, she dedicated herself to drawing and singing. Endowed with a very beautiful voice, the girl used to sing in the church choir, much to the delight of her parents and the priest, Don Mario, who was more than pleased to listen to her voice. As far as father Lollobrigida was concerned, he didn't mind the girl singing as long as it was in a church activity.

One memorable event related to Ginetta's voice took place during the war when Don Mario, searching for something to cheer up the townspeople, convinced the Italian baritone Tito Gobbi to perform in Subiaco's main square. As the show progressed, the guest singer expressed his desire to sing a duet with one of the young ladies in the audience. Don Mario immediately thought of Ginetta, who refused the invitation. After some persuasion, the girl gave in and together they sang an aria from Puccini's *Tosca*. It was a triumph for Ginetta and the priest congratulated her on the public debut as a singer.

Eleven years later Gina, then an international actress, repeated her success singing *Vissi d'Arte*, an aria from *Tosca*, in *The World's Most Beautiful Woman*, one of the actress' box-office attractions of the Fifties.

While zigzagging around the twisted roads of Subiaco talking at random with old folks who knew Ginetta (who doesn't know her there?), my image of Gina as a child was reconfirmed by my first interviewee, signor Ricci Gregorio, owner of a small clothing store near Piazza San Andrea where a Cathedral of the same name stands. The gentleman informed me that Ginetta was a happy, clever and very lively girl who was, on occasion, mischievous; she was a child of strong character who knew what she wanted. I asked signor Ricci if Lollobrigida's role in *Bread, Love, and Dreams* reminded him of Ginetta. He laughed.

"Exactly. That film was made for her because the part she played had much of herself." In the picture, Maria (Gina), nicknamed

# 33--Imperial Gina

Bersagliera, is the village spitfire. She's so named after Italy's well-known corps of assault troops, distinguished for their double time marching and for the flamboyant feathers in their hats. A snapshot of Ginetta riding a donkey at the age of 13 provided subtle foreshadowing of her carefree Bersagliera role.

Not too far from signor Ricci's shop stands the old Palazzo Romano on Via Papa Braschi II where Ginetta was born and where the Lollobrigidas lived until they moved to a more spacious house in Valle Principe Umberto. The palazzo survived the bombing and stands firm as a monument to the Lollobrigidas.

As I left the building I walked into a street that came out of nowhere; there I asked two old ladies if they knew the Lollobrigidas. Despite their desire to help, they didn't know much about the family but they did remember Ginetta as one of the most beautiful daughters of Subiaco. "Era bella, molto bella" (she was beautiful, very beautiful), remarked the ladies, adding that Ginetta resembled her mother.

Ginetta possessed the magic formula: beauty and a mind of her own. As a matter of fact, individuality and a fighting spirit were cornerstones of the Lollobrigidas' character. One of Ginetta's uncles was a doctor who believed he was also a great poet. If the story is accurate, he wrote prescriptions in rhyme, and not being pleased with Dante's *Divine Comedy*, rewrote it and declared his final version superior to the original.

Ginetta's father once carried on an anti-profanity campaign and went angrily around Rome tacking up posters on the well-known graffiti-covered landmarks.

One day Ginetta saw her future endangered when she returned home to find her house occupied by three German soldiers. Religious and historical Subiaco had become in the autumn of 1943 the home of fascists. "Our houses had practically been invaded by the Germans," declared a Subiaco citizen. With German soldiers occupying their homes and Allied bombs being dropped in the spring of 1944, the Lollobrigidas decided to leave town. Their house in Valley Principe Umberto (now Valley della Repubblica) as well as the family furniture shop were destroyed and the family sought refuge in the north.

\*\*\*

In that fateful spring of 1944, the family fled northward towards Florence (as Ginetta suggested to her parents) since they had friends there. They took whatever they could and slept in the open air while bombs fell around them as they walked along with retreating Germans. They ate what they could get from trees or abandoned homes. The family never made it to Florence, and on the eleventh night of their journey they stayed in a house partly occupied by German soldiers who left the next day. The family, however, wasn't aware that the house was mined and if it weren't for an American unit that arrived hours later, they would have been killed. Ginetta was discovered hiding somewhere in the house by one of General Mark Clark's GIs.

The Lollobrigidas' adventure continued. They arrived in Todi (Umbria), an ancient Etruscan city famous for its ruins from the Middle Ages and the Renaissance. A year after their arrival there, signor Lollobrigida decided to move with the family to Rome where they settled in a residence in Via Taranto. The first few months were hard on them, as work was difficult to find and the family had to do all sorts of odd jobs to survive. Gina's sisters Giuliana and Maria were employed as usherettes in a cinema, work that probably didn't leave their parents overjoyed, but a job was a job and money wasn't easy to come by. Ginetta, who had previously sung for Italian troops stationed in Subiaco, now strolled among US Army men offering to sketch the GIs. Spirited by nature and an incessant fighter, the girl wasn't easily overcome by the hardships and, together with the family, made the best of the unsatisfactory situation. Nevertheless, like thousands of other Italians who were suffering the consequences of the war, the Lollobrigidas dealt at times in black-market cigarettes, US Army blankets and "C" rations, and ate at the local charity kitchen.

Sometime in 1946 the family situation improved, and the Lollobrigidas moved their belongings into an apartment in Via Montebello. With some of the money Ginetta had saved from sketching, she soon had enough to pay for singing lessons at the Liceo Artistico where she won a scholarship, easing the financial strain.

One worry, however, gave way to another, as Ginetta's Sabine beauty caused one of her instructors to fall so desperately in love with her that the institute was forced to transfer the poor fellow. The episode gave a new meaning to the phrase déja vu; in the following six months Ginetta had no alternative but to change her teacher six times for the same reason.

The easy way out had never been part of Ginetta's philosophy of achieving success in life, and she lived by that rule when she became the queen of the international cinema. With a beautiful countenance and gorgeous curves, she could have had the world at her feet faster and easier if she had so desired. But no. She wouldn't have success handed to her on a silver platter by a singing instructor, or a husband eager to become her producer. It was probably because of the hardships that Ginetta experienced during the war and her parents' example that Gina developed the strong character of a woman who believes that success follows hard work.

Women like Gina born under the sign of Cancer are extremely persistent and dedicated to their work up to the point of employing super-human means to achieve their goal. Endowed with creative talent and incredible imagination, Cancer women often make extraordinary progress in their careers.

Astrology is a subject that I know very little about; nevertheless I have always found it amusing and I believe in it to some extent. Since I live in the East, I often enjoy reading about the Japanese [fortune] calendar which was borrowed from China. The Chinese zodiac is based on a cycle of twelve years with an animal assigned to each year. The Chinese believe that people born in the year of the tiger, for example, will have the same characteristics enjoyed by that animal.

Virtuous, reserved, financially lucky, talented and ambitious are those born in the year of the rabbit, which fell in 1927 when Luigia Lollobrigida was born. Furthermore, Gina considers herself to be "tenacious, stubborn, enthusiastic and impulsive," and life for her can be summed up in her own three words: "work, love, and fantasy."

Work. She strove tirelessly to get where she wanted, molding her career practically alone. She fought to her teeth to make producers and directors understand that she wasn't just a beautiful body beneath an empty head; she was an actress. Well-known for constantly suing those who tried to tarnish her reputation, Luigia Lollobrigida became actress Gina Lollobrigida with a scandal-free career.

Love. Faithfully married to handsome Doctor Milko Skofic, she played the role of a good wife as long as their love lasted, never ceasing to adore Milko Jr., her son. She devoted constant care to the well-being of her parents, sisters, and most close friends, while working on her films with unceasing dedication as a true professional.

Fantasy: What other career could offer someone more make-believe than that of show business? To live on the celluloid a life which isn't your own, to receive the applause and admiration of the public at film festivals and to be loved by millions of unknown faces is indeed a world of fantasy. Furthermore, Gina is also an accomplished singer, a skilled painter and sculptress, an enthusiastic archaeologist, a brilliant TV actress and a professional photographer. The actress' second career, photography, has provided her with the proper setting for a colorful life capturing exotic places and V.I.P.s around the globe with her cameras.

***

Postwar Italy was facing difficult times. Yet it was in the midst of a nation in chaos that Silvana Mangano, Lucia Bosè, Gianna Maria Canale, Silvana Pampanini, Gina Lollobrigida and Sophia Loren were discovered.

In 1943 Italy was a hungry, desperate and defeated nation. This grief stricken tableau was clearly depicted in films that made people burst into tears because of the extreme realism that was portrayed; these pictures, a faithful mirror of a dramatic period, were successful the world over.

Rosselini's *Roma città aperta* (Open City) was probably the first of its genre; also, it was the beginning of the criticized and sensational long love affair between the Italian director and Ingrid Bergman. The impact the film caused on the Swedish star awakened in her the desire to work at least once for the acclaimed Rossellini; but that "once" brought much pain to many lives.

When the Germans left Italy in 1944 Italian film makers organized themselves in order to protect the industry. The new movement gave birth to the neorealist period acclaiming Rossellini as its father and champion.

Another veteran of those days, actor-director Vittorio De Sica, transmitted the human reality of an Italy in tatters in works such as *Sciuscià* (Shoeshine Boys, 1946) and *Ladri di biciclette* (Bicycle Thieves, 1948), films of sentimentalism and compassion.

The first neorealist films were produced between 1944 and 1945. The plots: simple and melodramatic. Actors were non-professionals in order to give a particular touch to the functional dialogue. It wasn't unusual for neorealist producers and directors to choose a passerby for important roles. Improvisation was also a common practice. Such working policy left Ingrid Bergman completely astonished when she left Hollywood for Rome to film Rossellini's *Stromboli* (1949).

These neorealist pioneers wished to destroy the complacent image of the Italian cinema as it existed during the time of Mussolini; a total reaction against the glowing fantasies of the fascist Italian movie industry. It was neorealism that made the fame of actors Massimo Giroti, Aldo Fabrizi, Ralf Vallone, Vittorio De Sica, Amedeo Nazzari, Alberto Sordi and actresses Lucia Bosè, Elena Varzi, Silvana Mangano, Giulietta Masina, Gina Lollobrigida, Sophia Loren and others.

A very, if not the most, controversial director of this era was Pietro Germi, who explored a new aspect of Italian life. His most well-known films were *Gioventú perduta* (Lost Youth, 1946) and *In nome della legge* (In the Name of the Law, 1948). It was the former that accorded Germi international fame as a director. Germi's *La città si difende* (1951), starring Gina Lollobrigida, received awards in Venice and Rome; he also achieved enormous success with *Divorzio all'italiana* (Divorce Italian Style, 1961). Another outstanding director of the mid-Forties was Luigi Zampa with whom Gina worked at the end of the decade and into the Fifties.

Towards the end of the Forties, the Italian cinema opened its doors to a new movement called pink neorealism. As the title indicates, this rose-colored era wasn't totally pessimistic. The films continued to feature all the regalia of neorealism, e.g. the poor youth unable to enjoy the same comfortable life as his rich neighbor, the good in heart, the rundown apartments and general obstacles of daily life. Still, rosy-realism was less serious, and life presented a light of hope. It was during this movement that Gina became a famous star; she gave the best of herself as an actress to this new direction of the Italian cinema and in return, saw her name gain recognition all over the world.

As the gypsy Adeline in Christian-Jaque's *Fanfan la Tulipe* 1951
(© Films Ariane)

# Chapter 3

## From Soprano Lirico to Movie Star

There were no paparazzi for Luigia Lollobrigida on Via Veneto where she strolled with a friend on that April day in 1946. To Luigia's surprise, a gentleman approached her asking if she'd like to appear in the movies. Suspicious of his intentions, she told him in an unfriendly manner that she wasn't interested. The caballero, however, insisted that she could earn two thousand lire a day; seeing that he couldn't persuade her, he gave the young lady his address and went on his way. Afterwards, Luigia found out that the man was Stefano Canzio, a very respected movie director; she had lost an excellent opportunity to make some easy money that could very well have been used to pay for her singing lessons.

Not too long after the Via Veneto experience, Luigia was at a party organized by the Latium Sporting Association when one of her colleagues from the Liceo introduced Luigia to her cousin, a young movie producer. She promptly told him of her lost golden opportunity, which he countered with an offer of his own. "Would you like to be in the movies?" he asked her, adding that he knew of a director who was looking for extras and that if she was really interested she should mention his name to the director. She wasted no time. The next day Luigia met with Riccardo Freda who immediately cast her as an extra for *Aquila nera* (Return of the Black Eagle, 1946) starring Rossano Brazzi. The shooting of her scenes with Yvonne Sanson (a budding starlet who would later appear in major roles) lasted for four days and she was paid one thousand lire per day.

The Lollobrigidas didn't demonstrate much enthusiasm at the thought of their daughter becoming a movie actress, and Luigia herself continued to yearn for an identity as a soprano lirico. Nevertheless, as she accepted an increasing number of small parts, her life began to follow another route.

The account of how Gina Lollobrigida was discovered and how she came to know Riccardo Freda is recorded in Franca Faldini's and Fofi Goffredo's *L'avventurosa storia del cinema italiano* (The Adventurous History of the Italian Cinema) but the source fails to mention Stefano Canzio. As recorded in *Time* magazine (August 16, 1954) Lollobrigida was discovered by director Mario Costa in 1947. The version which I believe is complete appeared in Maurizio Ponzi's *The Films of Gina Lollobrigida.* According to the author, Gina's first venture with the cinema came from her encounter with Stefano Canzio in 1946, after which she was again stopped in the street with a proposal by director Mario Costa, which yielded a very small part in Costa's *L'Elisir d'amore* (This Wine of Love, 1947).

Between Gina's first appearance on the screen and Costa's film, she worked as an extra in four other pictures. The order of events remains somewhat of a puzzle. In Gina's account of how she began in the movies, as quoted in *L'avventurosa storia del cinema italiano*, during the four days in which she worked on *Aquila Nera* she met Mario Costa, who assigned her to a small part in a film in which future star Silvana Mangano also appeared as an extra. Somewhere in interviews and articles about Lollobrigida the information was apparently unintentionally misinterpreted.

Piero Ballerini's *Lucia di Lammermoor* (1946), a musical based on Gaetano Donizetti's opera, introduced Gina again as an extra. However, picture making was still for Gina a means of making money. She didn't take seriously the minor parts which boosted her financial situation since she was also the provider for the family. Her mother, probably for financial reasons, had urged Gina to quit her voice lessons. The extra parts saved her. Nineteen forty-six wasn't Gina's golden year but it was her best since the arrival of the Lollobrigidas in Rome.

A treasure chest of memorable surprises lay ahead for Gina in the future; nevertheless, it was only towards the end of the Forties that the thought of becoming a movie star entered her mind. Until then, she never ceased to assume that she'd soon return with more dedication to singing. Meanwhile, Gina's pursuit of painting and sculpturing at the Academy rounded out her experience in the Fine Arts.

As far as continuing in the movies was concerned, mamma Lollobrigida didn't like to think that her Ginetta could be one day the sexual fantasy of millions of men. Of her daughter's films she most preferred *The World's Most Beautiful Woman*, a picture that made as much money as Fellini's *La dolce vita* (1961). On the other hand, Gina's father stated that she should star only in films like *The Song of Bernadette*.

\*\*\*

While still an art student and an extra in films, Gina met a handsome Yugoslavian physician, Dr. Milko Skofic, at a New Year's Eve Party (1946) given by mutual friends. At that time Dr. Skofic, having fled Yugoslavia during the war, was the senior medical officer at the International Refugee Organization (IRO) camp which had been set up in the Cinecittà Studios on the outskirts of Rome.

Born in Austria, little Milko had moved with his parents to Yugoslavia when he was one year old. Years later, after the Skofics had established themselves in Rome, young Milko continued the medical studies that he had begun in Zagreb.

When Gina and Milko met it was love at first sight. According to American columnist Lloyd Shearer, the actress recorded her meeting with the doctor in her diary with these words: "January 1, 1947. New Year - new boyfriend. Last night I met Milko, a doctor. He is good looking and 26. My infatuation with Bob is now only a sad memory. Milko never left me even for a moment. He understands me. He likes me. He is the husband type. I hope we will get engaged real soon. I am sick and tired of single life."

Dr. Skofic found Gina extremely beautiful with her dark hair flowing down her back, a detail he never forgot because his mother thought Gina's hair was too long. But she didn't deny the girl's beauty. The physician recalled in an interview that Gina was so lovely that it was just impossible not to fall in love with her.

On their first date following the New Year's Eve party, Gina brought a friend along with her, Silvana Mangano; Dr. Skofic also came with a friend, a Yugoslavian soccer player. When the time came to take the girls home Milko was afraid his friend would leave him with the other girl. He had no reason to worry, for nothing would have changed the final result, as Gina had decisively further written in her diary that she was going to marry the handsome doctor, and when Gina had set her mind on something, the probability of making her change was infinitesimal.

The Skofics were married on January 14, 1949 and a few years after their marriage Milko gave up his career to become her business manager. In Shearer's article, *The Star and the Shadow* (from an unidentified 1955 British paper clipping), the "shadow" is an allusion to Gina's husband who, in his new position, watched over his wife's well-being and success around the clock. Gina declared then that "Milko is more than my husband. He is my physician. He is my favorite reporter. He is my tennis coach, my business manager. Above all, he is the guardian of my happiness."

Back in 1947, Gina was still adorning the screen as an extra. *Il Segreto di Don Giovanni* (When Love Calls) marked the debut of Silvana Pampanini, a potential competitor of Lollobrigida in those days. A former Miss Italy, la Pampanini was lucky enough to have her first film distributed by one of the seven most prestigious American studios, 20th Century-Fox.

The film has been erroneously registered as Mario Costa's in both *L'Annuario del cinema italiano* and *Catalogo Bolaffi del cinema*. This production, in which la Lollobrigida, la Bosè and la Mangano appeared as extras, was directed by Camillo Mastrocinque. Reflecting on her colleagues, la Pampanini once proudly stated that she had never worked with Gina Lollobrigida "On the contrary, she worked with me." (Sophia Loren and Eleonora Rossi Drago also appeared as extras in another Pampanini film.)

A new extra part came for Gina in Alberto Lattuada's *Il delitto di Giovanni Episcopo* (Flesh Will Surrender, 1947) starring Aldo Fabrizi and Yvonne Sanson. Gina and Silvana Mangano are shown together in the sequence of a New Year's party featuring Lollobrigida's first screen close-up.

*Vendetta nel sole* (A Man About the House, 1947), a British-American production, has remained a puzzle in Gina's filmography. The actress doesn't recall having made it and the title isn't listed in any of Gina's mini studio biographies. Nevertheless, one of the issues of the magazine *Fotogrammi* (1947) carried an ad for the picture and Gina's name was included in the cast.

Silvana Mangano, who soon became famous with De Santi's *Bitter Rice* (1949), was cast for the third time as an extra with Lollobrigida in Costa's *L'Elisir d'amore*. Again, my findings unearthed a certain inconsistency with the Costa-Lollobrigida beginning. *Time* magazine reported that the actress went to work for Costa but failed to mention the title of the film, while Ponzi's work introduced *L'Elisir d'amore* as Gina's first film for the director in a series of three pictures done consecutively between 1947 and 1948.

My understanding of the subject was clouded when I read in *L'Avventurosa storia del cinema italiano* that when Gina met Mario Costa she worked for him in a musical for forty days, earning 40,000 lire. (With the earnings Gina bought an overcoat and an umbrella.) Following the forty days shooting, my findings indicate that the actress was given a part in Costa's *L'Elisir d'amore* which would then make her second film for him. The protagonist is Adina who appears with five girlfriends played by Loretta Di Lelio, Fiorella Carmen Forti, Flavia Grande, Silvana Mangano and Gina Lollobrigida. Here the source says the actress was on the set for ten days earning two thousand lire a day, a total of twenty thousand lire. Author Ponzi suggests that the pay was fifteen thousand, forty with extra hours, and that Gina acquired the coat and the umbrella with her wages from the film.

Couldn't these two films have been the same? Both have almost identical plots and the character Adina appears as Dina in one of the sources. The misinformation originated, I believe, in the number of shooting days, the actress' wage, and the lack of a title for the film in *Time* magazine. While the correct data is confusing, the important factor is that Mario Costa was the man responsible for launching Gina Lollobrigida, whose career dragged on in comparison to that of some of her contemporaries. Costa gave Gina significant parts, saw her potential as an actress, and counseled her. Among other things, he told Gina that if she'd take acting seriously, she'd have a brilliant future. "You're photogenic and have an actress' mind."

Costa was right. Gina was a potential starlet but her heart wasn't in making movies; when she finally made the decision to exploit the actress that was within her, she made sure that she would be THE ACTRESS and she managed it beautifully. Lollobrigida rose to the top and gloried there as the most popular Italian - and then international - actress of the Fifties and Sixties. Between 1955 and 1962 she was voted the most popular star in Germany and Belgium, and regularly headed exhibitor and audience polls in France, Italy, and many other countries. Gina became a household word everywhere.

Aside from her minor participation in films in the mid-Forties, Gina also signed a contract with the magazine *Il mio sogno* (My Dream) sometime in 1947. She posed for a photoromance titled *In fondo al cuore* (At the Bottom of My Heart), published in a series of 23 issues from March third to October fifth. For this modelling job she used the "nom de plume" Gina Loris. (In Robyn Karney's *The Movie Star's Story* the name was registered as Diana Loris.)

These photoromances were very popular in Italy and were called "fumetti" (the plural of "fumetto," meaning "smoke"), referring to the familiar balloon of speech emerging from the characters' mouths. The term "fumetti" was applied to all of comic-strip magazines which were very popular and served as a convenient vehicle to make oneself known.

In that same year a photographer-film producer with a studio in Via Margutta, the Roman Montmartre, came up with the idea of making photoromances inspired by famous songs. He invited Gina to pose as the heroine of *O sole mio*.

Like many starlets, Gina also participated in beauty contests. In 1947 she won second place in the Miss Rome beauty contest; the winner was a Sicilian, Nini Du Bac. However, the public, displeased with the result, applauded Gina for nine minutes and forty seconds; the judges saw no alternative but to include Gina in the Miss Italy contest to be held at Stressa, a popular resort. There, she took third place, while Lucia Bosè and Gianna Maria Canale came in first and second, respectively. Eleonora Rossi Drago placed fourth. La Drago never won a beauty contest. She had the misfortune of having her face ruined by a slightly misshapen nose and rose in her career the hard way. (In 1954 she won the "La Victoire" prize, and in the same year, while in Paris, had her nose attended to by a French surgeon.)

In a replay of Gina's first beauty contest, the public expressed its disapproval of the jury's decision. But for the Subiaco girl and movie producers, the final word was the public's, and from then on scripts never ceased to find their way into her hand. The fact that Gina wasn't elected Miss Italy didn't disturb her; she was positive that her talent, enthusiasm and beauty would speak for her when the time was right.

***

# 45--Imperial Gina

There was fierce competition for supreme popularity among the new Italian stars of the postwar neorealist Italy. The earthy Italian beauties, reflecting a new type of Mediterranean glamour exquisitely produced under the Italian sun, brought light to the screen.

Of the top ten, six had been chosen in beauty contests and Gina Lollobrigida was competing against what one onlooker described as a "series of busts." This bouquet of lovelies included, among others, Silvana Mangano, Silvana Pampanini, Eleonora Rossi Drago, Rossana Podestà, Gina Lollobrigida and Sophia Loren.

After being elected Miss Rome (1946), la Mangano, measuring 36-25-36, worked as an extra in a few films and accepted modeling jobs until she landed an important role in De Santis' *Riso amaro* (1949).

Green-eyed, black-headed Silvana Pampanini (37-24-36) came in second in the 1946 Miss Italy contest. In the early Fifties, before Lollobrigida's rise, it was this daughter of a Roman typesetter who received the heaviest fan mail of all Italian stars. La Pampanini, however, always complained that producers wanted her to do scenes in the near-nude.

Unlike la Pampanini, green-eyed, redheaded Eleonora Rossi Drago (35-24-33) was in no position to assert her superiority above other Italian beauties, but she declared: "I would give up everything for my career, and I mean everything."

Rossana Podestà (35-21-33) was the Italian Terry Moore. La Podestà was born in Tripoli and was cherishing a dream to become a doctor when a moviemaker discovered her in a swimming pool sometime in 1950. She did sixteen pictures in the following five years and was assigned the title role in *Helen of Troy* (1955).

Sophia Loren (38-24-37), always considered Gina's number one rival, appeared in *Aida* (1953) but her first chance came the following year in De Sica's *Gold of Naples*. The supposed feuds between her and Gina created a lot of publicity.

Gina Lollobrigida (36-22-35) retains her own special qualities from these endowed muses; she possesses that "something" necessary to rise to the top, the qualities of a true star. "Gina is the cinematic animal," affirmed a movie director, "as specialized as a hunting dog. She is governed by a perfect instinct of what she does. She gets up in the morning and thinks of movies. She works at them, and at lunch she talks about them. She knows nothing whatever about ordinary little details of life... how much a ticket from Rome to Paris costs, or what time the train leaves. She would think nothing of it if you told her you had paid $500 for a Cadillac. But she knows how much a good scriptwriter should get, or what the going rate is for a technician, or what any given cameraman's strong points are."

Sometime after the 1947 Miss Italy contest, producer Maleno Malenotti asked Gina to have a series of photos taken to see if she could get a part in Costa's *Folie per l'opera* (Opera Fans, 1948).

The photos, taken at Gina's future brother-in-law's in the Parioli District, got her the part. Her name was credited after the protagonist, Aroldo Tieri. In the US she was billed as Lollo Brigida. The misspelling didn't alter the final result for Gina was being exported not only to America but to Russia as well. (The film was the first postwar Italian production to be distributed in the USSR.)

Musicals were in vogue in the Italian cinema and singers were called upon to act. The public loved to hear a well-known canzone or musical score and didn't demand much of a plot or setting. Italian musicals were restricted in number and quality, most of them being biographies of musicians and filmed operas.

A musical comedy of a certain originality in which the combination of singing and acting worked quite well was Costa's *Opera Fans*.

To attract moviegoers to the theaters, three of the most well-known Italian opera singers of those days joined the cast: Tito Schipa, Gino Bechi and Tito Gobbi with whom Gina had sung an aria from *Tosca* in Subiaco's main square during the war.

The critics were rather indifferent to this Costa film and Lollobrigida was referred to by a critic as a very beautiful Roman girl in an unglamorous role.

***

When Mario Costa approached Gina with the role of Nedda in *I pagliacci* (Love of a Clown, 1948), she accepted it with enthusiasm, but when she found that the female lead was that of an exuberant and passionate gypsy, Gina flatly refused the part, objecting that her Latin nature wasn't enough for it. "I'm sure you can do it. Let's shoot a scene and see who is right," countered the director.

Gina couldn't think of a way to politely refuse the logical suggestion, so she decided to ask for an outrageous fee - one million lire - with the thought of discouraging Costa. To her astonishment he said the part was hers with shooting beginning the following day. She had to memorize the score and all her singing gestures would be synchronized. Gina found it to be a very tiresome job. She had never seen Leoncavallo's melodrama that Costa had adapted for the screen, and her heart wasn't in it. Nevertheless, this was Gina's first big offer; she'd receive top billing and again appear with Tito Gobbi. At the same time she felt guilty for having asked for such a high salary. But she was still helping to support her family, and the money would go a long way. However, she'd have been happier with a good singing part than with a million lire.

Gina's performance yielded poor reviews. While some critics limited themselves to praising her exuberant beauty as perfect for the role, others predicted she had no chance as an actress.

Gina was tired of being constantly referred to as a beautiful body with no acting capacity. Since Italian stars were dubbed (according to the Italian system of the era), interpretation of parts was rendered separately by others or by the stars in some cases.

The practice was well illustrated in Truffaut's 1973 Best Foreign Film Oscar winner, *Day for Night*, starring Jacqueline Bisset; Truffaut himself plays a movie director trying to film a love story. Italian actress Valentina Cortese is the desperate aging star (in the film) who can't remember her lines, thus requiring take after take. She hopes to solve the embarrassing situation, telling the patient director that she could just say numbers instead of lines and dub the dialogue later, for she used to work like that for Fellini. She demonstrates by saying a series of numbers to her leading man, Jean-Pierre Aumont: "24-56-42-63-11-51-71" etc. The director, feeding her despair, says that it is "impossible in this country."

In the early-Fifties when Gina was reaching stardom, she had a clause added to her contracts saying that her voice couldn't be dubbed in Italian, French and English speaking movies. The success that Mario Soldati's *La provinciale* (The Wayward Wife, 1953) brought to her name allowed the actress to take that step.

With the mortifying reviews of *I pagliacci*, Gina decided from then on to give the best of herself to prove that she wasn't just a beautiful face, but a woman who could really emote if she put her heart to it. On top of the criticism, Milko had told her that these first movies she had been making were no good at all. "My husband tried to dissuade me from going into films. He did not believe I would be a success." Gina, who wasn't born a loser, promised to show him that she could perform. It became something of a bet and it was here that she made a resolution. "I had almost decided to quit the movies when Milko told me I never could become a fine actress" and she vowed to go on. Years later Dr. Skofic sighed when he went to the theater with Gina and suffered a hundred pair of opera-glasses directed on them.

\*\*\*

After Gina had met her beau at that New Year's Eve party in 1947 the young couple were inseparable for the next two years, the time limit signora Lollobrigida had advised them to wait before taking their vows.

During their dating period Gina used to visit Milko at his small apartment to cook his meals and sing for him. In fact, she so lost herself in singing that there was often no time to prepare the meals.

On January 14, 1949 in a little church 6,000 feet up in the snowfields of Mount Terminillo, bride and groom wore ski outfits at their wedding ceremony. Witnessing the marriage were the American Commander of the D.F. camp and Gina's colleague, Yvonne Sanson. (In Allan Weber's mini studio biography of the actress, the writer lists Professor Royce of the University of Pennsylvania, the American Commander of the refugee camp and Captain Kurata of the camp as witnesses.)

The Skofics established themselves in Via Sambucuccio d'Alando, near piazza Bologna, where they led a simple and well-organized life. Before and after their marriage the Skofics were never the focus of scandals. Gina's impeccable reputation on film sets dates back to the very early days of her career. The charismatic Errol Flynn was bothered by her cool and distant behavior while shooting *Crossed Swords* (1953); the American billionaire, Hollywood mogul Howard Hughes, found no response to his advances when he invited her to film in Hollywood. Gina wanted no part in his harem, into which Ida Lupino, Ava Gardner, Lana Turner, Carole Lombard and others had fallen victim. (Actress Janet Leigh joined Lollobrigida as one of the few who expressed an aversion to the legendary Hughes.)

Gina's life - before and after her marriage - was always private, the betrothal and the wedding far from pompous. That seemed to be symptomatic of the decorum of Italian stars of those years. There were, of course, cases that reached the top of the scale in world-wide scandals. Roberto Rossellini (then having a love story with celebrated Anna Magnani) had a highly publicized adulterous affair with Ingrid

# 49--Imperial Gina

Bergman. Another tumultuous case involved Lea Padovani and Orson Welles. But Gina Lollobrigida and Dr. Milko Skofic belonged to the list of well-behaved notables. During their 17 years of married life there were no known lovers, one of those rare cases in the show business world.

Gina's refusal of romantic entanglements with producers and directors was, to a very large extent, the cause of her slow beginning as an actress. By that I don't mean that all overnight successes passed the couch test or the one-night stand with a potential movie-maker. Gina's best weapons in the struggle for stardom were her talent, her stunning Mediterranean beauty and her willpower.

Several of Lollobrigida's contemporaries were luckier. In addition to their curves, they had someone to give them a hand. Silvana Mangano married producer Dino De Laurentiis after the shooting of *Bitter Rice* and Sophia Loren became the protégée of Carlo Ponti who "helped her obtain bit parts in numerous movies and a lead role in *Aida* (1953)." Sexy Elsa Martinelli was discovered by Kirk Douglas, who launched her career in 1955. A new star in the Lollobrigida mould emerged in the early Sixties: Claudia Cardinale, protégée and then wife of talented producer Franco Cristaldi. But by the time la Martinelli and la Cardinale appeared on the screen, Gina had already been number one for many years.

Unlike the above examples, Gina's husband gave up his career to become his wife's business manager; nevertheless, the physician didn't have the resources of a De Laurentiis or Fellini - the latter married to Giulietta Masina. Gina Lollobrigida led her career to the top practically alone.

\*\*\*

Three years had passed since Gina had been on the set of *Aquila Nera* and no particularly excellent parts had come her way. Nevertheless, her international recognition began in England in the summer of 1949 when she was in the British capital to shoot an episode of *A Tale of Five Women* with Marcello Mastroianni.

Gina's first day in London was a busy one. She was at the studio at 8:30 a.m. to film a scene with actor Bonar Colleano that continued until 7:00 p.m. However, it was a quiet day insofar as Gina was unable to speak English then. Before leaving Italy she had memorized some English words and sentences but found it difficult to remember them and usually asked for help from Miss Mary Alcaide who had travelled with her as an interpreter.

Unfortunately, the film didn't help Gina to fulfill her commitment to show the critics that she could act. An Italian critic stated that "in the Roman episode which direction was offered to Rossellini who declined it, appear Gina Lollobrigida and Mastroianni, young and charming in the most superfluous performance of their careers." The film nevertheless worked to Gina's benefit since it introduced her to British audiences, but it wasn't the sort of picture to which many of them flocked.

Following her unsuccessful overseas experience, she was cast in Luigi Zampa's *Campane a martello* (Children of Chance, 1949), a Carlo Ponti production. Lollobrigida disliked working for the renowned producer. She was in five other Ponti films in the Fifties but that didn't change her impression of him. His constant complaining about the lack of talent in Italian stars who, unlike Hollywood's, were incapable of acting, singing, and dancing displeased her. "I must say," declared Gina years later, "with him I made my worst pictures. He didn't believe in my possibilities."

Ponti, on the other hand, claims he gave Gina a start in her career, but when he produced better parts for her she was already a famous and international star. Before she did *The Wayward Wife* for him - a significant film - she had already achieved fame with *Fanfan la Tulipe*, *Times Gone By* and *Beauties of the Night*.

Despite Gina's unappreciative comments on Ponti, not all films she did for him were that awful. *La romana* (Woman of Rome, 1954) probably was the producer's best offer to Gina, but at that stage she had already worked for John Huston opposite Humphrey Bogart in *Beat the Devil*(1953) and reached stardom with *Bread, Love, and Dreams* that same year.

*Children of Chance* had been written for Anna Magnani, but thinking of saving a few million, Ponti thought it'd be better to star Gina because she was beautiful but unknown. Speaking of lire, Lollobrigida's income in those days was so low that she couldn't afford a car or a better apartment. Italian movie people didn't think much of her as an actress; Gina pretended to ignore them and continued to work harder to improve her acting. When stardom and world popularity were finally hers she became the most expensive Italian movie actress in the Fifties.

# 51--Imperial Gina

*Children of Chance* tells the story of two prostitutes who, upon returning to their hometown, discover that the priest to whom they used to send their earnings for safekeeping had spent everything building an orphanage.

Zampa's rapport with the cast was good and he felt that actor Eduardo De Filippo needed no direction in the priest's role; Zampa had to work a little with the two ladies but it wasn't a particular problem.

The movie was simultaneously made in two versions, English and Italian. In the English cast were actresses Patricia Medina, Yvonne Mitchell and Manning Whiley in the role of the priest. There were two scripts in the two different languages and as soon as a scene was shot in Italian, the British cast took their positions on the set indicated by marks on the floor and repeated the same action. It was a long and tiresome process; however, it wasn't a unique case. When Mauro Bolognini did *L'ora della verità* (1952) with Jean Gabin and Michelle Morgan, actors Walter Chiari and Daniel Gélin alternated in scenes for the two versions of the film.

In this first Lollobrigida-Zampa encounter, the actress revealed some of her acting potential at least in one sense, she was at ease and fresh. Nonetheless, a movie critic wrote that the film exploited Gina's and Sanson's breasts rather than analyzing the human condition of the two "signorine" and the factors that led them to such a way of life. Most critics weren't pleased with the tone in which the subject of prostitution had been approached and considered this Zampa film "sketchy and superficial."

Notwithstanding, it was a good opportunity for Gina to work with Zampa, then a highly praised director. His *Vivere in pace* (Live in Peace, 1946), had received an award from the New York critics as the best foreign movie of the year, and by working with him, Gina's prestige would improve.

A change from most of her previous films, Gina rendered a good performance in *La sposa non può attendere* (The Bride Can't Wait), her last picture of the Forties, and a very successful one with the critics (if not with the public). The comic genre brought out another side of the actress who, until then, had only attempted dramatic roles. She revealed herself to be a fine comedienne. With this Gianni Franciolini film, Gina moved a big step forward co-starring with Gino Cervi in the part of the groom who is late for his wedding when he saves a suicide from drowning.

By the time Gina began her next film, *Miss Italy* (1950), she had become an established star with eleven films to her credit (the first five as an extra) even though many were so unsubstantial that Gina herself prefers to forget them. "My first pictures were terrible, I know. But I feel it's better to make bad pictures first and get better in time. Otherwise, if you start at the top, where do you go from there?"

After seeing Gina in Giorgio Pàstina's *Alina* (1950), the Italian film critic Mario Landi commented that the actress had made some progress since *La sposa può attendere*, but that she still had much to learn. *Alina*, however, also starring Amedeo Nazzari, presented Gina with a screenplay unworthy of her efforts.

A couple of other poor Lollobrigida films are somewhat of a mystery. *La prigionera dell'isola* (The Island Prisoner, 1947), directed by Marcel Cravenne for Lux Films, is one of them. The picture is listed in the actress' filmography in the *Dizionario del cinema italiano 1945-1969* and in *Las Estrellas* (The Stars), but Vinicio Marinucci's *Tendencies of the Italian Cinema* excludes Gina from the cast. Ponzi's *The Films of Gina Lollobrigida* ignores it.

*Tocsin* (1948), also for Lux Films, has been listed in a couple of studio mini biographies as another Gina picture but no other source has documented it. Therefore, according to Ponzi's work, the official number of Gina's pictures between 1946 and 1948 is eleven. The following 22 years saw Gina Lollobrigida in 49 productions and the actress proved to both the public and the critics that she was good in both dramatic and comic parts, many of which received worldwide recognition.

In Luigi Comencini's *Bread, Love and Dreams* (1953) (author's collection).

Gina as Esmeralda in Jean Delannoy's *The Hunchback of Notre Dame* (1956). Paris film and Panitalia. Courtesy of Ado Fujita (Kobe).

# Chapter 4

The World's Most Popular Actress

(The Glorious Fifties)

"Remember, I am an actress, not just a body!"

The postwar Italian cinema had entered a new era, and Gina Lollobrigida flourished with it. Apart from Anna Magnani, Italian show business presented an unglamorous façade until Lollobrigida ascended the stage. For the Italian public, the emerging actress became the personification of feminine beauty; a healthy, ravishing Sabine woman.

The neorealism era was turning Rome into the Mecca of the cinema with Italian pictures receiving awards in European capitals and in New York. Italian film production expanded from fifty-four films in 1948 to one hundred and forty-five in 1953, with one third of them in color. Meanwhile, 5,000 movie theaters were closed in the US, while the number of new venues in Italy jumped to 9,778 from a previous 6,500. Box-office sales also increased from $8.8 million to $48 million. (*Time*, August 16, 1954).

It was at this time that Hollywood stars, a delicious attraction to the Roman paparazzi, began to swarm in Via Veneto. Celebrities like Kirk Douglas, Claudette Colbert, Linda Darnell, Hedy Lamarr, George Sanders and Shelley Winters were working for Italian directors filming the great epics of world history.

As Hollywood stars flocked to Rome, their Italian counterparts became favorite exports along with caffè espresso and Vespa, and Gina headed the list as the most popular and most highly paid Italian actress. Few other stars were as esteemed by the overseas public as was Gina. A few exceptions were Giulietta Masina, Anna Magnani and Silvana Mangano. La Loren, la Martinelli, and la Cardinale were strong contenders but la Lollobrigida remained the most celebrated.

Claudia Cardinale played very good parts, but in the words of an American critic, "she never really made great impact."

Even though Gina never worked under the direction of the three most famous neorealists - Antonioni, Fellini and Visconti - the actress achieved national and international fame working for Zampa, De Sica, Blasetti and Castellani on the domestic front, and Christian-Jaque, René Clair, John Huston, Sir Carol Reed, King Vidor and others no less prestigious on an international scale.

Duilio Coletti's *Miss Italy* a Ponti production, introduced Gina in her third starring role receiving top billing. (The other two were *Love of a Clown* and *Children of Chance*.) Alberto Lattuada had also thought about making a film with a Miss Italy plot but the project was abandoned. Gina's presence in the cast gave a touch of credibility to the plot since she had been a Miss Italy candidate herself. The film was regarded as trivial by the critics.

Another Ponti production directed by Zampa came along again and offered Gina a somewhat less witty character than she had rendered for them before. *Cuori senza frontiere* (*Hearts Without Boundaries* or *The White Line*, 1950) paired Gina with Raf Vallone who had his debut in *Bitter Rice*. Wearing an apron and a head-scarf to portray a humble character, Gina was her beautiful self, but the film received lukewarm reviews and suggested there was much to be desired from Zampa.

Sometime in 1950 Fellini co-directed *Luci del varietà* (Variety Lights) with Lattuada, a comedy involving a vaudeville troupe with Giulietta Masina, Carla Del Poggio and Peppino De Filippo. When Fellini and Lattuada asked Ponti to produce the film, his reaction was negative, saying that the plot wasn't good. Later the two directors discovered that Ponti was shooting *Vita da cani* (A Dog's Life), a similar script, with Gina. The film wasn't well-received.

\*\*\*

If anything ever spelled trouble for Gina Lollobrigida it was Howard Hughes. The actress' nine-year saga with the movie mogul began when Milko took a series of his wife's photos with a Leica which Carlo Ponti had given them as a wedding present. The photos were issued to magazines free, under the condition that proper credit should be given. One of them showing Lollobrigida modelling a bikini ended up in Hughes' hands and he decided to summon her to

# 57--Imperial Gina

Hollywood. Even for Gina, who had been waiting for her big break, a Howard Hughes invitation for a screen test was probably more than she expected. The 23-year-old actress was supposed to fly to the United States with her husband, but at the last moment only one of two promised plane tickets arrived. Dr. Skofic trusted his wife and didn't stop her from going alone, sure that she'd be faithful. She was.

On July 22, 1950, Gina left Rome for Los Angeles with all expenses paid. She was met at the airport by Hughes' agents who "shooed reporters away" and escorted her by limousine to a luxurious hotel in Hollywood. There, in her golden American cage replete with a swimming pool, a secretary, a chauffeur, an English coach and voice teacher, Lollobrigida experienced one of the worst adventures of her life. She was practically imprisoned, and was shuffled from imposed English lessons to rehearsals to "oorible RKO peectures." She felt lonely and thought much of her husband who phoned and sent her telegrams constantly.

The language barrier contributed to her loneliness and frustration. One particular day she looked for a bell in the room to order breakfast. After discovering that it was necessary to call room service, she phoned and ordered coffee and a "brioche." The attendant had no difficulty in understanding "coffee" but she had to repeat "brioche" several times. A few minutes later when she was brought coffee and a tooth brush, she broke down and wept.

For the two and half months she was at the mercy of Mr. Hughes, she received no screen test. She was given a script to rehearse - a divorce scene. Was Hughes giving her a hint? He was well-known for his thirty years of constant pursuit of Hollywood film stars. "He dated many famous movie actresses but seemed more interested in collecting them than establishing a serious relationship." The 6' 4" slender, dark-skinned Texan, however, didn't know that he was playing with fire this time and that he was no match for Gina Lollobrigida. For Hughes, actresses weren't classified as good or mediocre, beautiful or ugly, but as hot and cold. Naturally, he was drawn to the "hot." Jean Harlow, Ava Gardner, Terry Moore, and Carole Lombard were associated with him.

Gina wasn't aware that the Hollywood czar was a problematic man living under intense stress. By the time they met at the Town House Hotel, Hughes had already suffered damage from a plane crash that required facial surgery and had been through at least two nervous breakdowns. He was suffering from serious mental disorders which explains, to some extent, his awkward behavior with Gina during those two months, and for the following nine years that he tried to prevent her from working in America.

When Gina returned to Italy, she gave an account of the Hughes episode to the papers and the story was constantly reprinted, sometimes in its full context or in parts, by the world press. The actress related the unpleasant event saying that the American billionaire usually visited her at 2:00 a.m. and asked the hotel orchestra to keep on playing while they danced until dawn. The charade went on for six weeks until Gina called a halt. Even though the screen test never materialized, she was asked to sign "a paper" that she couldn't read. Was it a contract? "I never signed a contract with him. It was an option," Gina informed a French columnist in Paris. "I was just starting," she continued, "and he had me come to Hollywood for two and half months. The option was in English and I asked for a translation, as I couldn't read English then. They translated it to me. Then I went back to Rome to get my things to move back to Los Angeles. But when they sent me the contract, it was not the way they had explained it to me at all. So I decided not to go back. Ever since then Mr. Hughes has prevented me from working abroad." (One of the clauses in the document was that Hughes should use Gina in a picture, but he never sent her a script.)

Gina Lollobrigida wasn't the only star brought to Hollywood to go through weeks or months of frustration and anger at the hands of movie moguls who kept young and aspiring starlets under payment without a script and delayed screen tests; some of them endured major physical changes like hair dyeing, dental capping, forced diets and who knows what else.

Meanwhile, back in Europe, Lollobrigida was becoming a famous actress working for Italian, French and American producers despite lawyers' threats that Hughes would sue them if the pictures were shown in America. The threats were ignored and while the film world battled, newspaper headlines gushed over Lollobrigida's beauty and popularity. Police had to control crowds in airports, squares and stations; everywhere she went, people wanted to see her.

In 1955 Hughes sent her word that he was going to draw up a new contract for her participation in four pictures at $280,000 each to be paid during the period of ten years at the rate of $2,000 per week. In the 1950 agreement her services were worth $20,000 per picture, which indicated that in only five years her name had soared fast. The new deal was executed by Gregson Bautzer, representing Hughes, and Charles Schwartz as Gina's agent. But she never made a film for Hughes. Between 1950 and 1955, they tried to reach some mutual understanding, "but you can't come to an agreement with Howard Hughes because you can never find him," said Gina. After Gina met with him in Hollywood, their paths never crossed again. There was an occasion when both parties were close to reaching a final decision, but Hughes was in Florida while Lollobrigida was in New York. He proposed that they meet in Los Angeles, but Gina wasn't willing to make the trip. So the problem continued unsolved.

During the time that Gina was unable to work in America, she never received a cent from Hughes, and as he continued to claim that he owned her, no Hollywood studio was willing to chance a court battle with him. Lollobrigida's temper raged because she felt no obligation to him and she was ready to sue.

So in 1959, after she had finished filming *Solomon and Sheba* in Madrid, she arrived in Hollywood for her first American film made in the States. Nine years had passed and she was positive that she was through with Hughes. Gina had nothing that could prevent her from working for any American studio. Unlike the unknown starlet who had come to Hollywood in 1950, the actress arrived this time with great pomp. The American public had already seen her in several productions including *Fanfan la Tulipe, Beat the Devil, Bread, Love, and Dreams, Trapeze,* and other films from among 36 she completed in the first 13 years of her career.

*** 

When Gina returned to Rome on October 12 (1950) after her regrettable encounter with Howard Hughes, she was cast in the role of Daniela in *La città si difende* (Four Ways Out) giving probably the best performance of this first period of her career. With Pietro Germi (one of the most controversial neorealist directors) and a screenplay by Federico Fellini, Tullio Pinelli and Luigi Comencini, the movie was chosen as the best Italian film at the XII Exhibition of Cinematographic Art in Venice in 1951.

Despite Gina's laudable performance, it was *Enrico Caruso, leggenda di una voce* (The Young Caruso, 1951) that produced the strongest box-office success. The picture ranked ninth among 118

Italian films shown between 1951-1952. Gina's performance as Stella, Caruso's first love, was a hit with the critics.

After the film's success, Italy was shocked by the death of the leading man, Ermanno Randi, who fell victim to his lover's jealousy. For the first time Italian newspapers had to speak openly about homosexual relationships. During her career Gina worked with other leading men who were also involved with homosexuality. Errol Flynn, who starred with her in *Crossed Swords* has been referred to as bisexual by author Charles Higham in *Errol Flynn: The Untold Story*. Tyrone Power, who was filming *Solomon and Sheba* with Lollobrigida when he died of a heart attack, has been similarly described. In 1985 the world was taken by surprise when Rock Hudson finally came out of the closet to reveal that he was dying of Acquired Immune Deficiency Syndrome (AIDS). Hudson starred with Gina in two memorable comedies: *Come September* (1961) and *Strange Bedfellows* (1964).

***

Fame also has its price, which Gina soon learned after the release of Carlo Lizzani's *Achtung! Banditi!* (Beware of Bandits, 1951), a film dedicated to the partisan war. The actress had always been aware that her curvy figure had constantly drawn the attention of men and made many women jealous of Mother Nature's generosity to her. She was understandably annoyed when critics wrote about her physical attributes and glossed over her acting, and it infuriated her to read derogatory remarks about her body. In such cases, Gina sued and usually won. At one time in her life she was involved in almost ten lawsuits. "I think everybody in life has the right to defend themselves. I don't permit anybody to push their foot on my hat; and if somebody tries to do this, I just answer him," she declared.

That was exactly what she did with Enrico De Boccard, a writer for Rome's weekly *Meridiano d'Italia*. The columnist had reviewed *Achtung! Banditi!* in the following terms: "The only thing of any continuity (in the picture) consists of (Gina's) breasts... Those breasts, which appear... to be rather praiseworthy, are presented in all possible ways, in long shots, medium shots, close-up and every close-up, and to give them particular prominence, they have been subjected to a perpetual trembling and wavering."

# 61--Imperial Gina

Gina was particularly outraged about two things. First, De Boccard neglected to mention that she was decently clothed in all scenes and second, when referring to her bosom the writer used the vulgar Italian term "zinna" which is reserved for the udder of cows. She took the man to court for defamation. De Boccard's lawyer defended the culprit, explaining that the columnist admired Gina's beauty and that the term in question referring to her bosom was an old Italian word that appears in Machiavelli's bawdy comedy, *Mandragola* (1524). The defense was rejected and both writer and publisher, Franco Mario Servello were fined $176 plus costs. "All the money I got from lawsuits I give to the poor, so nobody can blame me for what I have done." The actress was, above all, determined to make it clear that "Gina Lollobrigida is an honorable woman."

Slanderous columnists and loss of privacy are probably a star's worst enemies, and Gina Lollobrigida had plenty of them despite her respectable life style. It was her high standards that tempted malicious critics and even priests to find some fault in her. Gina always refused to appear nude or expose her breasts on screen and in photos. Whenever a scene au naturel was required, she had her skin-colored tights on hand.

\*\*\*

The best thing that could have happened to Gina after her ill-fated visit to Hollywood was co-starring with Gérard Philipe in Christian-Jaque's *Fanfan la Tulipe*. Thanks to director-producer Giuseppe Amato who had met Gina on the set of *A Man About the House*, the actress was cast as Adeline, a plump armed gypsy type in a peasant costume. Amato was positive that Gina was the perfect star for the role. For three years he had promised the actress that when a good part appeared, he'd consider her. His experience had convinced him that she was able to play popular characters well, and that her former parts had been unsuitable for her.

*Fanfan la Tulipe*, set in 18th-century France of Louis XV introduced Gina wearing the corsets of the epoch, thus giving a special touch to the bust which made Lollobrigida's figure more beautiful than in any other role she had played to date. But it wasn't just her Bohemiène costume that helped her to achieve success in the part. Her acting had improved to a great extent and she gave an outstanding performance portraying the picaresque Adeline.

Gérard Philipe, a handsome and very popular French star playing the swashbuckler of the title role, couldn't have been a better match for the Italian star. Their rapport on the set was first-class. Philipe pleased Gina with his politeness and consideration, teaching her French and making her feel comfortable in the setting. In general, there was a very happy atmosphere among the cast and Gina has beautiful memories of the time they were shooting the film. The happy atmosphere that prevails in the movie seems to be genuine.

When *Fanfan la Tulipe* was released in the early Fifties it achieved international fame. Several factors contributed to its triumph: two superb stars, an absorbing plot involving court intrigues, and plenty of sword fighting. The reviews in France and Italy were excellent and Lollobrigida's popularity in France saw no limit. After the picture had been running for a week in the theaters along the Champs-Elysées the distributors had all posters altered to feature Gina's name larger than her leading man's, and posters of her completely covered the walls like Coca-Cola ads. "My name was suddenly very big on the theater. And for this reason I am very loved in France. They adopt me as a French star, because the public there really made me popular."

Before the film's release, there hadn't been the usual film propaganda, but within a week of projection, Gina had become the darling of the French. "If her compatriots adore her," wrote a critic, "the French have a secret preference for her."

The "Lollobrigida phenomenon" was born in Paris and the French called her "Lollo." This was the first time, I assume, that the term was used in reference to Gina Lollobrigida and it soon penetrated languages around the Globe. Was Lollo a simple abbreviation of the actress' name? Yes and no. "Lolo" (spelled with one "l") is a popular onomatopoeic for "lait" (milk) in children's vocabulary according to the *Petit Robert dictionnaire alphabétique de la langue française* (1977) and *Cassell's New French dictionary* (1966). In the 1969 edition of *Petit Robert*, "lolo" was also entered as "sein de femme" (woman's breast). In the *Larousse de la langue française* (1959) we learn that the term appeared from a confusion of the French noun "lait" and the French "l'eau" ("the water"), pronounced "lo."

Lollobrigida didn't mind being referred as "Lollo" then, but despite the reciprocal admiration between the actress and the French in the past four decades, writer Henry-Jean Servat more recently quoted the actress as saying that she "detests" the term.

# 63—Imperial Gina

*Fanfan la Tulipe* was released in the States in 1953. Regrettably, American reviewers, like those in most parts of the world, greatly publicized Gina's curves and ignored her talent. The *L.A. Times* read. "Number One in Europe, Gina Throws Curves at U.S." portraying the actress in her decollete Adeline costume. The columnist described her measurements and her income, mentioned a film she was making with Errol Flynn, but said nothing about her rapport with the camera, her spontaneous acting, or her matchless pairing with Gérard Philipe whose name was unfairly omitted.

Gina reacted typically. "I don't take serious the critics. What I take serious is the reaction of the public. The last judge is always the public." More important than the critics at that point in her life was the fact that her name was making headlines in American newspapers, a plus for her career and a lesson to Howard Hughes.

Now that Gina was on the road to becoming an international actress, she had to learn English and French. (Her voice in *Fanfan la Tulipe* had been dubbed by Adriana Parrella.) For an Italian who had never spoken English before, she was doing very well in her American interviews. Reading several of them printed verbatim, her English was perfectly clear even though the phrasing was 'cart before the horse'. By the mid-Fifties her command of the language had shown immense progress.

Lollobrigida, however, loves to speak French and finds it easier than English. This is understandable since French, like Italian, is a romance language.

The victory of Gina's first encounter with the French camera brought Lollo back to Paris where she was paired with Gérard Philipe in *Les belles de nuit* (Beauties of the Night, 1952). From then on the actress was part of the French cinema throughout her career. Still in the Fifties she did a remake of *Le grand jeu* (Woman and the Flesh, 1954) with Jean-Claude Pascal; *The Hunchback of Notre Dame* (1956) with Anthony Quinn and starred with Yves Montand and Marcello Mastroianni in *La Loi* (Where the Hot Wind Blows, 1958).

Awards began to shower on Gina not very long after her first two French movies. In 1953 she was awarded the "Victoire," France's highest tribute to a foreign actress. The event repeated itself in the next two consecutive years, rendering her ineligible for further competition; in 1955 Gina Lollobrigida became an honorary judge of the "Victoire" council. Three decades later, "French Minister of

Culture Jack Lang awarded the veteran actress with the French Order of Arts and Letters". Do the French still love her?

La Lollo's popularity in the Fifties was such that at the 1952 Cannes Film Festival people were shoving each other to see her pass. They threw flowers at her and rushed to touch her. The actress, however, wasn't very fond of this sort of demonstration. In America, her popularity soared after *Bread, Love, and Dreams* was released in New York in 1954, and her prestige as a top class actress has continued among the American people through all these years. In 1985 she was nominated for the "Golden Globe" for her performance in the CBS soap opera *Falcon Crest*.

Contrary to what many movie critics opine, Gina's fame didn't evaporate after the glorious Fifties. Twenty years after *Bread, Love, and Dreams* she was still receiving fan mail from all corners: Germany, Finland, South America and Japan.

In spite of the admiration of her fans around the globe, the affection that France bestowed upon la Lollo was incomparable; Paris had become her second home. Gina bought an apartment there, and in 1960 it became her main residence. The Italian cinema was then going through a shaky period and Gina thought that Paris would be more accessible to the world of movies than the Appia Antica. The luxurious apartment was decorated with some of her antique collection (Gina loves archaeology and has a large variety of rare Greek and Etruscan pieces), and the furniture was flown over from Rome.

*** 

When Lollobrigida returned to the Eternal City after working in *Fanfan la Tulipe* another fantastic opportunity awaited her. This time the star was fortunate not only in having a fine part - short though - in Alessandro Blasetti's *Altri tempi* (Times Gone By, 1952), but also in working with one of the most outstanding Italian actor-director, Vittorio De Sica.

The year 1952 was particularly propitious for Italian comedies of all kinds, and *Times Gone By* presented an unusual and delightful collection of eight episodes adapted from well known authors, which the director transferred to the screen using a changing style appropriate for each individual author and his stories. The episode *The Trial of Frine* was particularly chosen with Lollobrigida in mind. However, before going in front of the camera for Blasetti, Gina appeared in

# 65--Imperial Gina

Giorgio Bianchi's *Amor non ho... però... però*, (Love I Haven't... But... But, 1951), an ambitious and humorous picture, but poorly shot - a work of no consequence for the actress' career. On the other hand, Blasetti's film brought Gina enormous notoriety.

Blasetti's peculiar filming technique contributed to Lollo's spontaneous performance. Acting each character's part as he wished them to do, Blasetti then had the cast repeat the master's performance, allowing them freedom to add through their own talents whatever was necessary for the development of the role.

For the rib-tickling episode of *The Trial of Frine* Blasetti thought the Gina-De Sica formula couldn't go wrong. At first De Sica refused the part but after repeated persuasion, he finally gave in.

The well-known Neapolitan actor started in show business on the stage back in 1922 as an extra with the company of Tatiana Pavolona, moving to the cinema in 1931 where he launched a brilliant career with his debut in *La vecchia signora* (The Old Lady). Blasetti's choice of Lollobrigida playing opposite De Sica was a combination of his recognition of her popularity and her status as an established actress.

The pairing of the two prestigious stars delighted Italian audiences. De Sica's reputation soared high and Lollobrigida was acclaimed a diva of first grandeur. But to her disappointment, a gossip columnist quoted De Sica as saying in a London newspaper that la Mangano, la Pampanini and la Lollobrigida were all curves with no talent. Gina hotly responded that the three of them were recognized actresses with script offers from major international directors. De Sica denied having made the statement, maintaining that it was a problem of translation at the time of his interview with the London journalists. It was only during the shooting of *Bread, Love, and Dreams* that Gina forgave De Sica, who then declared to the press "Gina è molto brava," (Gina is very clever.)

\*\*\*

*The Trial of Frine* was based on a Greek legend concerning a well-known model, an extremely beautiful woman who is indicted before Athen's supreme court for going further than the assumed limits of her calling. The story solidifies on the screen, where Blasetti shows Gina as the beautiful prostitute (Frine) who is absolved through her lawyer's (De Sica) inspired tactics of praising her physical attributes to the courtroom.

Unlike her part in *Fanfan la Tulipe* and her future role in *Bread, Love, and Dreams* Gina wasn't a rambunctious tomboy. Her outfit wasn't that of the gypsy Adeline but a well-designed frock featuring a full length skirt with a tight, long sleeved bodice revealing a diamond--shaped opening in the front. The trial scene was the highlight of the film, and De Sica and Lollobrigida were much commended by the critics. Even though Gina's part was relatively short, her presence in the picture caused much of an impact on both the critics and the public.

*Times Gone By* was responsible for the critics dwelling on Gina's curves, highlighted by De Sica in the trial scene. Speaking in her defense, he underscores the accused's beauty by calling her a "maggiorata fisica." The term is conveyed through a play on words: "Ma d'altra parte, non e questa stessa nostra legge che prescrive siano assilti i minorati psichici? Ebbene perchè non dovrebbe essere assolta una 'maggiorata fisica' come questa formidabile creatura?"

My English failed me when I tried to render a decent translation of the passage, and I requested the help of my colleague, Professor James Kirkup, who suggested the following: "But on the other hand, isn't it the same thing, our law prescribing that mental defectives should be acquited? Well, then, why should not she, too, be acquitted, a physical phenomenon like this formidable creature?"

According to Kirkup the play on words here is "impossible to translate - the slight resemblance of 'psichici' and 'fisica,' the contrast between 'minoriti' and 'maggiorata,' suggesting 'minor' and 'major' but actually meaning something else - 'minorati psichici' means 'mental defectives,' 'maggiorata fisica' means something like 'physical super woman,' containing the idea of 'profusion, overabundance' etc."

The label "maggiorata fisica" accompanied Gina for a long period of her career, much to her displeasure. She was constantly being referred to as a "sex symbol," or the "Italian bombshell," concepts the actress never acknowledged herself.

Three decades later, while talking to *Clarín Espetáculos* in Buenos Aires Gina was quoted as saying that she had never felt like a sexual object because she thought of herself as an actress. She knew she was an extremely beautiful woman and that her figure was provocative, but she never exploited these attributes that Mother Nature had cast upon her; she'd rather be considered a talented actress struggling for good parts than a "maggiorata fisica."

# 67--Imperial Gina

Lollobrigida was, however, concerned about what looked good on her: costumes, hairdos and make-up, for example. Therefore when Blasetti asked her to part her hair in the center for the film, Gina was against it, suspecting that it wouldn't look good. It took the director and Milko to convince her that she'd still be attractive with that different hairdo. She finally gave in, and was actually pleased when she saw herself on the screen. "You were right," she told Blasetti, who considered Gina an intelligent actress with good intuition about what she should or shouldn't do.

When Gina came to Hollywood in 1950, she was practically unknown. Few Americans had seen her in Costas' *Love of a Clown* and the name Gina Lollobrigida probably wouldn't have rung a bell for most moviegoers then. The scene began to change after the public saw her in *Fanfan la Tulipe* and *Times Gone By*.

"*Times Gone By* is the Italian Film Export picture with Gina Lollobrigida that recently stirred big interest during a 20-week Beverly Hills showing, though it hasn't as yet played in other parts of the country," wrote Edwin Scharllet for *The Los Angeles Times*. "The lush beauty of the feminine star," he continued, "was flashed at audiences in the courtroom sequence, where she was on trial, with Vittorio De Sica, who ordinarily directs, appearing as an actor in the role of an attorney. Miss Lollobrigida was the accused, and bound because of her attractiveness to be declared innocent in this satirical sequence."

Two years after *Times Gone By*, Blasetti hoped for a similar happy outcome with *Tempi nostri* (Our Times). Much to his disappointment, Gina refused the part because she was occupied pouring over the English script for Huston's *Beat the Devil*. Too, Robert Siodmak had requested her to star in a remake of Jacques Feyder's *Le grand jeu*. With an English script in one hand and her French in the other, she didn't have time for an Italian part despite the short shooting schedule of only ten days. When Blasetti telephoned Gina from playwright Vitalino Brancati's house, she explained that her international engagements forced her to turn down his offer. Blasetti gave the part to Lea Padovani opposite Vittorio De Sica and Marcello Mastroianni.

On September 3rd, 1951, Gina adorned the cover of *Life* and in 1953 her figure was to appear on the cover of forty magazines - eight in one week - all over the world. Philippe Halsman (who photographed numerous movie celebrities including Anna Magnani, Silvana Mangano, Elizabeth Taylor and Gina Lollobrigida) concluded that Gina "probably has the best figure of any actress I've ever seen."

\*\*\*

After Gina's triumph in *Times Gone By* she was paired again with Gérard Philipe in René Clair's *Beauties of the Night*. In this French masterpiece of the Fifties, Clair satirises those who believe in the "superiority of the 'good old days.'" To achieve this purpose, he makes use of dreams with cleverly interlaced stories. In *French Cinema*, author Roy Armes presents a fine portrayal of the picture. "The film is neatly constructed and the balance between dream and reality is always held. All the dreams of the music teacher hero (Gérard Philipe) grow out of his everyday life and all the women in them are romanticized versions of people he meets everyday. The various epochs in which these dreams are set - Paris in 1900, the Algeria of 1830, the French Revolution and the age of the Three Musketeers - are linked by the recurring figure of an old man whose continual reminders of the superiority of the 'good old days' serve to trigger a new jump back in time. The sounds which plague the music teacher are balanced by the lighthearted rhythms of the music by Georges Van Paris and the carefree tone is preserved throughout."

Gina's role in the film is that of a cashier in the café where the piano teacher usually goes. In his dreams she appears as Leila, an odalisque in Algeria, and he falls madly in love with her as he does with the other women in his dreams, including Edmée (Martine Carol), mother of one of his students.

When the movie was released, the press - as usual - focused on Gina's curves. A New York columnist commented that Gina "in a very scanty harem costume, which reveals that she sure isn't kidding, is a formidable attraction all alone." The actress indeed looks gorgeous in the film, however the only revealing parts of her odalisque attire are from the lower abdomen to the shoulders with the breasts fully covered by a beaded cloth brassière. The legs are completely concealed by long puffy pantalons, presenting her attractive hourglass figure most respectably on screen.

In 1971, the *L.A. Times Calendar* (Sunday, August 29) wrote that Gina had been seen totally nude "by many including the Queen of England at the start of her career in a film called *Beauties of the Night*, and that the American version had omitted the scene. Gina, in an interview with *Cue* (October 23, 1954), declared that the nude

# 69–Imperial Gina

odalisque in the bath scene "was a girl who pretended to be me. But now, I do not allow even somebody else to do nudes for me."

\*\*\*

Mario Camerini, the Roman René Clair, was considered as one of the best Italian directors of the 1930-1940 era. In 1952 he cast Gina as Ottavia in *Moglie per una notte* (Bride for a Night), an adaptation from Anna Bonacci's play *L'heure blouissante* played in Paris in 1944.

In the film Camerini undertook the difficult task of creating an unglamorous Lollobrigida, with the actress sporting spectacles and a mousey hairdo. But the director was an expert in this type of farce and as the plot in the comedy developed he introduced a fascinating Gina to the audience.

Twelve years after the release of Camerini's film, Billy Wilder adapted the picture for Hollywood as *Kiss Me Stupid!* The production had been planned for Marilyn Monroe but he part was finally given to Kim Novak, who was becoming a screen goddess.
(Miss Novak had received a contract from Columbia in the early Fifties to replace Rita Hayworth and, at the time, rival Marilyn Monroe. Miss Novak is probably best remembered for her performance in Hitchcock's *Vertigo* in the late Fifties.)

Following Camerini's film Gina was involved in a very complex lawsuit with Michelangelo Antonioni and his *La signora senza camelie* (The Lady Without Camelias), a production that dragged on for two long and complicated years.

The film was meant to be a satire of the Italian cinema depicting the story of Clara, a salesgirl with no talent who becomes a famous movie star "via face and physique" but fails in serious acting and then submits herself to parts exploiting her physical charms.

Lollobrigida had already signed for the part when she walked out of the picture charging that the movie was a farce of the Italian cinema of her day, and she was being forced to belittle the world she worked for. Gina felt the film was a parody of Italian producers and actresses she knew and a satirical portrayal of herself. She strongly objected to the plunging necklines and maintained that her role was so morally low that she was afraid it might falsely reflect on her private life. Gina asked for changes in the script but she was told there was no time for it.

The film in its final form didn't seem offensive to the actress, but she felt that it differed from what she had seen earlier. When she walked out of the film, producers sued her for 200 million lire and Gina countersued, claiming the film was a ridiculous insult to the Italian film industry. Antonioni claimed that it wasn't. The public sided with la Lollo and the judge ruled in her favor.

Without Lollobrigida in the film, Antonioni was forced to search for a substitute. First he thought of an extra at Cinecittà, Sofia Scicolone - later Sophia Loren. But the producers wanted a well known star instead and signed Lucia Bosè, Miss Italy 1947.

The film was a fiasco with the public and the critics. But "all's well that ends well" and Antonioni made peace with Gina some time later.

***

The first of five films Gina did in 1953 was Steno/Monicelli's *Le infideli* (The Unfaithfuls). A Ponti-De Laurentiis production, the picture was favored by both the public and the critics. The other adulterous ladies - in the picture, mind you - were May Britt, Irene Papas, and Marina Vlady. A maid who commits suicide was played by Anna Maria Ferrero who, in real life, sparked the discord between Italian actor Vittorio Gassman and Shelley Winters while they were married and living in Rome. The film's international cast also included Milko Skofic as Guido; it was the only time husband and wife appeared together on screen.

Probably the best awards a star can receive throughout his/her career are popularity with the public and favorable reviews. Awards in their physical form are mere symbolic representations of the reaction of the critics and not the public in general. Nevertheless, the two of them sometimes go hand in hand; if a picture is popular and the star is good, there is little doubt that nomination for an award will follow. But no mediocre star receives prestigious recognition for a picture which is just popular with the public. Gina Lollobrigida first won the vote of the public, then the critics' approval, and finally international awards.

At St. Vincent she received the "Grolla d'Oro" (Golden Beaker) for her performance in *La provinciale* (The Wayward Wife). She also received awards from the French and Belgian Press, from the Cinema Industry of the Argentine and from German journalists. And in every country she visited she was the poupular representative of the Italian Cinema.

Based on Alberto Moravia's novel of the same title, the screenplay of *The Wayward Wife* directed by Mario Soldati provided sounder acting material for Gina. It was her first dramatic role depicting a Moravian woman and her performance showed that she had a deep understanding of the character.

Most Italian critics expressed that Soldati's film offered the actress one of the best roles up to that time, and her dramatic accomplishments indicated she had much improved and was capable of rendering a fine performance. Furthermore, Soldati had made a literary film introducing the public to a more diligent and responsive Lollo than in some of her earlier movies.

The plot of the Moravian novels involve contemporary intellectual and sociological problems in modern society. The bourgeois environment in which *La provinciale* takes place presents the story of a beautiful country woman, Gemma (Gina), who dreams of a marriage that can free her from the limited milieu of her daily life. She falls in love with a rich young man, Paolo (Franco Interlenghi), and when she thinks that the day has finally come, her mother reveals that the man she loves is her step-brother.

Disillusioned, she agrees to marry a mathmatics teacher, Franco (Gabriele Ferzetti), a boarder in her mother's house. When the husband neglects her for his studies, Gemma finds some comfort in the friendship of a Rumanian countess who convinces her to give in to the advances of an old friend of hers. The countess then blackmails Gemma, aims to make a prostitute of her, and moves bag and baggage right in with Gemma, who pounders Franco's lukewarm but honest affection and tries to drive her "friend" out. The disturbing occurrence opens Franco's eyes, and he immediately expells the countess from his house and forgives his wife.

Gina's leading man, Gabriele Ferzetti, began his acting career two years after Gina launched hers, and in this first film with the actress he shared her glory in being awarded the Nastro d'argento (Silver Ribbon). Later he played again opposite Gina in Bolognini's *That Splendid November*, (1968).

Lollobrigida's confidence in herself as an actress was strengthened with both the reviews and the award. Her self-confidence took a further step when she performed in English in her next two films, co-starring with the legendary Humphrey Bogart in *Beat the Devil* and the charismatic Errol Flynn in *Crossed Swords*.

Huston's *Beat the Devil*, Gina's first English speaking movie made in Europe, offered her the opportunity to work for an acclaimed American director with a screenplay by none other than Truman Capote. The fine international cast led by Bogart included Jennifer Jones (who had won an Oscar in 1943 for her saintliness in *Song of Bernadette*), Robert Morley, Peter Lorre and Edward Underdown.

When Claude Cockburn (who used the nome de plume James Helvick), a friend of Huston's for many years, found himself short of money during the war, wrote *Beat the Devil* as a potboiler. Claude welcomed the cash that a motion picture rendered him. That was when Huston phoned Bogart about the book. Bogart had founded a film company with Morgan Maree and Romulus-Santana, and had bought Claude's work for $10,000. (John Huston, *An Open Book*).

Huston didn't want to write the screenplay, so he asked Peter Viertel and Tony Veiller to do the job. The final result wasn't very good. But before the script was finished, the complete picture was cast and the crew was about ready to start filming. It was at this stage of Huston's adventure that Truman Capote entered the story. The writer happened to be in Rome and Huston, who hardly knew the man, asked for help. Huston and the cast were pleased because, in the director's opinion, they "could never have made the picture without him."

Actual shooting began in Ravello, south of Naples, with excellent matching work in Shepperton Studios. Deep inside, Huston felt the picture was going to be a fiasco, and confided to Bogart: "We haven't got a script, and I don't know what the hell is going to come of this. It may be a disaster. In fact, it's got all the earmarks of a disaster."

After much trouble, the final script with Capote's dialogue was ready. It told the adventures of two couples, Billy (Bogart) and Maria Dannreuther (Lollobrigida) and Harry Chelm (Underdown) and his wife Gwendolen (Jennifer Jones), who are involved with four ridiculous thieves: Petersen (Robert Morley), O'Hara (Peter Lorre), Ravello (Marco Tulli) and Major Ross (Ivo Barnard). The couples are planning to buy some land in British East Africa that they think is loaded with uranium. Meanwhile, Billy, who works as a go-between for the four thieves, falls in love with Harry's wife; in turn Billy's wife is smitten with Gwendolen's husband. And from this rather complicated situation develops the action that is presented in 89 minutes.

# 73--Imperial Gina

Filming *Beat the Devil* was a positive experience for Gina. The actress grew fond of Huston, Bogart and Lorre. Her respect for the American director and her leading man was such that the star joked that "the only people I never sue are Humphrey Bogart and John Huston. They are so nice."

Bogart, discussing women, marriage and actresses back in 1953, either before or after the making of *Beat the Devil*, referred to Lollobrigida and a couple of other actresses in a definitely "not so nice" fashion, and I wonder if Gina was ever aware of it. Bogart, then happily married to Lauren Bacall, disclosed to *The Hollywood Reporter* that stardom "ruins so many people - particularly actresses. Ninety percent of them are the dullest broads in town." The legendary *Casablanca* hero further expanded the topic saying that those actresses had no appeal to him at all, "and that goes for Marilyn Monroe, Jane Russell and Gina Lollobrigida. In fact, the only actress in town with any true allure is Lauren Bacall... I don't go for those top-heavy dames at all. That isn't sexy to me, but then, I'm not a bosom man. Now, Bacall has everything: charm, wit, looks and talent. Most of those other actresses look alike to me. I can't tell the difference between them anyway!" Physical constitution and talent are remote from each other and Bogart wrongfully judged his co-star of *Beat the Devil*.

The Lollo-Bogart match, however, was an amusing one. When they first met Gina found him "frightening," but as she got to know him better she discovered he was a "tremendously fine person." Indeed, Bogart had a very good sense of humor and loved to tease Gina. In Verita Thompson's *Bogie and Me*, the authoress relates the happy atmosphere that existed between the two and says Gina too had "a delicious sense of humor." She usually mispronounced Bogie, calling the actor "Boogie," and "Boogie" retaliated with "Low Bridge." One day they were discussing the shooting of the film over lunch at the studio commissary, and Ms. Thompson could hardly eat for laughing.

Bogart once made the statement that Gina made Marilyn Monroe look like Shirley Temple in *Sunnybrook Farm*. The teasing one day got to a point where Gina tired of it and began to yell back at him in Italian and walked off the set. After that, said Gina, "he liked me very much, and he was very nice to me."

Gina was also high on Truman Capote. "He is a wonderful person. Just at that time I was just learning English and Truman used to love to hear me talk. So every night when he would write scenes for the next day, he would write in more for me to do, then he would bring it to me to read for him alone and he would listen and giggle crazy. So by time the picture is over, my part which start out to be just small one gets bigger and bigger. He is a wonderful."

As for Lorre, Gina mentioned that when he was working she always stayed on the set to watch him because she felt she could learn much from the veteran actor.

The easygoing atmosphere that prevailed on the set of *Beat the Devil* was transmitted to the screen, for "there was a general air of gaiety and lightheartedness throughout the picture," recalled Huston. He considered Helvick's novel funny "but the humor in the script was broadened further and the absurdities were accentuated."

It has been said that when Jack Clayton (the production manager), Huston and Truman looked at the rushes the three wondered if the audiences would think the film was as funny as they did. Well, some did but the majority didn't.

I believe the film works for its sparkling language and the irony involved in it. Probably the best gag in the picture comes from Bogart's interview with an Arab authority who provides him and his gang with a boat to return to Italy in exchange for a promised introduction to Rita Hayworth. Some of the lines and puns are surely too good to lose. For example, Ravello keeps calling O'Hara "Mr. O'Horror." The film's most memorable line is uttered by O'Hara when, in a boat scene, he sees Maria (Gina) painting a profile portrait of Harry (Underdown) and he says: "It-has-only-one-eye." (The painted canvas that appeared on the screen was actually one of Lollobrigida's works.)

Considering the combination of Huston's directing, Capote's writing and the talents of a super cast, the film's box-office failure was surprising. Lollobrigida felt that the film was released before the proper time, and Huston concurred with the following comment: "*Beat the Devil* was ahead of its time. Its off-the-wall humor left viewers bewildered and confused. A few critics hailed it as a little masterpiece...but they were all European. There was not an American among them. But slowly, despite its early reception, the picture began to attract audiences, particularly in university towns. Now it has a cult following. *Beat the Devil* has done well over the years. I only wish Bogie could have been around to see this happen." (Bogart and Huston had worked together in several other productions before this ill-fated release, their last picture together.)

# 75–Imperial Gina

Columnist Milton Luban for *The Hollywood Reporter* under the heading "Huston Turns Out Amusing Satire" claimed that the picture "is an intriguing off-beat film that is bound to become a controversial conversation piece. There will be no halfway opinions about this Santana-Romulus production. People will either love it or hate it. A clever, very funny satire on international crooks, it will be regarded as over-talky in some quarters, although the dialogue in the John Huston-Truman Capote screenplay sparkles with sophisticated wit." Philip K. Scheuer for the *L. A. Times* considered the film "far from Huston's best, but it has moments that are some of the best of Huston in it." Scheuer added that the picture was full of contradictions so "that one could say nearly anything about it and be right." The film, opined the columnist, was "one of the talkingest cinemas of recent record, yet one of the most pictorial. A melodrama in outline, it is nevertheless written and played as a kind of eliptical comedy that I, for one, found exhilaratingly funny. You may not."

The cast fared well. Lollobrigida was described as being "beautiful and smooth as Bogart's wife" in *The Hollywood Reporter* while *Variety* agreed that "Gina Lollobrigida gives a provocative portrayal." Ruth Waterbury of the *L. A. Examiner* marveled that "there is nothing anyone can do but rave over the beauty of the luscious Lollobrigida, who can also act." Her generosity extended no further. Although the columnist declared herself "ordinarily a cheerleader over the work of John Huston" she made "sashimi" of the picture.

Ten years after its release the movie was very popular, but back in the Fifties most critics and the public dismissed Huston's film as an "entertaining spoof thriller" and an "eccentric black comedy."

*Beat the Devil* was Lollobrigida's fifteenth film in the first three years of the Fifties, an average of five films per year. Her iron willed desire to improve and become a brilliant actress was overshadowing some of her earlier pictures. The term "maggiorata fisica," however, still followed her wherever she went and she continued struggling with the press and the public, which still insisted on ejoying her more as an aesthetic creature than an actress. The order had to be reversed.

Soon after *Beat the Devil*, Lollo was again the talk of the town starring opposite Errol Flynn for Viva Films. American show business critics indirectly proclaimed victory over Howard Hughes for Gina's second American film made in Europe.

Released in Italy as *Il maestro di Don Giovanni* (The Master of Don Juan), and originally called *The Golden Blade*, the film was finally shown in the States as *Crossed Swords*. The picture, written and directed by Milton Krims (co-directed by Vittorio Vassarotti), was created due to Flynn's enthusiasm following favorable reviews of his performance in *The Master of Ballantrae*.

Filming began in Naples sometime during the winter and the scenes that were "supposed to be taking place in summer heat were shot between flurries of snow falling from a black sky."

Flynn played the part of a Don Juan-like figure who introduces a younger Don Juan to the tactics of swordsmanship and love. Gina was Francesca, a temperamental beauty who marries Renzo (Flynn) at the end of the story.

The Australian star contributed fifty percent of the capital needed to realize *Crossed Swords* and Gina received 30,000,0000 lire ($48,000) for the eight weeks' work with Flynn. Her salary, however, jumped tremendously the following year and she became "one of the world's most highly paid actresses," commanding about $100,000 per picture.

Because Gina is such a responsible actress, teaming her with Flynn wasn't the best of ideas. The latter was infamous for his late entries and for his indulgences in alcohol and sex. For Gina, work was work and her behavior was impeccable anywhere she went with or without her husband. She "felt no sexual attraction to Flynn, and this bothered him. She was cool and distant and Flynn insisted she, like Olivia de Havilland, was something of a professional virgin." Gina's attitude led Flynn to label her "Lollofrigida," not a gentleman's comment.

Gina's lady-like remarks about him indicated that he was easy to get along with and that she enjoyed the picture with him.

As shooting progressed Flynn came down with hepatitis and was hospitalized. When producer Barry Mahon came to see him one day, he asked the nurse about Flynn's condition. "He probably won't live till morning," she replied. A worried Mahon exclaimed: "But he can't die before morning. He's making a picture with Gina Lollobrigida."

When the film found its way into the can Milton Krims wasn't entirely happy with it, foreshadowing its lukewarm reviews. George Morris in *Errol Flynn* wrote that the only worthy elements in the film were the presence of Gina Lollobrigida and the excellent photography of Jack Cardiff. In Jack's words Gina was "the nicest girl I ever worked with, the most cooperative and the most beautiful to photograph."

# 77--Imperial Gina

With *Crossed Swords* and the upcoming *Bread, Love, and Dreams*, both American movie moguls and the public became very familiar with the Italian star who had already conquered the hearts of millions. As the American press began to give full coverage to Gina's artistic and private lives, audiences finally had the opportunity to learn more about the actress.

The first thing Americans had to learn was how to say her name, pronounced "low-low-bridge-id-ah." For Americans it wasn't as easy or smooth as Marilyn Monroe, Lana Turner or Rita Hayworth. "Lollobrigida" was rather long and foreign, which made it twice as difficult. But her name soon caught on with her popularity. Dr. Skofic once offered a humorous comment on the subject: "For the movies, it's a good name, no matter who else is in the picture, Gina gets a line for herself in the billing. It's not only for her talent but for space."

Easy or difficult, Gina refused to change her name. After all, "Lollobrigida" wasn't quite as unworkable as Walter Matasschanskaya-ski (Walter Matthau). Gina's husband's name was also somewhat of a problem for Americans; he was quoted as Mirko Skopic, Milko Skopie, Milko Shopic and Miklos Skofic instead of Milko Skofic.

In her first interviews in the US Gina admitted that even if she did come to America for pictures she'd hope soon to return to her native land, because she asserted she was very happy in her married life and felt contented with the mode of living in Italy. Nevertheless, with the passing of the years, Gina learned how to appreciate the American way of life in many respects. She loved American efficiency, contrary to the rather improvised atmosphere that reigned in Italian studios. For an actress who worked hard, made movies twelve months a year, memorized entire scripts in advance, responded immediately to her director's advice and devoted meticulous care to her costumes and make-up, an American studio was an ideal place to work. Unfortunately, Gina's talent was rather misused in her first two movies in Hollywood.

A peculiarity in Gina's character as a public figure is that she demands personal privacy. After her villa was built in the Appia Antica, no business acquaintance was allowed in and only a rare friend was permitted to enter by the large green gate that I faced for hours. If you try to intrude on her life, chances are that you get a chilly reception. For Gina work was work and play was for children. But life for her in the early Fifties wasn't just work; she enjoyed a tennis match with Milko and loved skiing, but didn't care for swimming.

Serious, dedicated and warm, Gina Lollobrigida came and conquered America. If the French and Italians had run out of adjectives, hyperboles and similes to describe her beauty, America had a fresh store of them to shower upon her. She was described as graceful, intelligent, a good friend, affectionate, and a woman of electrifying quintessential Mediterranean beauty. Columnist Mary Hasenclever, writing for the *L. A. Examiner*, elaborated on the above qualifications saying that "Gina Lollobrigida, the most beautiful actress in Italy, might have inspired a Venus by Titian or a winged angel by Botticelli;" while Ryan Water expressed in *Cue* that "Miss Lollobrigida is the greatest thing to come out of Italy since Columbus."

Once - in one of Gina's countless interviews for the American press - she was asked if she would like to play historical heroines. La Lollo responded to the idea of appearing as Cleopatra, but she knew that it was a picture that should be made in the States, "where the money and facilities to produce it properly exist. It is much too difficult a picture for us to undertake in Italy, though we have, of course, made some very fine historical productions. I still feel that you in America have all the techniques as well as the vast experience that is necessary for anything so unusual and costly." The actress would never have foreseen, when she said this way back in 1953, that ten years later 20th Century-Fox would move the doomed Lady Cleo from the Thames to the Tiber where, after innumerable curses, it was finally completed.

Moreover, Gina never dreamed that the role of Cleopatra would be offered to her while the intended star, Liz Taylor, lay sick in a London clinic.

\*\*\*

The Italian public, tired of an overdose of reality from the neorealists, was demanding something to distract them from their problems. The neorealist philosophy that the cinema wasn't just entertainment but a means of reflecting reality was rather depressing for the Italian working class. It was then that the realistic film took a new form with Renato Castellani's *Sotto il sole di Roma* (Under the Roman Sun, 1948). This new facet of the genre became known as rosy realism - reality seen through rose-colored glasses.

# 79--Imperial Gina

In this "neorelismo rosa" hunger and misfortune were more palatable, poor men were handsome, and penniless girls were glamorous. Gina, defending the movement, explained that "there is a new kind of realism today which the public likes very much - optimistic realism - with a reasonable amount of gaiety. To be realistic does not mean it has to be dreary."

*Due soldi di speranza* (Two Cents' Worth of Hope, 1952) was a more successful Castellani film, followed by Luigi Comencini's exceptional triumph with *Pane, amore e fantasia*, which sparked a series of films of the same ilk.

Comencini began his life in the cinema while he was still very young, doing film research together with Alberto Lattuada and Mario Ferrari, thus creating the foundation of what one day would be the Italian Cineteca. In the postwar period he directed some documentaries, receiving the "Silver Ribbon" for *Bambini in città* (Children in the City, 1946). In 1948 he directed his first film, *Proibito rubare* (It's Forbidden to Steal), which explored the theme of forsaken youth. Although he received an award for *Tutti a casa* (Everybody Go Home, 1961), the most treasured prize of his career was the popularity achieved with *Bread, Love, and Dreams*. (Some sources register the film as *Bread, Love, and Fantasy*.)

When Comencini wrote the script for the film together with Ettore Margadonna, they had actor Gino Cervi in mind, but the role was finally offered to Vittorio De Sica. Comencini considered la Lollo for the female lead because he had been much impressed with her in *Times Gone By* and realized that she was the ideal actress to play the role of Maria De Ritis, the very poor and simple yet vivacious peasant girl nicknamed Bersagliera. Actor Roberto Risso was cast as Pietro Stelluti, the "carabiniere" in love with Bersagliera.

The film was shot in a little village not very far from Rome near the ruins where the shrine of the Goddess of Fortune has lain for centuries. At the time Gina was there riding on her donkey and acting the village spitfire, the Goddess of Fortune was very unlucky; those who passed by the shrine didn't stop to pay her homage, but went a bit further towards the nearest village of Castel San Pietro Romano to see a new Roman goddess in flesh and blood, a young woman dressed in sexy rags. The pilgrims were pleased indeed with their findings.

The plot of the film is easy to follow. A marshal of the "carabinieri" (Italy's national police), Carotenuto (De Sica), is assigned to duty in the small village of Sagliena. This good-hearted Don Juan type bachelor falls madly in love with la Bersagliera. The girl, however, has given her heart to Stelluti, who is too shy to reciprocate her honest messages of love. Carotenuto is also much interested in Annarella (Marisa Merlini), the very reserved midwife. Because of a quarrel with the jealous Paoletta (Maria Pia Casilio) the innocent Bersagliera spends a night in jail.

Realizing that she shows no interest in his advances, Carotenuto decides to court the midwife. Meanwhile, Stelluti declares his love for Bersagliera and wants to marry her. Annarella, on the other hand, is reticent and doesn't want to give in to the marshal's advances. Finally, she reveals to him that, in reality, she has a child out of wedlock. The news doesn't change his feelings for her. The four characters in the story are at last paired, although Stelluti is about to be transferred and has to wait to tie the knot with Bersagliera.

Gina had depth and understanding of her role, and rendered a splendid performance; audiences cheered for la Bersagliera as she tangled with the police and pitied her during the tempestuous night in jail. They loved the cruelly poor hillbily girl as she travelled about on her donkey, prayed in the village church and kept herself morally clean. In other words, la Bersagliera embraced all the traits of the rosy neorealist protagonist. Barefoot with her rags and pigtails, "la Bersagliera incarnates the poverty theme of the film and, as such, she becomes the key to Comencini's generic experiment in realist comedy."

Reviewers in America considered Comencini's film "a first-rate movie." The picture was mostly well-received at numerous film festivals from Cannes to Buenos Aires, while Italian and foreign critics exhausted their list of glowing terminology on Gina's acting; she was great in her timing. The picture was acclaimed the year's best in Italy and on July 5, 1954 Gina was awarded the "Silver Ribbon", the Italian Oscar equivalent, presented by the Syndicate of Italian Film Journalists.

An exceptional honour was conferred on the actress by the National Association of Bersaglieri which, after a special assembly, nominated Lollobrigida "Vivandiera ad honorem" with the right to wear the plumed hat characteristic of the bravest and most audacious Italian soldiers. This high honour had been conferred upon two other women since the founding of the corps in 1836: a nun, decorated with a medal for distinguished conduct during World War I and the Princess of Piemonte, Maria José, the future Queen of Italy.

# 81--Imperial Gina

De Sica also received very laudable national and international reviews. "One of the most sensitive bits of acting you'll ever see comes when Vittorio De Sica, as the commanding officer of the 'carabinieri,' goes to Miss Lollobrigida's hovel and sees for himself the miserable poverty of her family. There is no one else in the scene, and it is all acting, no words."

De Sica also received very laudable national and international reviews. "One of the most sensitive bits of acting you'll ever see comes when Vittorio De Sica, as the comannding officer of the 'carabinieri,' goes to Miss Lollobrigida's hovel and sees for himself the miserable poverty of her family. There is no one else in the scene, and it is all acting, no words." Before leaving the wretched dwelling, De Sica puts 5,000 lire in the pocket of an old Bersagliera dress. When her mother (Vittoria Crispo) returns to her cramped shelter and, to her astonishment, finds the money she believes it to be a miracle. She looks at the statue of Sant'Antonio (Apostle of charity and patron of marriage) standing on an old piece of furniture and thanks him; she then runs to tell the villagers about the miracle. Later we see a table outside the house with Sant'Antonio's image on it while the village women line up and, upon paying a symbolic fee, make their wishes.

The smash hit of the film surprised Comencini, who didn't expect much from it. The excellent reviews, including those of Alberto Moravia and the movie critics of Milan, were something he hadn't anticipated. According to Gina, however, "Comencini signed [the film] but it was De Sica who directed it, as well as *Bread, Love, and Jealousy*. There were precise agreements, it wasn't a mystery, everybody knew it." Contrary to Gina's statement, a movie critic expressed that the "most skilled of film directors in Italy, Vittorio De Sica, does not direct *Bread, Love, and Dreams* but plays opposite Gina in the leading male role." Lollobrigida, on the other hand, sustained that in the film there was the humour, heart and spirit of De Sica. As a matter of fact, Gina revealed that she made the film because De Sica was in it and with his help she could create the tragicomic character of Bersagliera. She believed De Sica was the best director with whom she had worked to date, and described the film as "good, healthy, and amusing." Indeed, it was one of those pictures that sent you home feeling that your time and money had been well spent. Unfortunately, the Italian cinema never created another Bersagliera type role for Gina or any of her colleagues.

After *Bread, Love, and Dreams* Comencini was inspired to do the sequel *Pane, amore e gelosia* (Bread, Love, and Jealousy, 1954) with the same cast. Another installment of the series appeared in 1955 with Dino Risi's *Pane, amore e...* (Scandal in Sorrento) starring Sophia Loren.

\*\*\*

On September 14, 1954, the Skofics arrived in New York for the première of *Bread, Love, and Dreams* and a four-week visit to America appearing on television, in newsreels, and at parties, motion-picture premières and charity balls. New Yorkers had the opportunity to see the actress in triplicate: as a lavishly costumed medieval noblewoman opposite Flynn in *Crossed Swords* playing in New York theaters; in her earthy forte as a tattered gamin in *Bread, Love, and Dreams*; and as her glamorous self.

While Gina was in New York, Marilyn Monroe and Ava Gardner were also in town and photographers were kept busy darting from star to star. Gina, who has never been in a hair-pulling match with another actress, moved around in gorgeous gowns promoting her career. When newsmen asked her about her bust measurements for comparison with those of the American sex goddess, Gina replied that only her dressmaker knew the answer and that she wasn't interested in the subject. "Marilyn is Marilyn, and I am Gina." When asked for comments on the new "flat-chested look" Gina answered: "It is horrible." (She was wearing a full-busted gown designed by Schuberth, a top couturier. The gown had been specially created for her trip to America.)

On September 20th, the Paris Theater in New York was showing *Bread, Love, and Dreams* and "the much awaited Italian movie" was a hit in Beverly Hills at the Beverly Cannon Theater. The film was shown to a vast American audience and reviewed by most major newspapers and film magazines in the country. *Films and Filming* wrote that the picture "which firmly established la Lollo as an actress has been the much lauded *Pane, amore e fantasia*, which has just had its triumphant New York première, and broken all records of the year in Italy and France." Gina was sure that the movie was going to be a success in America simply because it was good and the character she played was simple and true.

# 83--Imperial Gina

Still behind the camera, but receiving complete coverage of her national and international social engagements, Gina Lollobrigida and her husband were received by President Eisenhower in the White House. The meeting was arranged by Spyros Skouras, president of 20th Century-Fox, a friend of Eisenhower's. Also present were Renato Gualion, president of Italian Film Export, and Italian motion picture producer Dino De Laurentiis. The American President told the actress that he was much interested in seeing Italy a "prosperous and happy nation."

After their visit with Eisenhower on Sunday, October 17, 1954, the couple flew back to Rome where a cheering, waving crowd of fans was waiting for Gina as she stepped out of the plane.

Lollobrigida, however, wasn't a woman who only dreamed of fame and money. During the Christmas holidays that same year, the actress was seen consoling a wailing child at a Christmas social event in Piazza del Popolo where Italian movie stars distributed presents to poor children. Gina loves children, mainly babies. Once she declared that if she could, she'd like to bottle the smell of babies' fresh skin and use the fragrance as perfume.

\*\*\*

Gina Lollobrigida had made it. Nevertheless, the "maggiorata fisica" shadow still followed her and she had had as much as she could take of the avalanche of tributes to her bodice and its contents. True the press now talked as much about her acting, but if half of the remaining compliments had been directed at her talent, she'd have been more satisfied.

When the Skofics left New York the specter of Marilyn Monroe was there hanging albatrosslike about the remarkably Roman. American newspapermen had the habit of calling Gina the Italian version of la Monroe, but for the Subiaco girl, Marilyn was a pin-up and Gina was an actress. "I am not - how do you say it? - a 'maggiorata fisica.' No. No, no."

The year of 1954 led to a happy ending for the Skofics with their effective American trip. Now that the couple had returned to Europe the never tiring Gina was about to continue to make more films, accepting or declining scripts according to her interest. She had already refused Blasetti's *Our Times*, and Antonioni's *The Lady Without Camelias* and was willing to proceed crossing parts that offered little acting potential. Gina was in a position to ask for higher salaries and a say in her leading men, a prerogative she exercised in 1958 with *Imperial Venus*.

Meanwhile, away from the cameras, Gina and Milko led a happy life in their apartment in Rome; the villa in the Appia Antica was still a dream. Dr. Skofic played the role of the careful husband guiding his wife in her career. The handsome doctor (who had a physique of Tyrone Power) was also an ambitious man and enjoyed the cinema world. However, he wasn't a Huston or De Sica and wasn't able to create parts for Gina, but he did serve as her closest advisor.

When Milko Skofic gave up his job as a physician to watch over his wife's interests - he refused to settle down in Pittsburgh where he was offered an excellent position - a few people in the industry made things difficult for the Skofics. Once when Milko came to see Gina on the set someone called out "good evening, Mr. Lollo." Gina wasn't amused. "It was an insulting thing to say," she complained.

In the early Sixties when Dr. Skofic was no longer her impresario, he became a publisher of medical books. La Maison Salani in Florence helped him in his career change. His plans, however, differed from what life presented him. "One day," he said while still working as his wife's manager, "Gina will retire and I shall return to medicine and specialize, I hope, in children's diseases." Contrary to what one might have expected, the doctor wasn't unhappy with the way things turned out to be, and was very successful as a publisher of first class literature. Gina was proud of him.

During the Fifties, whenever talking to the world press, Gina's husband usually offered remarks with a good sense of humor. Like Gina, he spoke English fairly well and there was no communication problem. On one certain occasion, he told an American columnist that when they got married, Gina was a "little actress" and he was a "big doctor. Now she is big actress and I am little doctor. And when fans send her candy I eat it." Dr. Skofic also acted as his wife's photographer, taking her pictures on Fifth Avenue and at the top of the Empire State Building during their visit to New York.

***

On August 16, 1954 *Time* magazine featured Gina on the cover and gave full coverage to her life up to the filming of *Bread, Love, and Dreams*. This was the period when Hollywood luminaries Kirk

Douglas, Claudette Colbert, Linda Darnell, Shelley Winters and other stars attracted the paparazzi in the famous Via Veneto. The latter, then married to Vittorio Gassman, gave birth to a baby girl named Vittoria Gina Gassman.

Miss Winters chose Gina for her daughter's middle name to honor her grandmother and because "Gina Lollobrigida is also one of the most beautiful women I've ever seen."

Three months after Gina was featured on the cover of *Time*, she reappeared on the front of *Life*, which carried a detailed description of her wardrobe consisting of 300 dresses, all of them Italian-made by Rome's Emiglio Schuberth.

With such a large collection of summer coats, cocktail dresses, stoles, raincoats, suits, etc... the actress was having difficulty requesting her maid to bring her a particular dress. Gina worked out a precise chart of her elegant wardrobe. Using her excellent drawing skill she spent three days sketching, numbering and describing each piece, easily identifying what the maid should bring upon request.

Naturally, with the passing of the years, her clothes collection went through constant renewal and her list of items kept growing. A generous woman, Gina always chose what looked better on her and gave other pieces to her sisters. She wore some of them only on a few occasions. Back in 1954 Gina had 75 pairs of shoes to complement the 300 outfits. The actress also kept 15 beautifully leather bound scrapbooks containing newspaper clippings on her, and had 300 fruit trees in her backyard.

The Skofics also had a fire-engine red Lancia Aurelia and thousands of dollars as part of their growing treasure.

Gina Lollobrigida is an avid art collector. After the couple moved to their villa in the mid-Fifties, Gina had quite a fabulous collection of Greek and Etruscan pieces. An archaeology lover, Gina couldn't have chosen a better place for a villa than the old Appian Way, totally surrounded by ancient Roman ruins. Gina once said she'd like to dig in her own backyard to find old art objects because she preferred to find them instead of getting them cleaned up already in some antique shops. One day unexpectedly, she unearthed two gold earrings in her garden, the site of a Roman tomb.

Towards the end of 1955 after the last still of *Trapeze* was taken in Paris, Tony Curtis and his lovely wife Janet Leigh drove to Rome where they visited with the Skofics. The famous American couple were impressed with the villa and its surroundings, so well described

in Janet's captivating autobiography, *There Really Was a Hollywood.*
I quote with the actress' permission: "The mansion was grandly, yet
tastefully, appointed, but the grounds were spectacular. We explored
the entire premises. If a property adjoined the Appian Way, you are
not permitted to build closer than eight hundred feet, so the view
remained constant. They had tombs and urn altars in residence.
Often when they dug to plant a tree or whatever, they would find
bones, or earrings, or playthings, or utensils. The unexpected
discoveries were kept very hush-hush for if the government verified
these plums, the spot would immediately become a national museum.
With my thirst for history I was a kid in a candy store. All this in
your own backyard!" (I should have done some digging myself while I
was there with the hope of meeting the actress. A little treasure
hunting could have been an exciting experience.)

When the Skofics built their villa upon that hidden wealth, the
whole thing cost three hundred million lire. I wonder how much it is
worth today.

Throughout these three decades the villa has been visited by
celebrities and described in detail in Italian and international magazines. The villa was portrayed by an Italian columnist as Sicilian-baro-
que, and is surrounded by all sorts of trees and plants; there is also a
tennis court with a lawn from Argentina. The whole building consists
of two living rooms, a dining room, and a kitchen downstairs, with
three bedrooms and five bathrooms. All the rooms in this pink villa
are spacious and high ceilinged, elegantly furnished with antiques.
One living room displays a fourteenth century Venetian cut-glass
chandelier. The decor, from room to room, presents Spanish and
Chinese flavor with a mixture of baroque and classic; a few pieces of
furniture belong to the Ming Dynasty. There are Etruscan vases and
busts including a bronze sculptured head of Milko Jr. at age one or
two by mamma Lollobrigida. Sharing wall space with paintings by
Manet are engraved photos of Elizabeth Taylor, John Wayne, Jimmy
Carter and other well-known figures of the political, artistic and show
business worlds.

By 1963 the rich Skofics had about half a million dollars in
paintings and art objects; their villa had become one treasure built
upon another. As the place had become a target for professional
burglars, constant vigilance was necessary. Mario, the gardener who
was a former "carabiniere," Roberto, the chauffeur, and three German
shepherds joined a night shift policeman in keeping a sharp eye pulled

for intruders. Gina used to lock her bedroom at night and they had special care for their Milko Jr. In the early Sixties the Skofics also owned a house in Switzerland, an apartment in Paris, a Rolls-Royce, a Jaguar and a Fiat.

Away from fans and the paparazzi who could easily monitor the family's movements in their former address in Via Sambucuccio d'Alando, the Skofics planned to lead a quiet and private life in their villa. It wasn't so for a while. Obscene phone calls were frequent and profanity was sometimes scribbled on the green entrance gate by men who held the actress as a sex symbol.

\*\*\*

Gina Lollobrigida considered Gérard Philipe one of the top European actors and was looking forward to playing opposite him in Siodmak's *Le grand jeu* (Flesh and the Woman, 1954). Gina's desire to work again with her partner from *Fanfan la Tulipe* and *Beauties of the Night"* remained unfulfilled; she was paired instead with Jean-Claude Pascal.

Robert Siodmak (born in Tennessee to German-Jewish parents) was a well-known director with a film career spanning Germany, France and the US, where he had a prolific Hollywood period between 1941-1951. His psychological thrillers achieved great popularity with audiences and in 1946 he received his only Oscar for *The Killers*, an adaptation from the classic short story by Hemingway.

Unfortunately, Siodmak's remake of Feyder's work was a disaster; in fact, it was one of the films Gina said she'd rather forget.

Despite the difficulties of using her own voice for the first time in a French film, Gina also faced the arduous task of performing a double role. Pierre Martel (Jean-Claude), is involved in a love triangle with two women who are identical but have different voices. In the 1934 version, Marie Bell played the two women, but in one of the roles her voice was dubbed by another actress.

Involving passion, fate and self-destruction, the plot was considered absurd and conventional in both versions, receiving rather poor reviews in France and Italy. The picture's failure, however, didn't hinder Gina's career. The film was shown simultaneously with *Bread, Love, and Dreams* at the Cannes Film Festival and it was a wonderful day for the actress, who signed 1610 autographs in two hours. One unfortunate French policeman was less jubilant; his effort to control the pressing crowd sent him to the hospital with two broken ribs.

Gina was more fortunate with her next picture, *La romana*, co-starring Daniel Gélin. The cast also included two other fine actors, Franco Fabrizi and Raymond Pellegrin. Pina Piovani played the domineering mother who exploits her daughter's beauty to make fast money, forcing her to pose nude for a Roman artist. Adriana (Gina), the daughter, doesn't sympathize much with the calling, but money is short. (The only posing session in the film exposes a seated Adriana with her back stripped from the waist up to the camera.)

This last participation of Gina in a Ponti-De Laurentiis production featured her again as a woman of loose morals, but victim of circumstance. The part penned by Alberto Moravia offered the actress the opportunity to show her ability in emotional roles; she presented a laudable performance.

The production had been eagerly awaited at the Lido in the 1954 Venice Film Festival where Gina was received by a screaming mob of fans. To get to the cinema foyer Gina had to be lifted up by the police and carried above the heads of her delirious admirers, who chanted "la Lollo, la Lollo." The producer tried to fight his way through the crowd with clenched fists and clipped himself on the jaw. Gina and her entourage made it through the cinema's heavy doors which were immediately locked by the police. In the confusion, Milko was left outside and when the police opened the door to let him in, they shooed out a few fans who had squeezed into the foyer. The in-and-out tragicomedy continued, for the producer was pushed out by mistake with the fans. By that time Gina's nerves were frayed.

"I'd rather die than to put up with that again," said a sobbing Gina.

Despite the critics' appraisal of Gina's efforts to present a fine performance, the film was unsuccessful at the festival.

For the deception of both Gina and director Luigi Zampa, *La romana* received no awards. "But in fairness to Gina," wrote *Films and Filming*, "it should be pointed out that the failure of *La romana*, was due more to director Zampa, author Moravia, and co-star Daniel Gélin than to Gina herself, who revealed in her portrayal that she has learned a lot about acting since her last Moravia role, *La provinciale*."

Over and above, the 1954 Venice Film Festival wasn't an easy one. Celebrated directors, remarkable films, and distinguished stars had joined Gina and Zampa for the competition. That was the year

of Visconti's *Senso*, a film that has been considered the most important work of the post-neorealists; Kurosawa's *The Seven Samurai*,
Castellani's *Romeo and Juliet*, Hitchcock's *Rear Window*, Fellini's *La
strada*, Kazan's *On The Waterfront*, and Becker's *Honour Among
Thieves*. It was *Romeo and Juliet* starring Laurence Harvey and Susan
Shantal that was awarded the "Golden Lion". A film critic, however,
declared that with *La romana* Gina had moved "into the Dietrich-Stan-
wyck, Garbo-Crawford-Swanson class thus bestowing a very special
award upon Lollobrigida.

One day, while talking with Goffredo Lombardi, one of the
producers of *Bread, Love, and Dreams*, Comencini erroneously referred
to the film as *Pane, amore e gelosia* (Bread, Love, and Jealousy),
unwittingly giving birth to the second "bread and love" film. Because
the first had been a tremendous hit, Comencini thought that a second
picture was in order.

Gina was reluctant to play the same role a second time. On
principle, she didn't like to exploit the source of a previous achieve-
ment, and accepted the role only at De Sica's insistence. Her fee to
ride the donkey again was $96,000, twice what she had earned for
acting with the poor beast the first time. (The film was released in
America as *Frisky*.)

The second Bersagliera episode begins the day after Stelluti has
left the village and Carotenuto is making preparations to marry
Annarella. La Bersagliera now does the housework for the marshal,
thus setting herself up as the target for gossip-loving villagers and
inciting jealousy in the midwife Annarella. Stelluti returns and breaks
up with la Bersagliera, while Annarella finds herself in the arms of her
child's father who has come back to settle things with her.

Meanwhile, a group of strolling players comes to the village and
la Bersagliera plans to join them. Finally, Stelluti makes peace with
his girl, Annarella marries her man, and Carotenuto is consoled by the
new midwife.

"Bread-and-love" type films weren't expensive to make and yielded
handsome sums, 1.3 billion lire each. *Bread, Love, and Jealousy* took
second place among the Italian films shown in 1955; it lost to Mario
Camerini's *Ulysses*.

In early April 1955, the Los Angeles Times carried a column with
the following heading: GINA SUES PRODUCER - GINA TIRED OF
ACTING WITH DONKEY, SHE SAYS. Goffredo Lombardo had in
mind a third episode with la Bersagliera which the actress flatly

refused to do. The producer criticized Gina, saying that he was tired of her mounting demands for money. It was reported that Gina wanted exorbitant pay: $800,000. The actress retorted that Lombardo's criticism was "unfair" and that she never had any intention of doing a third Bersagliera film. Gina sued the producer. "I don't want a single centesimo for myself," she said. "Any wages I collect I will turn over to the Old Actor's and Actresses' Home." Dino Risi's *Pane, amore e...* (Scandal in Sorrento, 1955) kept Vittorio De Sica in the role of the simpatico but ridiculous marshal, transferred the setting to the resort town of Sorrento (Naples) and substituted Sophia Loren for Lollobrigida in the new character of Caramela. La Loren was still a relative newcomer in the cinema. She had already appeared in several films as an extra and in minor roles but it wasn't until De Sica's *Gold of Naples* (1954) as a volatile Neapolitan shopkeeper that she got international attention. It was once said that Gina gave Sophia the chance of her life by refusing the third "bread-and-love" film.

Both De Sica and Sophia are from Naples and the formula worked, but the first two films were more applauded and are considered among Gina's best ten movies, while the third is excluded from Sophia's top ten. The Illustrated History of the Cinema quotes *Pane, amore e....* as the most successful of the three, but my findings produced the opposite conclusion. La Loren's first outstanding screen effort was *The Key* (1958).

Another intended Lollobrigida part that was passed on to Sophia was Jean Negulesco's *Boy on a Dolphin* (1957). The script was offered to Gina during a dinner party in Paris in 1956, but Gina was already thinking of having a bambino and had future commitments to do *Trapeze* and *The Hunchback of Notre Dame.*

The happy outcome of the "bread-and-love" chemistry gave origin to other similar productions. Luis Lucia's *Pane, amore e Andalucía* (1958) starred Vittorio De Sica with Carmen Sevilla and Franco Brusati directed *Pane e cioccolata* (Bread and Chocolate, 1974), a mature socio-comedy with a touch of rosy realism in its plot.

In her discussion of the "bread-and-love" films, Millicent Marcus writes in *Italian Film in the Light of Neorealism* that "what is significant" in Brusati's work is the "omission of 'amore' from the rosy realists' conventional tripartite titles. Though love is by no means absent from his plot, the title's failure to include it may be Brusati's attempt to distance himself from his rosy predecessors' bias toward the overly sentimental." The film, set in Switzerland, exposed the plight of an Italian emigrant worker.

Following his *Pane, amore e...* Dino Rissi expanded the rosy realism horizon with *Poveri ma belli* (Poor But Beautiful Boys, 1956), *Belle ma povere* (Beautiful But Poor Girls, 1957) and *Poveri milionari* (Poor Millionaires, 1959). Stars Alberto Sordi, Vittorio Gassman and Marisa Allasio (the Italian version of Jayne Mansfield) were the major and popular protagonists of Risi's films.

***

Much had happened to Gina since the Lollobrigidas left Subiaco in 1944. In the last ten years, her life had drastically changed from sketching GIs for survival to becoming the world's most celebrated movie star. Just in the first four years of the new decade she had been toasted in Rome, Paris, London, New York and Buenos Aires. In the Fifties the Italian press unceasingly praised Gina's accomplishments, particularly her success in art and her beauty and grace in foreign lands. Consequently, her triumphs echoed in mountainous Subiaco, moving the town to invite Gina to a homecoming at her convenience. The high regard Gina's fellow countrymen had for her was reflected in the newspaper *Il Popolo* sometime in November 1954, expressing Subiaco's genuine delight in her talents, her outstanding artistic originality and the fact that she had swept the whole world off its feet.

The following December, *Il Giornale d'Italia* announced that although Gina's acceptance of the invitation wasn't official, it was "sicurissima" (certain); the town's Council would pay Gina a visit and set the date for her to receive the applause and a parchment from Subiaco.

There's an old saying that if you want to see the Pope you have to go to Rome. Well, on January 6, 1955 Subiaco came to Rome to see Gina Lollobrigida. The visit took place at her Roman residence where she graciously received Mayor Scarpellini (who offered her the parchment) and her old teacher, Professor Tiglié. There was a committee of some twelve members including the Mayor and the Professor, who in their two hour visit, exchanged precious memories related to Gina's childhood, her schoolmates, close friends and the town's priest. The delegation also expressed Subiaco's desire to have Gina live with the townspeople again - at least for one day.

The committee were very impressed with Gina's simplicity and warmth. The touching encounter was reported by columnist Mario Lollobrigida (a relative, I wonder?), and RAI (Radio televisione Italiana) recorded the event which was broadcast on Saturday, January 8 at 8:15 p.m. Gina's visit to her birthplace, however, didn't materialize until seventeen years later.

Gina's impression on her fellow-citizens has also been shared with relatives, close friends and columnists, who have chatted with the actress either in her villa or on studio sets.

They have usually found the actress to be tender to her husband and warm to her friends, but sometimes temperamental and angry when dealing with greedy promoters, fly-by-night producers and inept moviemakers. With the latter, Gina always fought to have things her way. In the early Sixties, Lowell E. Redelings, after interviewing Lollobrigida for *The Citizen-News*, concluded that the actress is "a sincere, straight-forward, outspoken person. She looks you squarely in the eyes, says what she thinks, and is not 'acting' while being interviewed, as it is the case with so many stars."

Gina Lollobrigida has always been known as a an authentic person very well aware of who she is and where she stands in her private, social, and artistic lives; flattery with her gets you nowhere. The actress "puts on no airs," testified reporter Kendis Rochlen while visiting Gina at the George V Hotel in Paris during the shooting of *The Hunchback of Notre Dame*.

Gina proved to be "friendly, intelligent and downright amusing and honest." Upon referring to herself the actress told Miss Rochlen: "I am me - Gina. The success, the work, all the attention haven't changed me. I am still Gina."

It was probably this sincerity in an environment as difficult as show business that gave Gina the reputation of being cold or indifferent to others. She often slipped into social events quietly, rather than making a grand entrance like a movie queen. She'd politely greet the host or hostess and then move on, accepting only soft drinks.

Another Lollobrigida trait that may have caused her to be less appreciated by some fellow-workers was her habit of referring to herself in the third person: "I am the expert on Lollobrigida," or "This is the last time Gina does a picture in two different languages." Since the actress knows "what's good for Gina," her make-up and hairdos looked impeccable in her films. If Gina thought something would look better on her or a particular scene would cause more impact on the audience if shot from a different angle, she was prepared to fight to have her own way. Gina's imposing manner, however, has a "raison d'être." She decided to take over Gina after her hair was burned and she escaped a bad eye injury due to a make-up accident. Complete professional courses in hairstyling and cosmetics turned Lollobrigida into an expert on Gina.

Unfortunately, this same self-reliance on her numerous abilities and talents has made her an island unto herself. But she isn't cold; she's a professional who has always known what she wanted.

With her laudable performances in the two "love-and-bread" films and *La romana*, Gina closed 1954 with triumph. La Bersagliera then discarded her tattered dress and got rid of the donkey to enter the stage as an opera singer wearing a handsome wardrobe in Robert Z. Leonard's *La donna più bella del mondo* (Beautiful But Dangerous), at risk of confusing it with the Jean Simmons movie of 1952.

Gina took two important steps with the new film: she co-produced it with Maleno Malenotti and Gina herself chose the director. She had first thought of Mario Costa and then Mario Soldati with whom she had worked at the beginning of her career, but finally opted for the former MGM director, the man responsible for the multi-Oscar-winning musical *The Great Ziegfeld*.

After his last work for Metro, *Her Twelve Men* (1954), Leonard left Hollywood for Italy to direct Gina in her new film, the biography of the Italian soprano Lina Cavalieri, a picture destined to reach a box-office peak. With *Beautiful But Dangerous* Gina had the opportunity to prove that she could also dance and sing, contrary to what Ponti thought of Italian actresses in general.

La Cavalieri (1874-1944), "the supreme testimony of Venus on earth," claimed Gabriel D'Annunzio, was a famous belle from Trastevere killed in an air raid. She started her career as a chorus girl, moved on to opera and finally made it to L'Opera de Paris as a superb performer. She was heard in many important European cities and in America she was applauded at the Metropolitan Opera House (1906-1907), the Manhattan Opera House (1908-1909) and the Chicago Opera Co. (1915-1916).

D'Annunzio's Venus of the turn of the century had a very tumultuous life with extraordinary adventures and many stormy love-affairs. (This aspect of the girl from Trastevere had nothing in common with her paisana from Subiaco.) During her tempestuous life, la Cavalieri had three husbands "and more boyfriends than the obituary writers could count after her death." Gina, however, never had any of that. Once she obtained her Italian divorce in 1971, she had a few candidates for a second marriage, including the famous surgeon Dr. Christian Barnard, but she dismissed all rumors of marriage.

The biographical screenplay melodrama begins at a small local theater where Lina has to substitute for her aging mother. It's during a performance that she meets Prince Sergio Bariatine (Vittorio Gassman), who protects her from a rude spectator. The nobleman gives her some money and a ring.

Meanwhile, Lina's mother dies, the girl sells the ring, and starts taking lessons from maestro Doria, who falls in love with her. When Lina feels ready to face a good audience she goes to Paris, and together with her friend Carmela, finds a position at El Dorado, where she does the Can-Can. There she is rivaled by ravishing and jealous Manolita (Tamara Lees) and a fencing duel between the two follows at dawn at the Bois de Boulogne. Lina's victory contributes to her popularity, and she becomes the darling of Parisians, with the doors of famous music-halls open to her.

Years pass and the Prince, unable to recognize her while visiting Paris, bets his stable of horses that he'll have the glamorous performer up in his room in no time. La Cavalieri, not aware of the bet, agrees to see the Prince, but upon finding out the scheme, runs away.

Following this episode, Lina announces her engagement to the tenor Silvani. Filled with anger and jealousy, maestro Doria murders his rival during a performance of *Tosca*.

Suspicion falls upon the Prince and Lina leaves France to avoid the scandal. During a Russian tour she meets the innocent Prince and they decide to get married.

Aside from the beauty attributed to Lina Cavalieri, there are biographical similarities to be drawn between the two stars. Lollobrigida, like la Cavalieri, began her career as a "C" level performer and reached stardom through hard effort.

Both belles took singing lessons from maestros who fell desperately in love with them. Even though Gina didn't realize her dream of becoming a professional soprano lirico, she too had her first victory in Paris, and like Lina, became the queen of Parisians and an international figure.

# 95--Imperial Gina

The film puzzled the critics and the public who weren't aware of Gina's singing talent. *Le Figaro* and *The New York Times* carried columns saying "too bad it's not Gina singing."

They should have read the credits more carefully. Gina sang her parts in the film including *Vissi d'Arte*, an aria from *Tosca*. "I sang with Mario del Monaco," protested Gina furiously upon reading that "it was a marvelous voice and what a pity she's dubbed." Even the great Maria Callas asked Gina: "Was that you really singing?"

Like the two "bread-and-love" films, *Beautiful But Dangerous* conquered Italy and achieved immense popularity abroad. It also took first place among all Italian motion pictures shown between 1955-1956, and it remains as one of Lollobrigida's most memorable efforts. Gina, then known as "Gina nazionale" (national Gina), was awarded the "David di Donatello" as the best actress of the year.

Suing and counter suing has remained a part of Gina's life during these four decades. (The actress' most recent lawsuit for defamation involved an Italian magazine in May of 1986.) Once *Beautiful But Dangerous* had been released in Europe, the International News Service and its Rome Bureau Chief Mike Chinigo distributed photographs of the actress doing the Can-Can in one of the scenes in the picture. When one of these photographs appeared on the cover of an Italian magazine, nobles and plebeians clearly noticed that the flash bulbs used in making the photographs had penetrated her lingerie, thus giving the appearance that Gina was wearing transparent panties. The Skofics were furious and Gina in vain tried to obtain the negatives. Dr. Skofic was very irritated with the whole thing and went to see Chinigo at his office to protect his wife's reputation. The visit wasn't a peaceful one; the accused sued the doctor for violation of domicile and uttering intimidating threats. Gina, always willing to fight to the end, sued Chinigo for "indecent fabrication," defamation of character and insults via telephone. Gina won the suit.

Following the Skofics-Chinigo case, Lina Cavalieri's only surviving brother, signor Oreste, was filling a petition in Rome for the destruction of the original film of his sister's life and for a ban on any copies of the picture. La Cavalieri's brother charged that the love scenes in the movie were "false, insulting and repugnant." He also charged that the shots of Gina doing the Can-Can were "impudent liberties" and that the duel scene where Lollobrigida, clad in black tights, slashes off Manolita's petticoat never happened. He added that the seduction episode in Paris where the Prince bets his stable of horses that he will get la Cavalieri to his bedroom was fictitious.

According to *Jours de France* (No. 44, 1955), a duel really took place between Lina and the belle Otero. In the film, however, the feud is with the popular singer Manolita, la Cavalieri's rival. The scene, I recall, was my favorite.

While signor Oreste was raising hell in Rome, Gina was literally swinging in Paris with Burt Lancaster and Tony Curtis for Sir Carrol Reed's *Trapeze*, and, although she had not yet received any legal papers, she'd have to defend herself in court upon returning to Rome.

As if Mike Chinigo and Lina's brother hadn't been enough trouble to Gina as she was working almost simultaneously in Rome and Paris, the Catholic Legion of Decency in Boston heaped further problems upon *Beautiful But Dangerous*. As the story went, Howard Hughes, still holding Gina under "contract," asked 20th Century-Fox to handle the picture in America while RKO theaters would show it. Hughes was in Boston to negotiate the première when he heard rumors that the picture was too hot to pass local censorship.

At any rate, the film, which was supposed to have its première on December 6, 1956 at RKO Keith Memorial Theater, was cancelled because it couldn't win the approval of the Catholic Legion. *Beautiful But Dangerous* was then rescheduled for showing in January 1957, but was again cancelled at the last moment because it couldn't get a Code Seal. It was only a year later that the film was okayed after a love scene had been cut. The unfair Legion made it clear that cuts or no cuts, the picture would be rated "C."

When Gina was in America in February of 1958 to see the final arrangements for the showing of the movie, the press asked about the Hughes-Gina "contract." "DOES LOLLO OWN LOLLO OR DOES HUGHES?" Gina openly declared that she was a free woman under no contract with anyone. A Hughes representative, conspicuously present when Gina met the Boston press, declared the contrary - that not only was she under contract with Hughes but that the option for her future services was also up to the boss. Then he added that as soon as Gina reached the coast, the Hollywood movie czar planned to discuss some pictures with her.

Gina hadn't done a single film for Hughes, and she had no plan to. In fact, she already had future engagements planned in Europe including *Solomon and Sheba* which she was co-producing with Edward Small and Arthur Hornblow. The veteran King Vidor would direct the picture and Tyrone Power would play opposite her as King Solomon.

***

On August 14, 1955, the 1200 persons who attended the benefit for polio victims at the Summer Sporting Club in Monte Carlo had the privilege to listen to Gina sing. The event, entitled "Nuit d'Aout 1955" (August Evening 1955), had been organized by Prince Rainier III who received the best "who's who" from Paris, New York, London, Rome and other major capitals in his tiny Mediterranean principality.

The V.I.P. list included, among other celebrities, Silvana Mangano, Françoise Arnould, Andre Cayat, Mary Pickford, Vittorio De Sica, Marlene Dietrich, Martine Carol and Kirk Douglas as master of ceremonies, sporting a red beard for his forthcoming role as Vincent van Gogh. Also in the audience were the former Queen Narriman of Egypt, Elsa Maxwell, Lady Docker, Christian Dior, Jack Warner and the Princess of Bourbon-Bavaria.

For the members of the hard-to-please international set, New York sent Darvas and Julia whom, in those days, Americans considered the best dancers then making $10,000 a week in Las Vegas; Paris sent them George Matson, a showman from the Lido. The Italian cinema was represented by Gina Lollobrigida.

American journalist Elsa Maxwell observed that the public of the Summer Sporting Club was the most famous and surfeit in the world. "Poor Gina," exclaimed Maxwell, "she is going to a dangerous soirée!" La Lollo, despite her understandable apprehension, provoked enormous applause when she appeared wearing a form-hugging white satin evening gown. Her performance revolved around three songs: *Amoureuse*, a 1900 waltz, *I Will Never Know*, and *Anima e core* in Neapolitan, receiving bravos and appreciative whistles.

Singing for Gina wasn't anything new, but since she was aware of the demanding public she was going to face, she rehearsed for two weeks prior to the event with Marlene Dietrich's accompanist, Jean Pierre Landreau. Kirk Douglas was another star attraction. Speaking in French, English and Italian, and drawing on his talent and humour, he easily melted the audience.

***

It wasn't until the mid-Fifties that the press tried to work up a feud between Gina Lollobrigida and the new rising star Sophia Loren. While Italians debated over the fame of their "Gina nazionale" versus la Loren's, Hollywood wanted to know who had the larger bustline. Gina disliked the columnists' attitude. Questions concerning popularity relative to bust measurements weren't welcome, but Gina usually answered them with diplomacy. Sophia was also the victim of reporters who placed her in a delicate position by comparing her to Gina.

The much publicized rivalry between them had awakened in me the desire to know more about the newcomer, and I went to several of her films, but la Loren didn't have the same magic that la Lollo had upon me.

Born in Pozzuoli (1934), a poor suburb of Naples, Sophia Loren saw her career to some extent parallel that of Gina. Both actresses came out of obscurity via small roles in rather poor movies, modelling jobs and beauty contests. Sophia was only fourteen when she won a competition, but Gina had already appeared in a few films when she ran for Miss Italy. Both girls were impoverished during the war, even though Gina had never been poor before. The two actresses played sultry peasant girls, ladies, prostitutes and Moravian women; they worked for famous national and international directors and co-starred with the most popular leading men.

On the other hand, their careers were also very different from each other in at least two important points. While Sophia had a mother pushing her daughter into show business, Gina walked in the hard way. The Neapolitan girl was still a teenager when she met Carlo Ponti, who opened many doors for his future wife. Gina's husband had no influence in the movie world.

In 1957 signor Ponti got Sophia a part in Stanley Kramer's *The Pride and the Passion* starring Cary Grant and Frank Sinatra. The role had been offered to Ava Gardner (who refused it), and Sophia accepted the part for $25,000. Then Carlo Ponti took Sophia to Hollywood where she did *Houseboat* the following year with Cary Grant.

Sophia's fame, according to some critics, lay not as much as an actress but as a rival to Gina. I disagree. There's no doubt that the supposed rivalry contributed to her popularity, but with time signora Ponti became a fine actress in her own sphere and deserves proper credit for her screen achievements.

# 99--Imperial Gina

The early Sixties saw the climax of Sophia's career. Nevertheless, she was no match for Gina, who had been at the top for nearly a decade. Films like *Two Women* (1961), for which la Loren received an Oscar, *Yesterday, Today, Tomorow* (1963) and *Marriage Italian Style* (1964) were among her most successful experiences. (In 1963 Sophia was ahead of Gina only in terms of magazine covers.) The critics, however, consider Sophia's most interesting role that of her own mother in the TV adaptation of her autobiography *Sophia: Living and Loving.*

Sophia's and Gina's fans were clearly divided in Italy and the same thing was about to happen throughout the rest of the world. Sophia's followers at home thought Gina was too cold; la Bersagliera's admirers said la Loren put too much stress on sex. In Paris, a poet said he could never write a verse from merely gazing at a portrait of Sophia, but for Gina he could write one with love even though he had never met her and probably never would.

Columnist Henry Thody described Gina with the following words: "Gina Lollobrigida is a natural beauty. Madonna-like features on a perfectly shaped body. With those large, liquid, luminous eyes, that mass of tousled dark auburn hair, those dresses which make no efforts to change her natural figure Gina Lollobrigida has the look of a smoky explosive vamp."

In her autobiography, Sophia relates the supposed rivalry between her and Gina. In the words of Mrs. Ponti, it was in 1954 that the issue first arose. She was in London with other Italian actresses - including Gina - for an Italian Film Festival. Sophia was still struggling with English and "questions and answers were rather mismatched" by the British press, claimed Sophia. The inconsiderate journalists asked the star: "Who's bigger, you or Lollo?" Sophia has no recollection of her exact answer, "but surely it was nothing like what appeared in the papers the next day. Under a banner headline, 'WHY LOLLO WAS MAD WITH ME,' there ran a verbatim interview in which I was quoted as saying that just because I was bustier than Gina that was no reason for her to be furious with me. Of course, I had said no such thing; I wasn't aware that Gina even knew who I was."

"Sophia is a very pretty girl but she cannot threaten me because she is incapable of playing my roles," read a quote released as Gina's by the press years after *Pane, amore e...* Sophia was then noted as saying: "Her personality is limited. She is good as a peasant but incapable of playing a lady." In the summer of 1960 an American magazine carried an article on Gina and wrote that "the only unforgivable sin is to mistake her [Gina] for Sophia Loren." Then it cited la Lollo as saying: "We are as different as a fine race horse and a goat." Probably neither of the two actresses referred to each other in the above terms, for both were victims of the vicious press in its constant search for sensationalism.

Much to the columnists' and paparazzi's disappointment back in the Fifties and Sixties, there was neither a public nor a private feud between the two stars. When Gina was about to go to Hollywood in 1959, a reporter asked her: "Now that you will be able to work in Hollywood are you planning to extend your battle with Loren to the international field?" Gina diplomatically pretended not to understand his question. "What do you mean - battle? What does that word mean?" After the journalist went through some synonyms for "battle" trying to explain his point, Gina said: "You are a very dangerous man. It is a difficult question. I have to have two weeks to think about it. My English is not so good. You must learn to speak Italian to ask me such difficult things."

On another occasion, frustrated reporters again came up with a goose egg. "I know the journalists have tried to work up a feud between us," Gina told them and concluded emphatically:" It is not true. There is no feud."

Once in a press conference with Metro agents and executives, Gina stated that "Miss Loren and I admire each other very much." Her words left those present unsure what to think. In the early Eighties when asked about Sophia's one-month jail sentence for supposed tax irregularities in Italy, Gina played it cool: "I really don't know too much about it. I live in New York now."

While in Madrid for a TV interview in early spring of 1989, Gina was asked if there really had been in the past a rivalry between her and Sophia. "We are two colleagues and respect each other mutually," declared la Lollo.

Throughout the five years that I worked on this book, I had the opportunity to talk about Gina and Sophia with people of all ages and nationalities. While those of my generation or older know both actresses very well, young adults are more familiar with Sophia Loren and know little about Gina and therefore assume that the latter was less popular. What they don't realize is that Sophia continued making movies until the late Seventies while Gina left show business in 1972, her last most popular film - *Buona Sera Mrs. Campbell* - dating back to 1968. Had Gina prolonged her screen appearances she'd also be well-known by a generation younger than mine.

One curiosity I stumbled upon regarding the two Italian stars is that some people become confused about which actress made which film. Despite the outstanding difference in their physical appearance, the mismatching does happen. A British friend phoned me one day to tell me that there was a Gina movie on TV and that he was sure I'd like to watch it. I ran to the "tube" and turned it on only to find Marcello Mastroianni with Sophia Loren in *Marriage Italian Style*.

A more humorous incident happened in a bizarre comparison when an old Japanese gentleman told me he had seen Gina Lollobrigida in *Bitter Rice* which in reality was a Silvana Mangano film. Perhaps the rice distracted him.

The rivalry mostly created by the press may have caused some of the confusion for many moviegoers, mainly for those not very familiar with the two actresses. Adding to that, there's also the fact that after Gina had starred in the first two "bread-and-love" films, Sophia did the third sequel. Both ladies did a movie on the author of Don Quixote even though their parts were as different as night and day. In *The Young Rebel* (1966) Gina played the part of a noble courtesan while Sophia was Dulcinea in *Man of La Mancha* (1972). Thus, even though Gina and Sophia have completely different lives and rarely cross paths, their careers and rise to stardom have repeatedly become intertwined. Had Comencini thought of making "Bread, Love and Rivalry" starring the two actresses, the film would have yielded box-office receipts far more extensive than the three "bread-and-love" pictures put together.

\*\*\*

In early 1955, Gina Lollobrigida announced that if it would be of service to anybody, she'd gladly take the role of good will ambassador to Soviet Premier Malenkov. She had already met President Eisenhower and General Juan Domingo Perón and had received the admiration of Yugoslav President Tito.

Later that year, Roman newspapers disclosed that either Gina or Sophia would head a delegation of film stars to a visit on Moscow for the Italian Film Festival in early September.

Sophia was probably unknown by the Soviets, but Gina's *Opera Fans* had been the first Italian movie distributed in the USSR after the war and chances were that at least her name was familiar behind the Iron Curtain. However, it was six years before Gina actually made it to the Kremlin for the Moscow Film Festival on July 15th, 1961.

Once an Italian school boy was asked who Gina Lollobrigida was. He answered, Italy; and because she was Italy, Gina usually represented her country on official visits to kings, queens, presidents and dictators. Why was a daughter from Subiaco received by dignitaries? There were those who protested that if Italy was to be represented officially, President Luigi Einaudi or Prime Minister Scelba should be sent. Novelist Alberto Moravia or industrial reformer Adriano Olivetti were also excellent candidates to act as Italy's agents. If the nation's emissary was to be an illustrious beauty there were other gorgeous Italian signorine with princely titles. The opposition felt the actress was the right representative just for film festivals; nevertheless, like the school boy said, Gina Lollobrigida was Italy and magistrates welcomed her.

La Lollo was genuine, never-ending Italy; the actress was straightforward, gracious and a fighter; she could speak and act for the young and the old, the flower-girl in the market and the aristocrat; there were "Ginas" all over Italy's churches and art galleries. La Lollo had become a national treasure and nobody better than she could mirror Italy.

A former art student, Gina was also the special envoy from the Goddess of Arts to 27 surrealists, romantics, abstractists, neorealists and other "ists" who for five hours on four consecutive days gathered in April 1955 at the Grande Hotel in Milan to portray Gina on their canvases. After Gina had first appeared in the movies she was dubbed "The Woman of Painters," and had she lived during the Renaissance she'd have inspired a Raphael or a Michelangelo.

Among the 27 artists that flocked to the hotel were the romantic Mario Togliani, the surrealists Gianpaolo and Thea Catalani, and the abstract Gianni Frassati painting side by side with some of the best-known names in Italian modern art, such as Bruno Cassinari, Giuseppe Migneco, Aligi Sassu and Silvio Consadori. All the works were displayed at a Milan art gallery.

Years later Gina was the subject of acclaimed Russian artist Glasunov, considered the Ievtushenko of Soviet painting. Glasunov had already created on canvas some of the great figures of the Italian show business: Fellini, Visconti and la Cardinale, but the Russian Da Vinci wasn't satisfied until he did Gina's portrait. (When his works were exhibited in Italy the new school of Botticellis acclaimed him a Russian genius.)

In 1955, Gina also took off to England for the Italian Film Festival. Britain's Elizabeth II and the International Movie Queen met at a royal cinema showing in London, followed by a dinner party at the Italian Embassy with the presence of Queen Elizabeth, Princess Margaret and the Duke of Edinburgh. At the event Her Majesty expressed to Gina her love for Italian movies because they are closer to reality. The first Italian film the Queen had ever seen was De Sica's *Bicycle Thieves*.

The highlight of the festival was Gina's *Bread, Love, and Dreams*. When the festivities were over, Gina left London for another film engagement, but her beauty stayed behind perpetuated in a work by Jacob Epstein, sculptor.

***

Nineteen fifty-six saw Gina's battle cry to Howard Hughes with her first American film made in Europe. *Trapeze* was Lollobrigida's evidence to Hughes that she could star freely in an American motion picture despite his insistence that she was under contract with him. *Beat the Devil* and *Crossed Swords* were co-productions (Italy/USA and Britain/Italy/USA respectively), but this Hecht-Hill-Lancaster film was of American origin distributed by United Artists.

To direct *Trapeze* the production chose one of the most respected British professionals, Sir Carol Reed, whose pictures won top Film Academy Awards in England between 1947 and 1949. "The Fallen Idol" (1948) and *The Third Man* (1950), two of Reed's most successful films, were nominated for the Oscar but it was for his musical *Oliver* (1968) that he took the coveted statuette home.

For circus lovers, *Trapeze* may well be an unforgettable movie for its remarkable action sequences and the fine screenplay by James R. Webb. "To give you an idea of how important we considered the script," explained Burt Lancaster, "we spent $100,000 for the writing of *Trapeze*. Among the people who worked on the script, based on Max Catto's *The Killing Frost*, are Sam Taylor who wrote *Sabrina*, James Jones (*From Here to Eternity*), Ernie Lehman (*Executive Suite*) and Ruth and Augustus Goets. Pretty good names, and a lot of money to spend before you ever get into production." Speaking of money,

Gina's salary was $160,000 (ten years earlier she had made $3.30 a day) for her actual work in the film plus all expenses for her and her husband for five months in Paris.

Hecht and Lancaster had met Gina previously to discuss *Vera Cruz* (1954) starring Gary Cooper and Burt Lancaster. The film, directed by Robert Aldrich, was one of the first hit Westerns in SuperScope but there was no outstanding female parts in it. Gina was already a big name and small roles - unless they were good ones - would probably digress her career. *Vera Cruz*, without Lollobrigida, co-starred Denise Darcel playing a French countess and introduced Spanish star Sarita Montiel as a mestiza village girl. The cast also included Ernest Borgnine, Cesar Romero and Charles Bronson.

When Hecht came to see Gina about *Trapeze*, he also mentioned the possibilities of classic roles such as Lady Macbeth and asked Gina what she'd like to make next. "I'd like to make a million dollars American," said Gina who was already worth that much. Hecht switched the conversation to a new focus.

Besides Lollobrigida and Lancaster, *Trapeze* also starred Tony Curtis, and featured Katy Jurado and Thomas Gomez. This was the first Lancaster film that provided a very familiar background to the actor, whose experience dated back to the early Thirties at the Kay Brothers Circus when he and his friend Nick worked for three dollars a week plus board. There's no doubt that Lancaster's understanding of circus life contributed to his excellent performance, rendering him and the film the 1956 Berlin Film Festival award.

Mike Ribble (Lancaster), plays an aerial acrobat injured in a fall and can no longer perform dangerous tricks. Tino Orsini (Tony Curtis), a trapeze neophyte, tempts Mike to coach him in the risky triple somersault and serve as his "catcher" (which Mike could easily do if his pride allowed him).

Against Mike's wishes, Lola (Gina), an opportunistic acrobat, joins Tino to successfully perform a nearly impossible trick without a net. When a love triangle develops Mike wants to leave the circus and Lola, who is apparently in love with Tino, chooses to follow Mike, her old flame.

The production hired the Ringling Brothers' Eddie Ward as a technical adviser for the film and as Lancaster's stuntman. The actor, however, just brushed up on his trapeze tricks and brilliantly executed most of his own stunts. Tony and Gina had to spend some time on a trapeze in order to learn enough tricks to minimize the need for actual acrobats. Lollobrigida had a special outdoor gym set up at her villa in Rome, where Lancaster's friend Eddie Ward tutored her. While in Paris she obtained a trapeze and had it rigged to her hotel suite. Gina went through considerable physical exertion for her role; she preferred the trampoline, as the trapeze made her dizzy. She also spent months learning the ropes. One scene required her to swing out in a horizontal line and then drop on the net 65 feet below. After doing the take three times, she was speechless.

Photos of the actress rehearsing at her villa and in the Cirque d'Hiver where all the circus scenes were filmed, indicate that she was willing to give her best to the performance, simply saying: "Remember, I am an actress, not just a body!" And thinking about every single detail for the perfection of her part, Gina designed her own wardrobe for the picture.

On the first day that Gina reported to the 100-year-old Cirque d'Hiver, snakes, elephants and lions didn't bother her; she even adopted a baby lion born during the four months' shooting. But she became apprehensive when Lancaster showed her the trapeze some 65 feet above her head. He failed to explain that there would be a net underneath, and therefore nothing to fear. Indicating the rope ladder they had to climb, Lancaster followed Gina up to the platform. When she looked down at the acrobats in the sawdust arena, she said: "To do this sort of act for a living one must be crazy." Lancaster countered acrobatics was precisely what he used to do. "Then you, too, must be crazy," she said, and promptly requested a double. One had of course already been hired for the flying scenes. Gina, nevertheless, demonstrated grit and courage in performing some of her own stunts.

Besides being courageous Gina also revealed her good sense of humour. Louis Berg, movie editor of *This Week Magazine*, was visiting the set when he was introduced to Zavatta, France's favorite clown. Even in that baggy suit there was something very distinctive about the clown's costume. Gina had rehearsed his gestures for four hours and fooled even her director. After Mr. Berg had seen the actress in her clown outfit, he watched her sail through the air singing on her trapeze. "She's a much nicer person on the set than in public," he concluded.

The day was beautiful and sunny in Paris when Gina Lollobrigida paraded behind six dappled circus horses together with Burt Lancaster and Tony Curtis; the entire cast of *Trapeze* joined the promotional event. According to Janet Leigh, who was pulled up on Tony's float, "there were over two thousand fans lining the streets." Tony and Burt were wearing the white tights and colorful capes in which they appeared in the film. Mexican star Katy Jurado, in pink tights, rode on Gina's float where the latter stood sporting a pink full-skirted dress instead of the pink tights she wore in the picture. The French and the tourists shouted "Gina" and didn't stop clicking their cameras.

The parade lasted for two hours, returning to the Cirque D'Hiver where it had begun.

The event was covered by *Life* photographer Milton Greene, who had also been assigned to cover the Curtises, his friends.

The Paris circus parade was also scheduled for the summer of 1956 in the United States as an advance promotion for the film. The cast would tour Chicago, New York and four other major cities via two special railroad cars on a transcontinental train.

Gina admired her *Trapeze* co-stars. "Tony - he is young manhood," she said. "I can understand why he is great love of those American Roberto-stocking girls." Later she explained that "Roberto-stocking" was the Italian version of bobby-soxer. Of Lancaster she declared: "That man has strength. I catch my breath when I think of him."

Discussing sex and her role in the film, Gina made it clear that for her, sex had gone far enough. "The public will think I can only love, that I cannot do the great dramatics. I am going to give them something to remember me by besides my figure. In *Trapeze* there is plenty of myself here for the public to look at. But I've got dramatics, too. A little something for everybody."

Indeed Gina had "a little something for everybody." Her beauty was exposed "in a CinemaScope screen filled with the most garish of color," while the Mike-Tino-Lola love triangle demanded her talent as an actress.

After the film was released in Europe and America, Gina's attractive short poodle cut became the craze for women who went to see their beauticians for a la Lollo "do," much like young ladies around the world flocked to salons for a "Di" (after Princess Diana) haircut in the early 1980's.

It's interesting to note that several Lollobrigida pictures caused a dichotomy of positive and negative reaction among the public; positive for her admirers and negative for those who abided by the strict censorship of the Fifties that governed the minds of puritans. Such was the case with the parish priest, Arturo Giovenzana of a small northern Italian town near Milan, who declared posters showing Gina in tights as scandalous. A theater owner, Angelo Bajetta, battled unsuccessfully in defense of Gina's right to be advertised in tights. The police ripped down the posters. The furious theater owner swore to sue the police and the town's Mayor, Aristide Cavalli. This was the second time Gina was persecuted by pious Catholic Church representatives. (The first censure came from the over zealous Catholic Legion of Decency in Boston over *Beautiful But Dangerous*, and the third with another priest concerning the anticipated *Solomon and Sheba*.)

Another controversy related to *Trapeze* arose when too little was shown of Gina. A still from the picture depicting Gina's torso clad in a tank top was completely retouched as ordered by the Johnston office, which enforced Hollywood's production code of self-censorship.

The original stills showed "too much cleavage," pronounced the censors. Gina angrily notified United Artists through her lawyers that "retouched pictures of her must not be released."

Now it was the actress who was furious when she saw the photos splashed across front pages. La Lollo wanted her public to see her exactly as she was with no more or no fewer clothes than she was wearing. She demanded the truth and not a false projection of her looks. In the past she had sued press agents who had published altered pictures of her wearing too little to the point of defamation. She was now defending the same principle from another perspective. She found the whole thing ridiculous, stating that the retouched photos made her look like Gary Cooper or Frank Sinatra with her head. There were some twenty negatives involved, and Gina had control over them as recorded in her contract. The real Lollo photo was then published in most newspapers next to the retouched one and they made quite a contrast.

(A poster of the original photograph welcomes visitors at the entrance hall of my apartment in Kyoto.)

*Trapeze* was Gina's first English speaking picture that achieved much success wherever it was shown; in August 1956 the movie was into its second run in four L.A. theaters: Orpheum, Hollywood, Uptown and Loyola, and was favorably rated by the critics. With *Trapeze* Gina's popularity increased in America while in Belgium, France, Italy and Germany, she was voted the most popular actress for four consecutive years, receiving more than 600 letters a day, usually addressed to "the world's most beautiful woman," "Gina Lola" or simply Gina Lollobrigida. (The Portuguese, consciously or unconsciously, refer to the actress as Gina Lola probably because of her role as "Lola" in *Trapeze*.)

\*\*\*

The Boulogne-Billancourt Studios (Paris) was Gina's next assignment. The rewarding experience of working at the Cirque d'Hiver with *Trapeze* was about to repeat itself with Dellanoy's version of Victor Hugo's historic novel *Notre Dame de Paris* (1831). "During the production stages, producers Robert and Raymond Hakim tried mightily and unsuccessfully to obtain from RKO the rights to the title by which the Hugo story is always called. Since RKO, however, refused to relinquish its copyright the Hakims called their version *The Hunchback of Paris* (and *Notre Dame de Paris* in France) until RKO suddenly reversed its original decision, releasing its grip on the title *The Hunchback of Notre Dame*."

The new adaptation of Hugo's novel was the sixth to be made in the history of the cinema. The story of the grotesque bellringer and the beautiful gypsy Esmeralda was first taken to the screen as *Esmeralda* (1906, French), followed by a remake, *Notre Dame de Paris* (1911, French) by Albert Capellani, who was well known for adapting the classics. *Darling of Paris* (1917, US, starring Theda Bara) preceded Irving Thalberg's *The Hunchback of Notre Dame* (1923) for Universal. The film remains a classic piece of silent film-making with Lon Chaney's performance as Quasimodo. RKO's version (1939), directed by William Dieterle, paired Charles Laughton and beautiful red-haired Irish actress Maureen O'Hara in the most brilliant screen interpretation of the work to date. (In the early Eighties Michael Tuchner directed a new version of Hugo's classic for TV viewers. The production was filmed at Pinewood Studios starring Anthony Hopkins and Lesley-Anne Down.)

Delannoy's *Hunchback* began shooting in April 1956 by Paris Film Productions at Boulogne-Billancourt Studios, where a five meter replica of the original 70 meter Notre Dame was built. The superb cathedral that took two centuries to be completed was reproduced in three brief months.

This was Gina's fifth motion picture worth her talent since *Bread, Love, and Dreams*; the screenplay by Jean Aurenche and Jacques Prévert provided Gina with a part as weighty as that of her leading man, Anthony Quinn. The film was shot in English and French, forcing Gina to burn the midnight oil studying her parts in these two foreign languages. The American script hadn't been finished yet, a frustrating experience for the actress, who was on the set without knowing what she was supposed to say until it was time to go before the camera. Each scene had to be shot twice, so it was like making two different films at once. "This is the last time Gina does a picture in two different languages," vowed Lollobrigida. Every night she returned to her hotel dead tired after a day's work in the studio, but she loved what she was doing and sensed that when she worked, she lived.

Known as a perfectionist, Gina, still on the set of the French studio, was very angry over the guitarist who was to accompany her in a song and dance in one of the scenes. The producer told her the musician was "the best guitarist in Europe; for you only the best." But Gina wasn't pleased with him. She affirmed that the producer "may know what is good, but he does not know what is good for Gina. Only Gina knows."

The audience's first glimpse of the fiery gypsy Esmeralda on the screen is during the gay Festival of the Fools where a bewitching barefooted Gina, wearing a low-cut, long red gypsy gown appears briefly searching for her goat. Esmeralda is admired by soldiers, beggars, and common folk, but mainly by the jealous and alchemist priest Claude Frollo (Alain Cuny), who orders Quasimodo to kidnap her. She's saved by Captain Phoebus (Jean Danet), who is stabbed by Frollo during an amorous encounter of the captain with the gypsy girl.

Esmeralda is accused of the crime while Phoebus recovers from the wound. She's sentenced to death for witchcraft and attempted murder when Quasimodo saves her from the hangman and keeps her in the belltower. The King sends his soldiers to fetch Esmeralda while the angered beggars storm the cathedral.

In the clash between the two forces, she is fatally wounded by an arrow. Quasimodo, who had learned to love her, kills the obsessed alchemist and goes to die near Esmeralda. (In Thalberg's version, Esmeralda and Captain Phoebus are reunited after the bellringer's death; public and press alike were pleased with the happy ending.)

The film had its Paris première on December 27, 1956. The love of the French for Gina, however, wasn't enough to control her disappointment when Victor Hugo received top billing for the event.

The author's name was up in lights twice the size of those allotted to both Lollobrigida and her leading man.

Despite some poor reviews here and there, the film was approved by the critics and received saturation booking in New York. The exquisite atmosphere of the Festival of the Fools, the private gathering of beggars and thieves in the Court of Miracles and the attack of Notre Dame by the enraged beggars rendered much of the pageantry in the picture.

With *The Hunchback of Notre Dame*, la Lollo completed her 34th film, an overwhelming output in ten years. Her medieval gypsy performance heightened her fame to the point that it was difficult for her to walk in the streets. One day in Paris, she had to be protected by the police and find quick refuge in a bar to escape the mob of fans that followed her. "The public reaction, it is very nice," Gina told columnist Kendis Rochlen for the *Mirror-News* at her suite at the George V Hotel. "But when I go out to walk on the street, the people keep following me so that I have to keep crossing back and forth in order to stay ahead of them. Sometimes I feel tired when all the people look at me. So I jump into a taxi and go home. But, of course, it's nice to be admired."

While working for Delannoy, "temperamental, friendly, intelligent and downright amusing Lollo" was interviewed for the *Citizen-News* via an international phone call directly from Hollywood. The actress mentioned her desire to visit the Mecca of the cinema in the future. Anthony Quinn had told her so much about the Land of Make-Believe that she felt she already knew the Grauman's Chinese Theater. During the interview Gina compared the rather small and inadequate European studios and dressing-rooms with the spacious sound stages and lavish Hollywood facilities that she had heard about. As a matter of fact, Gina's dressing-room was so tiny that it would have sent any American star into a temper tantrum. However, Gina made it clear that there was one thing which she liked about making films in Europe. "My photographs can remain without retouching, and I can appear to the public exactly as I am by nature."

One of Gina's concerns about going to Hollywood was that she was afraid the studios would make her over, and the last thing she wanted was to be a replica of another actress.

European studios let Gina do her own make-up and hair. "I am an expert on Lollobrigida. I do my own eyes and lips and hair before I leave the hotel for the studio. There are no complaints - they look all right." On another occasion she exclaimed: I've known myself for a long time, so who is a better judge about what is good for me?"

When Darryl Zanuck went to pay a visit to a self-asserted Lollobrigida in Paris, the American producer was more than eager to know who Gina's agent was because he had never seen so much publicity for one actress before. When Gina told him she had none, he couldn't believe it. The simple truth was that "agent Lollobrigida" worked hard to obtain the best deals for "actress Lollobrigida," who usually got a six-figure salary or a handsome percentage of the picture, which she usually invested in Rome real estate.

With her mission over in Paris, Gina thought it was time to stop flying, filming and suing for a while and concentrate her attention on adding a little someone to the family; and with that thought in mind, she stayed away from the studios until 1958.

*\*\**

The New Year had begun with joyful news for the press and Gina's fans all over the world. On January 3, 1957, Mrs. Skofic announced she was expecting a bambino. She hoped it would be a girl and decided on the name Luigia, after her own; a son would receive the father's name.

Meanwhile, when Gina was four months pregnant, she left with her husband for Austria. Unlike the American sex goddess Marilyn Monroe and glamorous Lana Turner, who loved keeping directors and audiences waiting for hours, Lollobrigida has always exhibited perfect British-like punctuality in her professional and social engagements. It was therefore most unusual that the Skofics arrived seven hours late in Vienna where 800 fans had been waiting since 5:00 p.m. to welcome her. The Austrian Artists Federation paced back and fourth in the actress' hotel while the police force that had been called to hold the crowd was at a loss for something official to do.

It was midnight when the Skofics checked into unobtrusive lodgings to avoid the crowd and the press; Gina wasn't feeling up to a confrontation with a swarm of people. When photographers and press discovered them, Gina had already retired to bed and Dr. Skofic wasn't in the best of moods after their ride from Munich. As a result, the City Council withdrew its invitation for the couple to a visit to the Town Hall, pronouncing that Dr. Skofic's statements the previous night were "not compatible with the dignity of a freely elected city government."

A series of misunderstandings seemed to have been the cause of the conflict. The following day Gina's husband apologized and promised that he and his wife would do their best to make peace with Vienna. Lollobrigida also said she was very sorry for the whole thing. According to reporters, the actress was scheduled to sing in the city for a benefit program to aid needy artists. Gina's story, however, was that the program had been planned without her being notified. She also explained that she had avoided the crushing welcome because of her pregnancy. The Viennese accepted the couple's apologies and the incident passed with no lingering resentment.

On March 24, a day after the Skofics' Cinderella-like arrival, the Italian Embassy gave a reception for them. Gina, looking beautiful but rather tired, said: "I am extremely sorry that a number of misunderstandings have occurred which prevented my husband and me from seeing the Mayor and Vice-Mayor. The misunderstandings were partly caused by the fact that we were not adequately informed about preparations made for our stay here. For instance, we did not know that tickets had already been sold for a concert tomorrow and especially that I was to sing there. This I cannot do because I am not feeling well."

At the artists' benefit concert Gina gave a brief speech to her local admirers who were thrilled to see the star. The walls shook with applause indicating that all had been forgiven and that her fans were just as true as ever. The press, on the other hand, was still discontent with the couple because they let Gina's fans down by checking into another hotel.

\*\*\*

From the moment the Skofics returned to Rome after their contretemps in Vienna, the Italian press and the unceasing paparazzi were restless, for they couldn't sleep until they knew where and when the stork would deliver the much expected bambino. Italians were more anxious about their "Gina nazionale's" big day than with government affairs or current events in general. Gina hoped for a very peaceful birth and avoided revealing details of the coming milestone.

# 113–Imperial Gina

Italian papers provoked Gina by saying that she was going to have the baby in Lausanne to avoid the fuss of the press, her fans, the paparazzi and the Roman summer heat. The false statement brought no reaction from the Skofics; were they to deny the reports, chances were that the news predators would conclude that the baby would probably then be born in Rome, or somewhere else in Italy. But where?

Gina's silence let the press to deduce that the Skofics were indeed Switzerland-bound. The newspapers then insolently wondered how she dared have the child anywhere but Italy. Gina wisely remained mute. Media men tried in vain to bribe her faithful gardener, and two weeks before the birth the paparazzi swarmed around the villa. The stork was but two days from the Appian Way and nobody knew where it would finally land. *Il Giornale D'Italia* interviewed the couple in their villa on the 25 of July, publishing the following day all possible details concerning the arrival of Milko Jr. or Luigia. During the visit, however, the reporters noticed a small suitcase containing infant's clothing and deduced that the national baby would make his or her entrée away from the villa.

"La mamma nazionale" was very well prepared for delivery. During the last few months of her pregnancy Gina methodically did muscular and respiratory exercises to ease the childbirth, read several books on childbearing and pediatrics, thus becoming perfectly aware of the signs, pains and pleasure of bringing a new being into the world.

On Sunday the 27 of July, the Skofics left their villa through an exit invisible to the paparazzi and drove across the field to avoid reporters. Four hours after their arrival at the American Salvator Mundi nursing home, Gina Lollobrigida gave birth to a dark-haired, 6-pound 11-ounce boy in the same suite in which Ingrid Bergman had her twins in 1952. The happy event that followed a period of heightened suspense had finally arrived. Andrea Milko Jr. had become a reality and Milko Sr., like most fathers, was overjoyed to have a baby boy. Gina was radiant with the bambino and forgot that she had hoped for a Luigia. She had given birth to a perfect child and that was all that mattered.

While the Roman gods reveled over the occasion, Dr. Skofic maintained an air of pragmatism, reminding everyone that little Milko was a baby just like any other who required feeding and changing every hour. The actress' fans seemed to have a different view. Gina's bambino was their "Caesar" and Gina their Roman goddess. Mamma and bambino "nazionale" were featured on the covers of numerous national and international magazines and made headlines in major newspapers around the globe.

The week following the birth, Gina received 3,000 letters including telegrams from Martine Carol, Christian-Jaque, and the Laurence Oliviers, among others. A fan wrote: "For us this is the national baby; Caroline of Monaco's isn't important." The declaration referred to the birth of Caroline Luise Marguerite born to Grace Kelly on January 23 of the same year.

The malicious press didn't let up after Milko Jr. was born, soon publishing columns suggesting that Sophia Loren envied Gina for having a boy. Sophia on her way back to Rome after a month's vacation in Switzerland, declared she didn't know that Gina had given birth to a baby, and when asked if she had any congratulations for Gina she asked the reporter "Why?" When she was told the news she simply stated: "I wish I could be her. I love much the babies, you know?"

Returning to the Appian Way was another ordeal the Skofics had to face. Knowing that the paparazzi would be haunting the clinic and the villa, they left secretly in their luxurious black Mercedes six days after the baby was born. Grandmother Skofic, a very superstitious lady, asked Gina not to return home on a Friday, so the couple left the clinic on August 2 at midnight, arriving at their villa on Saturday. Rosvita, a young German nurse chosen from hundreds of European girls, was impatiently awaiting the arrival of the famous child. Gina's motherly instinct, however, left her reluctant for anybody to touch her baby; she wanted to change him herself that night.

Papà Milko wanted to touch his son but was afraid, like many neophyte parents, that the infant would break.

The atmosphere at the villa had turned into the ideal set for a Comencini "Bread, Love and Diapers." The baby's parents had acquired three cradles, three prams and hundreds of toys. Gina had coveted an 18th-century lacquered wood cradle with a 20 million lire price tag, exorbitant even for a wealthy actress. The cradle which ultimately found its way into the villa, however, was brass with a white-laced canopy. Presents sent by friends and well-wishers filled the rooms. Some of the offerings came from a handicapped child and two prisoners. Gina was touched. Paramount Pictures wanted to give the baby a present and asked Gina what she'd like; she responded that she'd prefer the studio donate a certain amount to charity.

Paramount sent 500,000 lire for poliomyelitis research. Little Milko also received 300 diapers; Gina reserved a few of them as remembrances and gave the rest to the poor. Gina herself had made much of the baby's clothing with the patience of a dedicated seamstress.

Nourishing little Milko turned out to be a painful experience for Gina, who had hired 25-five-year old Celeste Cornici, mother of three children, to be the baby's wet nurse. Poor Gina hated the thought that every three hours her baby was being fed and during that time she yearned to be a mother like any other. Blessed were the phone calls that helped take her mind off the feeding. On August 14 Milko Jr. was baptized in a small church in Sabaudia on the Mediterranean coast. Spyros Skouras, president of 20th Century-Fox, was the boy's godfather. A Roman lady, Gina's close friend and counsellor, was the godmother; the woman, mamma of six and expecting another, asked the Skofics not to mention her name in the papers. Gina, who was radiantly happy, wanted her offspring to become either an atomic scientist or a doctor like his father. One thing for sure; she wanted her son to have a normal childhood going to school with boys of his own age and not a gypsy life like hers, hopping from one movie studio to another across countries.

Life for the Skofics was joyful at their roomy villa after all the hurly-burly that reigned over them before and after the baby was born. The Lollobrigidas and the Skofics loved the already chubby eight month-old bambino who gobbled up everything "like a small pig," as Gina confided to Louella Parsons, who interviewed her over the phone straight from Beverly Hills. Gina was a loving and tender mother and Milko Jr. was the apple of her eye. The family was seldom separated; Gina called her husband Mike, he in turn addressed her as Bimba, and both of them called their baby Bambolo and later Milketto.

Being an actress and a mother wouldn't be an easy job, and Gina was apprehensive about playing both roles simultaneously. She soon realized that her public was waiting and that money had been invested in new pictures; it was time to face the reality of work again. With her new roles in films, she'd have to teach Bambolo not to cry when she was away working. With the presence of the new family member, Gina would have to make fewer pictures in order to have time to stay with the child.

She worked out a kind of compromise with herself to be an actress by day and a mother by night.

\*\*\*

When Gina arrived in London ten weeks after the baby's birth, her 22-inch waist and 35-inch hips clearly indicated that bearing the child had not altered her sirenish figure. The Skofics told London papers that they wished to have another baby, and Gina was quoted saying that childbearing was "easier than making a good picture."

For the two-day visit with Princess Margaret, la Lollo brought three suitcases with 11 dresses and 25 pairs of shoes. Gina was in London with other celebrities including Italy's Mr. Cinema - Vittorio De Sica, for the opening of the New National Film Theater. While in the British capital, the couple stayed at the Savoy where Sophia Loren was due later that week.

While mamma Lollobrigida was away from the Appia Antica, Milko Jr. was being watched by Rosvita, the nurse, their chauffeur, Roberto, the gardener, and Djali, Tweldy, and Elck - Gina's three German shepherds trained in Munich.

Starring in a British film was part of Gina's plan for the future, but the question was raised whether British studios could afford her. Gina didn't think so much about the money as long as it was the right picture, either with Sir Carol Reed, for example, or Sir Laurence Olivier. Gina's wish to work in England was realized in 1963 in Basil Dearden's *Woman of Straw* opposite Sean Connery.

\*\*\*

The last two years of the Fifties were busy ones for Gina. She went before the camera for *Anna di Brooklyn* (Fast and Sexy) and *La Loi* (Where the Hot Wind Blows), both in 1958, and signed for three Hollywood pictures the following year: one for United Artists, *Solomon and Sheba*, and two for MGM, *Never So Few*, and *Go Naked in the World*. Not wanting to be always separated from her son, she had the boy with her on international sets whenever possible.

The beginning of 1958 took Gina on a Washington tour where she was guided by Republican Peter Rodino. On her way to America, she stopped over in Paris where there was a showing of the latest fashions, and Gina was branded as being out of date. The new line for women had flattened the bust, taken a hike in the hemline and loosened the belt. "Gina's bust is too much and it is badly displayed," opined the papers. By "badly displayed" they meant that her breasts weren't set off by long tucks which was de rigueur that year. Columnists also insisted that Gina's dress was much too long, only 13 inches from the ground, when it should have been 18. The belt was too tight emphasizing her waist. Belts that year were worn loose to define the front of the dress.

Always considered one of the best dressed women in Italy, Gina was indifferent to the criticism and dismissed the Paris incident. It was neither the first nor the last time the actress was criticized for not following pro tempore fashions.

Suing also returned to Gina's life within a few months after the birth of Milko Jr.. This time the lawsuit involved a vermouth firm in Turin which used her image for publicity purpose without her permission. She collected $1,600 in damages.

***

Produced by Milko Skofic, *Anna di Brooklyn* was an amusing treatment of a restless Italian woman (Gina) who returns to her native town after many years in America to become the townspeople's focus of attention. Directed by Carlo Lastricati, the film had the supervision of Vittorio De Sica.

As it happened with *Bread, Love, and Dreams*, De Sica also directed the picture but wanted no credit for it. Reginald Denham signed the English version, but again there was the strong presence of the Italian director in the film. This was Gina's fourth picture with De Sica, and he worked very closely again with her.

Gina's exhausting experience of making the same picture in two versions was repeated. "I did *Notre Dame de Paris* in both French and English, and before the end of the day I would get all mixed up with the two languages. The reason for that is that the first scenes are spontaneous, and the second become mechanical." (The situation was unavoidable unless her voice was dubbed.) Nevertheless, Gina was very enthusiastic about the new film and hoped it'd be popular in the States where it was to be distributed by RKO.

Dale Robertson, Gina's leading man, felt the picture should have been entitled "An American in Rome" or "Innocent Abroad" since his relationship with the Italian crew and the actress wasn't the best.

"Gina and I didn't have any fights. Some fantastic stories were printed, including one that I showed up at the airport with a black eye she gave me. There was nothing like that. But I will say we didn't hit it off too well."

Unlike Gina's assertion about how well she was treated in Hollywood when she came a year later to film *Never So Few*, Dale declared: "Those Italian film people aren't the warmest in the world." The actor complained about not having a dressing room of his own, that nobody was waiting for him at the airport in Rome, and that they were using a different script from the one which he had agreed. The lack of consideration for movie stars from the Roman studio was new to the American newcomer, who was used to the Hollywood star treatment that European counterparts didn't expect in their own lands. Gina herself had gone through the same problem until she began demanding things her way. The American actor was furious. "But it does seem funny," he told reporters, "whenever a European star comes here, they get the finest suites, uniformed chauffeurs and the works. Over there, they don't even meet you at the plane."

Dale (Walter in *Dynasty*) also claimed that there were 4,300 stills taken for the picture, but only those where Gina looked her best were used. Furthermore, when the production started on billing, he was told that his name would appear 75 percent the size of Gina's, and Dale burned with anger, demanding a 90 percent type to which they finally agreed. After the billing episode, Dale said he wouldn't make another picture in Italy under the same circumstances.

Contrary to Dale's disappointing experience, Gina received red carpet treatment on her arrival at MGM on April 14, 1959 with a cocktail party thrown in the executives' suite of the Thalberg Building. When asked how she liked Hollywood, Gina stated: "Everyone was so friendly and everything was so well organized - it is good, working without waste." Knowingly or unknowingly Gina confirmed Dale's conviction.

Despite the actor's clashes with the Romans, *Fast and Sexy* found its way into the can without major problems and Gina Lollobrigida proved once again to be a top-notch comedienne. The film, the only one produced by her husband, received good reviews and Gina was awarded a "David di Donatello" for her performance.

\*\*\*

# 119–Imperial Gina

Sometime in 1986 I wrote to the Italian Cultural Center (Tokyo) requesting its director, signor Giorgio De Marchis, to include some of Gina's pictures in their annual film festival.  Unfortunately, the features had already been programmed and any late changes were practically impossible.  That was when my search for Gina's movies released on video started.  At present, my Lollo library houses many of her shows, including her second 1958 film, Jules Dassin's *La Loi.*

When the picture was first mentioned in American newspapers, it was entitled *The Law*, a straight translation from the French, but it was eventually released as *Where the Hot Wind Blows.*

Based on Roger Vailland's Gouncourt prize-winning novel about the fiery people of South Italy, *La Loi* "meanders around the subject of legalized immorality in small Italian village." Two powerful men, Matteo Brigante (Yves Montand) and Don Cesare (Pierre Brasseur), have control over the villagers, who respect the latter and fear the former.   The piquant and provocative offbeat tale swirls around Marietta (Gina), a tomboy-like woman who is victim of intrigue and jealousy, coveted by men, but smart enough to get what she wants.  A subplot involving a love affair between the married Lucrezia (Melina Mercouri) and Brigante's son, Francesco (Raf Mattioli), completes the script.

The establishing shot introduces a hot, languid day in a Southern Italian village by the sea.  Marietta's neighbors unintentionally listen to her beautiful singing as she shines Don Cesare's boots in the veranda facing the rustic village square.  With one hand inside a boot and a brush in the other, she plays with them jestingly.  The scene, masterfully performed, reveals the woman's character through facial expressions and body movements that go with her singing (Gina's own voice); she emanates a sensuality and innocence exposed in her large and lustrous almond-like eyes.  She's sexually ripe, but not for just anyone.  When Tonio (Paolo Stoppa), one of Don Cesare's servants tries to touch her legs in the boot-brushing scene, she vehemently fights him back.

Gina's sex appeal has always been a controversial subject, for the actress never tried to exploit it on the screen.  "Sex appeal I do not do on purpose, I do it sincerely.  I am always dressed in my pictures.  The expression on my face I don't know about.  I am always surprised when the censor says, 'too strong'."  Later in her career, Gina appeared in some films in risqué scenes wearing suggestive outfits (*Solomon and Sheba, The Dolls*) or mostly covered by a sheet (*Imperial*

*Venus* and in her last major picture, *King, Queen, Knave*), but never completely undressed; and whenever possible she had her flesh-colored tights at hand. Gina isn't prudish, but she has high moral standards and plenty of self respect.

*Where the Hot Wind Blows* intermingles brutality with humorous episodes, the former being a theme that Dassin admired, respected and feared. He was usually attracted to very strong subjects which had a social comment, which explains the success of his first French picture, *Rififi* (1954).

In 1960, Dassin wrote, directed and co-starred in *Never on Sunday* with Greek actress Melina Mercouri, both receiving an Oscar nomination. After his disappointing *Circle of Two* (1980), he retired from show business after a long career with several studios - MGM, Universal and Fox - before he was forced to seek work in Europe for political reasons in the early Fifties.

Despite Dassin's screen achievements, Italian critics attacked both *Where the Hot Wind Blows* and Vailland's novel as fleeting and superficial with a moralistic ending that makes the whole story absurd and inconceivable. Upon Don Cesare's death he leaves his large house to his servant Marietta, who marries the agriculturalist (Marcello Mastroianni), the man she loves. Poetic justice culminates with Brigante's loss of power among the villagers for his wrongdoings.

Gina's first and only film for Dassin wasn't one of his best projects, but it offered the actress a part that she could play with convincing spontaneity. Her forte lay in Bersagliera, Marietta and (future) Mrs. Campbell type roles: "the urchin pure, simple, magnificent; the erotic ragamuffin; the elemental creature filled with a shrewd, radiant animality." Gina would have been marvelous had she played the hellish Katharina in *The Taming of the Shrew* or the volcanic Serafina in Tennessee Williams' *The Rose Tattoo*.

After Gina had completed her work for Dassin, she flew to Spain for *Solomon and Sheba*. If her hourglass figure looked dazzling in her first performance following the birth of Milko Jr., she was breathtaking in her second as the tempting and passionate Queen of Sheba causing a lot of trouble for poor King Solomon.

\*\*\*

From the early Fifties Hollywood had turned its cameras to the great historical epics stimulated by Italy's overwhelming output of the genre beginning with Blasetti's *Fabiola* (1949), followed by Pietro Francisci's *La regina di Saba* (The Queen of Sheba, 1952), Riccardo Freda's *Spartaco* (Spartacus, the Gladiator, 1953), Mario Camerini's *Ulisse* (Ulysses, 1954) and many others. But it was with Francisci's *Le fatiche di Ercole* (The Labors of Hercules, 1957) that the genre really achieved international popularity. The film grossed 900 million lire, making Francisci rich overnight and turning him into a popular director.

With one eye on cheaper labour and the other on easier tax rates, Hollywood embarked to Italy and Spain, where famous stars lived the lives of well-known Biblical and historical figures. Time and money, however, established the distinguishing characteristic between the Italian and the American epic. While the former was shot with tight funds and in high gear, the second involved millions of dollars and a generous shooting schedule.

These celluloid extravaganzas, in one way or another, exploited European resources and filled the screen with sweat, blood and tears in CinemaScope. Peter Ustinov, Deborah Kerr, Rossana Podestà, Charlton Heston, Sophia Loren, Kirk Douglas, Anthony Quinn, Silvana Mangano, and Elizabeth Taylor turned back the pages of time. Like her Italian colleagues, Gina shared her talent and beauty in the epic genre. Nevertheless, no actress reached Lollobrigida's "commanding performance of electrifying sexuality" in *Solomon and Sheba* (1959), not to be confused with Francisci's *The Queen of Sheba*. Movie experts asserted that la Podestà's performance didn't equal her beauty in *Helen of Troy* (1955), and that la Loren did better in movies exploring an authentic Italian milieu than in *The Fall of the Roman Empire* (1954) and *El Cid* (1961).

As recorded in 1 Kings 10:1-13 and 2 Chronicles 9:1-22, the Queen of Sheba had heard so much about Solomon's wisdom that she decided to test him with difficult questions. With her, she brought many attendants and camels loaded with gold, jewels and spices, which she presented to Solomon. During her stay in the Holy City she admired the King's wisdom and returned to the Land of Sheba with many gifts which the King bestowed upon her in return.

Another account of the legendary Arabian Queen is found in the *Koran*, where she appears as Balkis, the personification of Shamis, the Sun Goddess. The scripture also narrates that the Queen's sojourn to Jerusalem was to probe the King's wisdom.

The Holy Books tell that Solomon housed many women in his harem and, as the tale goes, was a man no woman could resist. This time, however, it was the King who found himself helpless before the Queen's sensual beauty. As a result of their love, the *Koran* registers that Sheba gave birth to a son and named him Ibn-el-Nakim, meaning Son of the Sun.

Comparing these versions, the latter seems to have been the source for Vidor's *Sheba*, for when the pagan Queen leaves Jerusalem, she's pregnant with Solomon's child. But neither one of the scriptures describe her as an enemy of Israel who planned to destroy Solomon through temptations of the flesh. Furthermore, neither the Bible nor the *Koran* record her supposed conversion to Jehova as we see in the film.

The dispute over the throne of Israel between David's sons in the screenplay is far from the story related in 1 Kings 2:13-25. Solomon, rather than his older half-brother Adonijah, had been chosen by God's will to succeed his dying father, David. After the old King's death, Adonijah went to visit Solomon's mother, Bathsheba, and requested her to approach King Solomon on his behalf to ask for Abshag, the King's favorite. This angered Solomon, who ordered Adonijah to be put to death.

In the Hollywood version, Adonijah is killed at the end of the story in a sword fight with his half-brother over the crown. His desire for Abishag is completely omitted and she dies in the temple when Jehova strikes it with lightning while Solomon is attending a Sheban ritual.

Moving still further from the ancient records, Solomon didn't turn away from God because of Sheba. Against the Israelites' and God's wish, the Old Testament tells that, the young King married many foreign women including the daughter of the King of Egypt; he wed a total of 700 princesses and maintained 300 concubines. These women from heathen nations led him to worship other gods, thus causing the Lord to leave him.

There's no doubt that the partially apocryphal screenplay presented the public with a more fascinating plot. By introducing la Lollo as a sensual and wicked queen, the script offered her more raw material from which to shape a performance than had she come merely on a diplomatic visit.

If Lollobrigida ever had trouble making a film, it was undoubtedly *Solomon and Sheba*, for it was a period of woes for everyone involved in the production; it was as if the Lord had cursed the film with the ten plagues of Egypt - from bad weather to the sudden death of Tyrone Power, Lollobrigida's leading man, two weeks before shooting of the final scenes.

The spectacle, filmed in Israel, Spain and Italy, faced most of its hardships in Spain. Battle scenes, shot on location between the military air bases of Zaragoza and Torejòn (near Madrid), were completely spoiled by overheard jet planes that zigzagged the skies leaving vapor trails - hardly an authentic special effect. Too, a total of 3,000 soldier costumes had to be totally altered to fit the 5' 8" Spanish extras. Young ladies from Zaragoza were responsible for the disappearance of hundreds of helmets which they took home as souvenirs and later had to be retrieved from them. Problems also arose with the scarcity of extras who could utter a few lines in English; to make matters worse, no Spanish families in the area were willing to let their daughters participate as extras since the prevailing attitude was that girls in show business were but a step away from being ladies of the night.

The production suffered unceasing rain, causing Solomon's temple to rot and mold on the set of Sevilla Studios (Madrid). The studio itself contributed to the reigning chaos with a lack of suitable facilities when compared to Hollywood counterparts; there were few sound stages, and appropriate dressing rooms and comfortable offices were but a dim memory for the participants. Finally, like the plague of the death of the firstborn, the crew and cast faced the shocking and sad news of the passing of Tyrone Power on November 15, 1958. The sword fight between Solomon and Adonijah (George Sanders) was being retaken for the eighth time in a row (at Sander's request) when Power abruptly shouted: "I've had it!" and retired to his trailer dressing room. He was tired, pale and shaking when he was rushed to the United States Torrejòn Air Base Hospital in Lollobrigida's Mercedes. He arrived DOA; Power had a heart attack during the ride.

After Tyrone's death, producers Edward Small and Ted Richmond had to take serious and quick steps to save the picture. They considered Robert Taylor, William Holden, Gary Cooper and Charlton Heston, but all were engaged in other projects. Yul Brynner, who in 1956 had executed an outstanding performance as Pharaoh in De Mille's *The Ten Commandments*, accepted the role. "No one who was asked to do such a thing could be able to say no," he expressed, referring to a performance in memory of Power. Brynner, as the new

King of Israel, played the other side of the cinematic coin, leading his men against the Pharaoh and his allies.

Brynner's terms, however, were twice as demanding as those of Power's. He'd pocket $700,000 (another source claims the sum was $1,000,000) plus 15 percent of the gross over $9,000,000. The picture became extremely expensive and since it had to be totally refilmed, "Fireman's Fund, the insurer, settled with United Artists for a total of $1,229,172, the largest insurance company loss in the film industry up to that time." Moreover, the picture had to be finished by February 15, 1959 due to Brynner's commitments with another studio.

With the new Solomon the film's international cast was complete again. Lollobrigida's Sheba and Marisa Pavan's Abishag were Italians, Brynner was Mongolian (born on Sakhalin Island not far from the Siberian coast); George Sanders and David Farrar (Pharaoh) were British, and Finlay Currie as King David, was a Scotsman. All being directed by a Texan. Lollobrigida and Brynner have accents which lent them credibility; Sanders and Farrar, have distinct British voices which are completely out of place in ancient Israel and Egypt.

The retake of *Solomon and Sheba* cost United Artists almost $6,000,000. When Tyrone Power died, only close-ups of King Solomon and Sheba remained to be shot and it was inconceivable to wrap up the last scenes with a new leading man. There were several problems involved. Power's performance was rather gentle, while Brynner's was virile; the former poetic, the latter "like someone about to crack a whip." Since Brynner and Power walked differently and Brynner had a larger build, all shots, even those with Power's back to the camera, had to be refilmed. Consequently, every single Lollobrigida power scene had to be completely retaken because even Brynner's wig didn't match in color with Power's. It was thought that the public wouldn't accept a Brynner with hair, but his success in the film proved otherwise. The actor is just as attractive and exudes as much physical appeal with hair as without. Brynner had shaved his head for his Broadway performance of *The King and I* and kept it that way even after the film version in 1956.

When the new Solomon arrived on the set, he was like a shot of adrenalin with his bright sense of humor cheering the gloomy cast, and helping Sheba to overcome her grief over the loss of Tyrone Power. "It was much an emotional experience. Both my husband and I loved Tyrone Power so much, and his death was a shock that it was hard to accept when he died so suddenly. He was such a gentleman, so kind and thoughtful of everyone," Gina recalled.

Notwithstanding the fresh atmosphere that the new King of Israel brought to the set, Lollobrigida didn't appreciate the manner in which he introduced himself. While she was immersed in the milky waters of Sheba's bath, (one of the five the actress takes in the picture), Brynner perched himself on a ladder and focussed the huge telephoto lens of his camera on her. Even wearing tights in the fancy tub, Gina usually loathed doing bathtub scenes, and she would have to take another one for the coming *Never So Few*. Referring to such scenes, Gina told a reporter that "they are just stupid. Just for the pleasure of the dirty ones of the public."

Brynner's approach, however, also had its positive aspect. Gina, who was already interested in photography, was familiar with the 8x10 negatives of studio still cameras, but she was particularly impressed with the very clear 35 mm negatives Brynner produced. He assured her the camera was easy to use and she borrowed one to see for herself. Soon, Gina had six cameras to her name including a Leica and a Hasselblad. It was, perhaps, through interaction with Brynner that Gina developed a liking for photography, eventually becoming a self-taught, expert lenswoman. Years later, collectors of Gina's photographs were also hunting for pictures taken by her. When the camera was not rolling on the sets, the Arabian Queen and the King of Israel were busy photographing each other off-guard with their concealed cameras.

Sheba's gorgeous and sexy costumes, however, left her at a distinct disadvantage in strategic hiding places for the weapons. Sheba's wardrobe and make-up were stunning. Gina wore a becoming dark wig that she modeled even off the set. Her eyebrows were given an Oriental upward slant at the temples, stressing her brown eyes. We first behold her as she speeds forward in her chariot towards a confrontation with the Israelites, her eyes ablaze, her entire body vibrating with energy. Her perfectly shaped nose and sparkling even teeth, contributed to the exotic image projected on the screen. Her face is alive with strength and character. She's a woman in control. Her exquisite 14 Middle East costumes in an array of colors and designs by Schuberth of Rome are tantalizing and exotic, producing a voluptuous, glittering Arabian in 70 mm. Technicolor-Technirama.

The only costume Sheba wasn't satisfied with was the one she had to wear for the ritual pagan dance. It consisted of a long gauzy skirt fastened with a golden belt sinking low over the hips, framing Lollo's navel which was, in true silver screen tradition, adorned with a jewel. The belt and the gauzy skirt firmly enhanced her waist. Above the midriff, Lollobrigida's scheduled wardrobe called for only a veil. The actress strongly objected. Producer Ted Richmond replied that he was sorry but she'd have to be contented with the costume as it was. Gina felt it'd be impossible to perform the ritual dance practically topless; the censors would reach for their pens the moment she turned to the camera. The following day when the Sheban orgy was to be filmed, Gina reported on the set wearing her flesh-colored tights and demanded a brassière. Richmond had no alternative but to agree with her, and a relieved Sheba spent part of the night working on a sort of pagan brassière with her own portable sewing machine. "I am the most nice girl in the world," said Gina. "If I think something can help the picture, then I do it." Later a calm Richmond voiced: "I find her irresistible, particularly when she insists on privileges which she cannot have. One has only one idea: to make her happy."

The flesh-colored tights and the brassière had already created friction between Richmond and Sheba, and both of them were careful to avoid future tension. Nevertheless, it didn't take long before the Queen went into another rage. Richmond hoped for a real erotic screen orgy in the pagan ritual scene but was afraid that Gina wouldn't give her best to an authentic pagan dance. Without Gina's knowledge Richmond hired a stuntwoman, a local belly dancer. La Lollo lost her temper and told the producer that she had to do the dance herself. She did it. The scene was staged twice, once for Europe and once for the States. The choreography by Jeroslav Berger and Jean Pierre Genet left much to be desired but it couldn't have been worse than young David's entrance in Jerusalem in Paramount's *King David* (1985) starring Richard Gere.

Despite the torrent of personal, financial, and other miscellaneous disasters, the film was completed. King Vidor, then 65 and well known for his *War and Peace* and for his five Oscar nominations, said that working with *Solomon and Sheba* had been no fun. The rain in Spain "and the repetition have done all of us in." For Gina it had been a very strenuous experience; from the death of her leading man to her clashes with the costume department to the threat of a lawsuit from Richmond for time lost if she didn't report to work on a particular day when she was working out her fury over her pagan costume.

# 127--Imperial Gina

Not everything was a disaster, though. Gina found pleasure in her suite at the Hotel Castellana Hilton which she turned into a nursery when Milko Jr. came for visits. As the boy began to grow, Gina had him brought to the sets wherever she went to work. By the time the baby celebrated his first birthday he had already become an international traveller, for Gina had taken him once to Paris.

Milko Jr. was very active, or a "terremoto" (earthquake) in his mother's words. One day, while on the set of *Sheba*, for example, the Queen of Bulgaria came to see Gina and while they were talking the 16-month-old bambino rushed to his mother with such force that he knocked her down. The Queen came over to help Gina and the toddler suddenly bumped into her and down she, too, went. Later when Gina recalled the episode, she was amused at the "funny scene;" but when it happened she was very embarrassed, particularly because someone caught the mishap on film. Luckily the Queen had a very good sense of humor.

On the set of *Sheba* Gina also found time to show her good spirits demonstrating her skill with a hula hoop in the studio. (She did a replay on the set of *Never So Few*.) And on the night of the Madrid première of *The King and I*, she happily accompanied Brynner to the event. So not everything tortured Sheba, but when plans didn't work out as she had hoped for, it took Lois Weber, the picture press agent, her dialogue coach Martha Labarr, King Vidor and Milko Sr. to appease the Arabian Queen's wrath.

Months before the location work reached its end, Gina felt that the film would be a fiasco and decided to sell back to United Artists her percentage interest in it. By doing so she lost several thousands of dollars. Nevertheless, the picture yielded Lollobrigida one of the largest American audiences ever; they enjoyed her convincing performance, underscoring Brynner's words: "She's a pro."

After the film was released in Italy, a priest wrote a newspaper column in which he attacked the actress saying that her performance as Sheba had been "immoral." He also stated that she had shown the film to her boy but had been careful to eliminate the pagan dance before screening it for him. By doing so she was protecting her son, but she didn't care if it corrupted others, he added. Lollobrigida exploded with anger, and wasted no time suing the priest. It was clear that he knew nothing of her repeated arguments with the film-makers over her skimpy costume and the dance itself. Most of all, Milko Jr. wasn't two years old yet and wouldn't have understood the picture

anyway had she showed it to him. And it would have been unthought-
ful of her had she done so since she knew the boy cried whenever he
saw her metamorphosed in Sheban costumes, and usually couldn't
recognize her. When Gina sued, the priest retracted his claims.

As Marietta from the motion-picture *Where the Hot Wind Blows* (1958)
- *Paris-Match* (Rizzo) - author's collection.

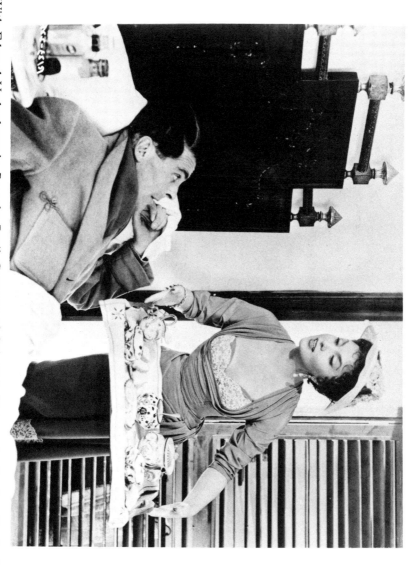

With Edward Underdown in *Beat the Devil*. Courtesy of Columbia Pictures (author's collection).

With John Huston during the shooting of *Beat the Devil*. Courtesy of Columbia Pictures (author's collection).

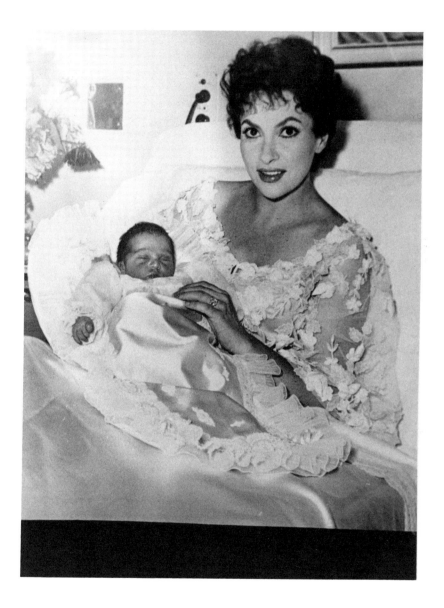

With baby Milko Jr. born on 27 July, 1957. Courtesy *Il Messaggero* (author's collection).

With Frank Sinatra in *Never So Few* (1959).  Canterbury Productions, Inc. and Loew's Incorporated (author's collection).

# Chapter 5

## She Got What She Wanted

With the commercialization of Italian films in the Fifties and Sixties, Hollywood moguls turned their eyes to the Mediterranean, eager to invite Italian stars to California. American movie studios had always welcomed international talent, and with the flourishing of the postwar Italian cinema Hollywood was more than happy to adopt Roman celebrities into its large family. Valentina Cortese, Alida Valli, Pier Angeli, Elsa Martinelli, Sophia Loren, and Claudia Cardinale all said "arrivederci Roma" in favor of the Dream Factory of the Western World, but Gina Lollobrigida's west-coast arrival was the most celebrated of them all.

When la Bersagliera finally made it to California, she had been preceded by her famed colleagues with exception of la Cardinale, who appeared later in the race. Nine years had passed since Gina had signed an option with Howard Hughes and for nearly a decade she was unable to work in America. But with *Trapeze* and *Solomon and Sheba*, she had established a foothold in the capital of the cinema world.

This new phase of Gina's career was the climax of her internationalization; it also enriched her savings with thousands of dollars and provided her with organization, something she missed in Italian studios where improvisation still reigned. For the perfectionist Lollo who normally got up at 5:00 and worked until 6:00 and read scripts for an hour before bed at 10:00, an organized studio was very important for good performances.

Unfortunately, Tinseltown was unable to bring forward good parts like the French and the Italian cinema had created for her. Apart from the two fine comedies she did with Rock Hudson - *Come September* and *Strange Bedfellows* - American producers had nothing special to offer Gina at that time. In the late Sixties, however, Melvin Frank's superb comedy *Buona Sera Mrs. Campbell* presented Lollobrigida with an excellent part that resulted in what the actress considered her best American film.

Gina's second journey to Hollywood, like the first in 1950, lasted a couple of months since she had further engagements in Europe. She arrived in Los Angeles accompanied by her husband and their 20-month-old Milko Jr.; along with the family came the child's nurse, and Gina's personal maid, Maria Teresa Morelli-Stefanelli. The Skofics were lodged at a bungalow in the Beverly Hills Hotel even though Gina thought a house would be more comfortable. (She got the house when she returned to Hollywood to do *Lady L* in 1961.)

While Gina was in town for *Never So Few*, and before she left Madrid after *Sheba*, she was constantly hounded by a voracious press which probed everything from a hypothetical new pregnancy to the ongoing headache with Howard Hughes, who still thought he owned the star. Again, Gina made it very clear that she had signed an option and not a contract with him. The option had expired in 1957 and the Hughes phase in her life was over. Gina considered her episode with the once "virulent anti-Communist, witch-hunt" movie mogul the worst experience of her career.

***

Based on a novel by Tom Chamales, *Never So Few* was a rather unsuccessful picture directed by John Sturges. Comparing the film to other Sturges efforts such as *Gunfight at the O.K. Corral* (1957) and *The Magnificent Seven* (1960), the critics wrote the picture off as a "dim war drama," an "undistinguished war film," and "an uneasy mixture of comedy and action drama" that sold well on the strength of its cast. Despite the participation of Frank Sinatra, Peter Lawford and two rising stars, Steve McQueen and Charles Bronson, the film was indeed an unfortunate choice for Gina's Hollywood debut.

I sometimes wonder whether the $400,000, plus a healthy percentage of the film's profits (some sources register $250,000 against ten percent of the gross) was worth the part when compared to some of Gina's former better roles. But Gina had to show to Hughes that she could work for American studios in the States regardless of the obstacles he had created for her. Nevertheless, according to reviewers, Gina didn't belong in the picture. It isn't clear whether her role is simply that of a kept woman or an Allied spy involved in the story of a few Burmese guerrillas against 40,000 Japanese.

Carla Vesari (Gina) a countess out of the East, appears in a sub-plot as the love interest of Captain Tom Reynolds (Sinatra) without any connection at all to the war intrigue. Maybe the producers just wanted Gina to decorate the picture or perhaps they had no idea what they wanted, for Gina's part was constantly being rewritten as the story developed. "Some scenes, they gave it to me just the night before. This is not enough. For me this is not funny," complained Gina.

This ongoing overnight rewriting upset Gina's habitual pattern of reading and memorizing entire scripts, particularly those in a foreign language. "When I am acting in Italian," she explained, "I can improvise, but in another language I must learn my lines so well that I can forget the words. In this film it was impossible. Every night they rewrote the script so it was impossible to learn by heart and Sinatra too was liable to put in his own words."

The lack of time to properly digest her lines resulted in a "singularly wooden" performance. Ranald MacDougall, who later directed Gina in *Go Naked in the World*, concluded "that she was saying something without knowing what it meant and consequently was unsure what to indicate. This becomes a blank stare sort of thing."

Working with Sinatra, a one-take man, caused an additional burden on Gina, who counted on rehearsal time and asked for retakes whenever she felt she could do better. Too, the constant rewriting of scenes caused Gina to make mistakes, necessitating even more retakes. Impatient Sinatra could give a convincing performance without either rehearsal or retakes, which caused more friction between the actress and her leading man, with whom she played most of her scenes. In retrospect, Gina said that "Sinatra was very kind and never said anything but I could tell he was annoyed and irritated though he did his best not to show it."

Contrary to Marilyn Monroe, who required take after take, Gina preferred not to repeat the same scene unnecessarily. The American sex symbol redid a certain scene 59 times in *Some Like It Hot* (1959), although her only line was "Where's the Bourbon?" Howard Hughes may have made a world record when he demanded 103 retakes of a specific scene in his 1943 *The Outlaw*.

Aware of Sinatra's aversion to retakes, Gina knew she had to be at her best the first time around, and she worked as much as possible in advance on her lines. Sometimes she'd work far into the night in order to avoid retakes the next day. One morning, Gina, exhausted, reported to the studio on time; Sinatra arrived an hour and half late. Gina, not knowing of his hypersensitivity to criticism, announced that he should have told her he'd be late so she could have slept at least an extra hour. Sinatra walked off the set and disappeared for two days. They later made peace and things went more smoothly with Sinatra consenting to occasional retakes.

They got along well after the incident and she liked his tender compliments like "walk slower, baby, so we can enjoy it longer." Gina considered Sinatra "a very good actor because he doesn't even pretend to act." Although relations improved, Gina's constant language awareness and effort to avoid retakes put too much stress on her. Later in her career she considered *Never So Few* an "awful" experience but "I was new and could not be fussy," she said. What Gina meant here, one concludes, was that she was a Hollywood neophyte, for the star had on several occasions demanded - and gotten - exactly what she demanded from European studios.

Gina regarded that movie stars working together had to like each other in order to deliver convincing performances. Whenever she could choose her leading man, she looked for a sensitive, warm actor who could understand her. Rock Hudson, it later became known, fit the bill most perfectly.

Always eager to know her co-star better before going in front of the camera, Gina confided to Louella Parsons that she was delighted Sinatra had invited her for dinner before the shooting of the picture got underway. The gossip columnist wrote that at the MGM lot the cast and crew of *Never So Few* had concurred that Gina was "completely professional and cooperative."

\*\*\*

After her Hollywood debut, Gina returned to Europe where a Dino De Laurentiis film for Paramount, *Jovanka e l'altri* (Five Branded Women, 1960) awaited her that summer. The picture was to be filmed in Italy, Yugoslavia and Austria with Gina starring opposite Van Heflin.

# 137–Imperial Gina

The screenplay was based on a true story about five women whose heads are shaved a la Yul Brynner by the partisans after they consorted with the Germans. "I will be beautiful in the picture, too. My hair will not be cut off for every scene. I look completely different when it happens - like a young boy," enthused Gina.

Months before shooting began, Gina mentioned that she was very disappointed that the picture wasn't going to be made in Yugoslavia after all. "It's so foolish for the country to forbid us to make it there when it's a true story and not any political discussion." Problems were eventually sorted out and the film was partially shot in Yugoslavia as originally planned. Before then, however, someone proposed to change the film title to *Five Women*, but Gina insisted that if she did the picture it'd be called *Jovanka*.

The film, minus Lollobrigida, was ultimately released as *Five Branded Women*; Silvana Mangano, De Laurentiis' wife, had stepped into the leading role. There were rumors in Roman newspapers that Gina had objected to shaving her head. The actress, wrote the papers, wanted to wear a contrivance that would make her appear bald. De Laurentiis mentioned nothing of it in his announcement to the press, instead stating that for reasons beyond his control, Gina wouldn't be in the picture. Studio sources disclosed that the actress' doctor had advised Gina that she had been overworking and needed at least a couple of months' rest. The Lollobrigida household staff stated that Gina hadn't been feeling well and that the Skofics had left their villa on the Appian Way for a rest.

\*\*\*

Sometime in May 1959 Gina had her debut on Italian TV in one episode of *Il mattatore* (The Entertainer), also featuring Vittorio Gassman. Gina's portrayal of an obscure busybody actress in the show was a hit. Other TV performances in Italy, America and England throughout the following years further illuminated Gina's talent.

In the preceding decade which closed with Gina's triumphant arrival in Hollywood, the actress had presented moviegoers with 28 motion pictures shot at home and in international studios. Gina Lollobrigida had undoubtedly become the world's most popular actress. Her drive to prove that she could render a fine performance for a De Sica, a Huston or a Vidor lifted her above the pin-up girl class of the late Forties and early Fifties into the ranks of the world's leading actresses.

During the summer of 1959 in Hollywood, three of Gina's pictures were still to be seen: *Fast and Sexy, Where the Hot Wind Blows* and *Solomon and Sheba*. Possible Lollobrigida films on the horizon were *The Image Makers* for Columbia - which she didn't make - and *Cleopatra* for 20th Century-Fox. The studio had considered Joanne Woodward, Joan Collins and Susan Hayward to portray the exotic Queen of the Nile, thus avoiding Elizabeth Taylor's exorbitant $1 million request. Liz Taylor finally got the part, but when she was confined to a London clinic with a temperature and other ailments that continued for more than a month, Spyros Skouras, the 20th Century-Fox President, was eager to have her replaced. The actress' illness was already costing Lloyd's of London $2 million, and the insurance company also wished to see another star in Cleopatra's gowns. Marilyn Monroe, Kim Novak, Shirley MacLaine and Gina Lollobrigida were suggested as possible candidates.

On the grounds that the pay wasn't worth all the work she'd have to go through, Gina refused the script. She also didn't feel like working with Rouben Mamoulian. When the Egyptian Queen was then moved to Rome, the production had Mamoulian replaced by Joseph L. Mankiewicz due to artistic disagreement.

While *Cleopatra* seemed to be drowning in the Thames, Gina was also approached with the role of Emma in Fellini's *La dolce vita*, but her husband turned it down and the part went to French star Anouk Aimée. Lollobrigida was also offered to play Annie Girardot's part in Visconti's best cinematic novel, *Rocco e i suoi fratelli* (Rocco and His Brothers, 1960), but Gina had already signed for *Go Naked in the World*. It was most unfortunate that she didn't work for two of the most prestigious Italian directors at the time. The parts she missed could have immensely magnified the actress' already sensational career. There was also a rumor that Gina was going to be the protagonist in Luis Buñuel's *Veridiana*, (1961), but she never worked for the Spanish director.

\*\*\*

In mid-February of 1960 Gina presided as the guest of honor at an MGM party upon her return to the studio for MacDougall's *Go Naked in the World*, a picture that rendered Gina a quality dramatic role which was far preferable to what Sturges had offered her.

# 139—Imperial Gina

The actress' presence again in Hollywood was proving to Howard Hughes that she hardly ever lost a battle. It's true that MGM would have been liable had Hughes sued the actress; but the studio, against la Lollo's wishes, had already settled with him for her services when she did *Never So Few.* Gina stated that the studio had taken that step because it was afraid of the movie czar. "Metro can be afraid of him, I'm not," she remarked. "If he continues claiming that I belong to him I am going to sue him in court."

But while Lollobrigida was in town for her second Hollywood picture, something unexpected happened. The Screen Actor's Guild went on strike, putting the production on hold. With shooting temporarily suspended, Gina went back to Europe where she had further commitments. When the strike was over, she returned to the MGM lot and *Go Naked in the World.*

Like her first Hollywood screenplay, this second film was also based on a Tom Chamales novel. It tells the story of Nick (Anthony Franciosa) who falls in love with Giulietta Cameron (Gina). As the plot develops, Nick finds out that the woman he adores was a high priced call girl. Pete Stratton (Ernest Borgnine), Nick's father, had been one of Giulietta's clients and understandably opposes his son's desire to marry the girl. After numerous father-son confrontations, Pete finally approves the marriage in order to regain his son's love. The father's consent comes too late for Giulietta; tired of the absurdity the situation has created, she throws herself into the sea at Acapulco.

Metro had great expectations for the film. Gina, who normally despised roles portraying her as a prostitute, considered Giulietta "a very good part" demanding the best of her as an actress. "Wear the skin of the woman you're playing" advised Gina's coach, Zina Provendie. At the end of a day's shooting Gina was invariably exhausted and found it difficult to be herself again; there were times that she thought she couldn't go on with the picture. Her efforts, however, were worthwhile. The critics applauded the film, preferring it over Sturges'.

The high class call girl theme was beginning to bloom, and MGM starred Elizabeth Taylor in her Oscar performance *Butterfield 8.* It's curious that the studio was shooting two similar themes with two famous leading ladies in the same year. Like Gina, Liz was less than thrilled to be cast as a prostitute. When work on the film began in New York in January 1960, Liz told the press that the film "stinks."

***

In April of that same year Gina was in Karlsruhe, Germany, where she received the "Bambi" award for leading the popularity list in a poll by a German fan magazine. It was also in that same spring that the Skofics announced to the press that they were planning to establish residence in Toronto and receive Canadian citizenship. Gina's Italian fans were disappointed. It was practically impossible to grasp the idea that their "Gina nazionale" would forsake her Italy; nevertheless, there was a solid reason for such a step in the actress' life.

Born in Austria, Milko's parents moved to Yugoslavia when he was a year old. In 1943 he escaped to Italy, but complicated legalities left him ineligible for Italian citizenship. Since he was considered stateless, when Gina applied for a passport for Milko Jr., the boy was refused Italian citizenship and was left in the same boat as his papà. "I was very surprised and hurt," confided Gina to the papers, "when my own country's officials would not give my son my nationality."

Milko's brother, Peter, who had become a Canadian citizen and was the executive of a steamship line in Toronto, offered to sponsor the family. Gina had formerly thought of becoming an American national, but there were such technicalities about a sponsor; with her husband's brother as a Canadian resident the red tape would be less frustrating.

There had been increasing rumors that Roman officials had refused Italian citizenship to Gina's son because of some tax entanglement involving the Skofics. Lollobrigida angrily denied her decision to move to Canada to avoid high taxes in Italy. (The Roman officials didn't bother to find out that taxes were higher in Canada.) "They are all lies," said Gina. And while she was in Hollywood during that spring of 1960 she told the press that she paid very high taxes in her native land. "I pay. Oh, how I pay! I pay more than anyone else in the entertainment field." She didn't, to be sure, remit them happily. "I would do so if I knew that everyone else paid what they should. But the industrialists - they pay only a fraction of what they really owe," continued Gina. "No one criticizes them because they control the newspapers." Gina's complaint could well be justified since her objection is a familiar one, mainly in Latin countries.

The Skofics had received Canadian immigration visas and were planning to fly to Canada sometime in the spring of that year, depending on how events developed with *Go Naked in the World*, which at that time was still unfinished. Once the picture was wound up, the couple would then leave for Rome to pick up Milko Jr. and then head for Toronto. Nevertheless, they didn't make it to Canada until the summer.

Meanwhile, Lollobrigida shared with Louella Parsons that she had no plan to become a Canadian citizen. Stateless Dr. Skofic, I suppose, wouldn't object being a Canadian subject as long as he had a nationality. Gina, on the other hand, loved Italy and was willing to move to Canada only for the sake of her husband and son. A globetrotter like Gina would establish residence in North America and film in Hollywood, Rome or Paris without abandoning her Italianness. "I never intended to make Canada my home," she insisted.

When the Skofics arrived in Toronto they had a civic reception and Mayor Nathan Phillips welcomed the family, naming a street after Gina. The mayor, well-known locally for refusing to kiss celebrities and for mispronouncing names as well, addressed the actress by her married name and got it wrong the first two times, calling her Mrs. Skofie and then Mrs. Skopic. After the reception, the Skofics moved into their $1,600 a month apartment. The residence soon was surrounded by fans who wouldn't leave until a policeman came to disperse the crowd. The family escaped for a weekend in the country.

Immigration law required that the Skofics live part of each year in Canada, and Gina was planning to move from the Toronto apartment to a 200 acre farm some 30 miles distant from the city. However, in early 1962, Gina was again living in her Roman villa. Meanwhile, the Italian government finally recognized that there had been a mistake on their part and decided to grant Italian nationality to her son. With that Gina cancelled her plans for Canada and stated: "I am all Italian - too much so to become a Canadian. Milko will still go ahead with his Canadian citizenship - but I and the baby will stay Italian. I am glad, to be quite honest. Very glad."

The former planned move to Canada and the switch to Hollywood studios had worked against Gina's popularity in Italy. In the mid-Fifties her fan club in Rome was over 50,000 and all her films sold out everywhere in the country, but after her first two pictures made in America, Italians saw her as a glossy star, an Italian import remodeled to American standards. But the Hollywood episode in her career was a necessary one for Gina's personal growth, and it was an experience she profited from in spite of the criticism she received from her people.

It was also during this Hollywood-Toronto adventure that Italian gossip columnists created all sorts of stories to damage Gina's popularity. These people couldn't accept the fact that the actress had been happily married for ten years and were unceasingly trying to find the Achilles' heel of her conjugal life. From time to time the papers averred that Gina was in the midst of an affair with one leading man or another, but the Skofics usually ignored the overzealous scandal sheets. One of the false stories then was that Gina was going to Canada to divorce Milko. Another malicious fabrication was of a 13-year-old illegitimate daughter born either of an American or British officer. The tale sounds like the plot of *Buona sera Mrs. Campbell*.

\*\*\*

Modeling returned briefly to Gina's life sometime in May, 1960. But Lollobrigida was no longer the girl who posed for the photo romance *Il mio sogno* in 1947; now she was the model of models posing for *Epoca* with the text by Alberto Moravia.

*The Roman Women* (not to be confused with the film *Woman of Rome*), depicted some extraordinary women in Roman history and Gina agreed to metamorphose repeatedly for the illustrated pages. Gina incarnated such personalities as Cornelia, Lucrezia Borgia, Lina Cavalieri (whose life Gina had so brilliantly taken to the screen in 1955), and Paolina Bonaparte (an aristocrat portrayed by Gina in Delannoy's *Imperial Venus* in 1962).

Gina's next assignment was to star in Robert Mulligan's *Come September* (1961) for Universal. The picture was Gina's strongest box-office attraction of all her Hollywood films to date. The $3 million CinemaScope-Eastman Color production tells the story of a millionaire American businessman, Robert Talbot (Rock Hudson), who takes his "major domo" Maurice Clavell (Walter Slezak) by surprise appearing at his Italian villa in July for his vacation rather than in September as usual. This is bad news for Maurice who, for eleven months of the year, turns Talbot's villa into a hotel, "La Dolce Vista." Lisa Fellini (Lollobrigida), Talbot's fiancée, has given up on him and is about to marry another man. Six Americans staying at the "hotel" add romance to the plot.

At the time the picture was being shot in Portofino and Cinecittà, Hudson had been voted the world's favorite actor and casting him opposite the world's most popular actress couldn't have been anything but a happy outcome. Hudson's fame in the 1959 comedy *Pillow Talk* with Doris Day repeated itself with Gina Lollobrigida, who was thrilled to have him for her leading man. On top of that, the actress loved to perform in comedies, always feeling "happy and up-beat" when making one. "*Come September* is a good comedy," she told Hedda Hopper. "When you see the picture you feel we enjoyed ourselves," she concluded.

Hudson remarked that "because of Gina, this has been one of the happiest companies I've ever worked with." Gina loved the picture so much that she appeared on the set even on days when she wasn't working, viewing the interlude as a good, long holiday. Co-stars Sandra Dee and Bobby Darin became husband and wife during the shooting, which brightened the atmosphere even more. In the film Darin sang *Multiplication* (words and music by Mr. Darin), a pop hit in the early Sixties.

Lollobrigida and Hudson got along like peaches and cream on the set. When the American beef-cake was approached with the script and told that his leading lady would be Gina Lollobrigida, the handsome actor could hardly wait to meet her. He prepared himself for the event to ensure that Gina wouldn't have a poor image of him. He had seen several of her films and thought highly of her; when they finally met, Gina saw in him the perfect gentleman. "When I am starting a picture with a new partner everybody usually say to be careful - and say things about him, but with Rock Hudson nobody told me something bad." Later, recalling her experience working with him, she emphasized her impression of the actor, saying that "Rock Hudson was an American sex symbol, but most people don't know he was especially sweet and kind."

The public thoroughly approved of the Lollobrigida-Hudson formula, and Gina was eager to make another picture with him. The chance came in 1964 with the hilarious comedy *Strange Bedfellows*. To express his admiration for Gina, Rock presented her with a camera featuring a huge 180 mm. lens. A gold plate engraved with her name was attached to it.

*Come September* offered Gina's fans the opportunity to see her in a wedding gown for the first time. For Gina herself it was also a new experience; if the reader recalls, her wedding ceremony took place at a winter resort area, with the bride and groom clad in ski outfits. In the film, the bride was unexpectedly followed by her three-year-old

Milko Jr. who made his film debut innocently walking after his "mamma nazionale" into camera range. He stole the scene!

The love symbol image Gina unwillingly spread around the world still followed her, and to her dismay, has never dissipated. After a mambo lesson for a scene with Hudson, she went to the commissary with the dance teacher and a half-dozen crew members followed them. During lunch she asked the teacher how she had done in the lesson. The maestro praised her instinct for dancing, adding that her extraordinary curves helped a lot. The crew who had followed them were eavesdropping on the conversation and broke into boisterous peals of laughter at the maestro's open admiration of her physical attributes.

To avoid undue ogling during rehearsals, Gina always wore very bulky clothes as she did that day in the commissary. On the sets of films like *Come September* where she could forget herself, Gina usually behaved like a tomboy so that the men around her wouldn't think of her exclusively as a sex symbol. That, however, was impossible when rehearsing scenes about to be filmed. In one particular take she had to be photographed from the rear as she walked up a rather long staircase and as she rehearsed it, the crew annoyed her with their shouts and whistles. She made the mistake of politely asking them to be quiet so she could work; within moments, Hudson and the other co-stars joined in the good-intentioned fun.

Lollobrigida's siren's figure and remarkable face have often brought her much pain and loneliness. Her English coach, Martha Labarr, once perceptively observed that she didn't begrudge Gina her beauty because it marked the actress as too different from others, making true friends a scarcity. Gina's life has never been easy; while men think of her as a love symbol, women envy her.

*** 

While Gina was in Rome for *Come September*, she was noticed driving a silver-grey Rolls-Royce; this unusual gift delivered to her door was for her work in *Solomon and Sheba*. Sure that the picture would be a flop, Gina had sold her percentage back to United Artists, but the picture made a fortune at the box-office and Gina probably forfeited over a million dollars. The studio cushioned the loss by presenting her with a Long Wheelbase Silver Cloud Rolls-Royce from Harold Radford, Ltd. in London. The car was originally to be delivered to the Skofics in Canada, but duty and Federal tax would consume more money and Harold Radford thought it would be wiser if the couple came directly to London to take the car. Final transactions between Radford and the studio, however, indicated that the car was to be driven to Rome and delivered to Gina.

Women, for one reason or another, have always had a poor reputation behind the wheel and Gina was no exception. "I am not a very good driver," admitted Lollo, who was also frightened to maneuver the Rolls-Royce. Columnist Roderick Mann for the *Sunday Express* wrote "[Gina's] friends in Toronto had reported that once behind the wheel, Miss Lollobrigida was the nearest thing to a Japanese kamikaze suicide pilot."

Conscious of her limitations, Gina considered her driving a little dangerous, but she didn't think she'd risk smashing up her Rolls yet. However, on February 16, 1969, she came within inches of death when the car hit a patch of ice and smashed into a cement wall.

\*\*\*

In the opinion of experts, Gina Lollobrigida is "a highly skilled painter and an ingenious photographer." Back in the early Sixties, photography was a developing hobby for the actress. By the time she left the cinema in 1972, she had become an expert shutterbug with her several cameras and made headlines in the press with her Photo Studio Lollobrigida in the Appia Antica. While working on a film - and also between new movie projects - maneuvering a brush or focusing the lens of her cameras seemed outlets for Lollobrigida's creative overflow. Her paintings were realistic; she worked with oil mostly, turning sometimes to pastels or sketches in pen and ink. The result of her studies at the Accademia di Belle Arti in Rome transformed her villa into a store of oils by Lollobrigida. The actress, reluctant to part with her works, worried about having enough space for them.

Photography, Gina's second brilliant career, brought an immense feeling of self-accomplishment. "In films I am not my own boss," said signora Lollobrigida in the early Seventies. "With photography," she continued, "I can say what I want." Her knowledge of photography was also helpful in her screen career. Gina, who never felt the need of a light meter, knew how to make the most of lights on a studio set or in the open. While in Acapulco for *Go Naked in the World*, an American magazine had sent a photographer to cover her stay in the exotic Mexican resort port. During an outdoor portrait session, the lensman set up a reflector, but after a dozen of rather unsuccessful shots Gina suggested he use a bed sheet to substitute for the foil panel. The photographer was dubious, but after seeing the proofs he realized Gina was right.

\*\*\*

Sometime in early 1961 Gina was in Hollywood to star in George Cukor's *Lady L*, based on a novel by Romain Gary. The script was being rewritten and Gina could hardly wait to start working again. "I think their intention is to have something really excellent, not just good," Gina remarked during an interview with Hedda Hopper. And while the rewriting continued, Gina enjoyed the comfort of the Beverly Hills home, complete with swimming pool, which MGM had found for her.

There were scenes in *Lady L* where Gina had to look 80 years old, requiring four hours with her make-up artist. The transformation left her unrecognizable. One day, during a visit to the studio, Sir Carol Reed saw Gina as the neo-octogenarian and didn't recognize her until she laughed; at the commissary nobody knew who that old lady was.

Lady Lollo spent several months in Hollywood and received $250,000 for a movie she never did. Constant rewriting finally sent Tony Curtis, her leading man, walking out because the final script had considerably minimized his role. The *Lady L* disaster was a turning point in Gina's life; from then on everything related to her career was divided into "pre-Lady L" and "post-Lady L."

Metro called Peter Ustinov to rewrite the script for the picture but when George Cukor also dropped out along with Curtis, the studio assigned Ustinov to direct the rejected "Lady." When the film was finally finished it had a new cast starring Paul Newman and Sophia Loren. Metro called David Niven to replace sir Ralph Richardson in the role of Sophia's husband, but the picture, produced by Carlo Ponti, was doomed to be a fiasco. Not even the stars' box-office draw could attract full houses.

The two most well-known Hollywood gossip columnists, Louella Parsons and Hedda Hopper, loved Gina. The pieces these two ladies produced about the actress were colorful and free of unwanted probes into her private life. Lollobrigida was usually very "courteous and gracious to co-workers and the press but never familiar," which was probably the key to her sterling reputation on sets. Nevertheless, she "is capable of a sharp retort, a lawsuit, or a delaying tactic where her star interests are involved," warned Hedda. Through her contacts with the Italian actress, the columnist was able to see both Ginas, the professional star and the loving wife and mother.

Once when Gina walked into Louella Parson's house, all the writer could think of was the song, *Did You Ever See a Dream Walking?* Straightforward and charismatic, la Lollo knew what she wanted and answered her interviewers with conviction. Concerning *Lady L*, before the picture was doomed, Gina insisted she wanted Bill Daniels as her cinematographer. Bill had worked with her in *Never So Few* and *Come September* and Lollobrigida was very pleased with his work. When Hedda Hopper asked her if she had his name mentioned in the contract, she simply and emphatically said: "I did not have it written but I say I want him."

La Lollo's drive was probably one of the key factors in the success of her careers. This personality trait in the actress comes from early in her life. "Even when I was young, my friends were always men and I was the boss. I always wanted to be the leader. And everything I wanted I got."

During this new Hollywood adventure Gina didn't hesitate to express what she felt about cultural differences she had noticed between Italy and the States. Introductions made her feel uneasy for the simple fact that she was never sure whether she should shake hands or not. "I don't know what to do always when I meet somebody. It's natural for me to give hands, but there they do not give hands. So I am thinking: should I give hands or not."

Concerning American women, Gina observed they aren't as feminine as their Italian counterparts. "An Italian woman," she said, "likes to feel protected, they like to be women. Here the women like to lead the men. In Italy the husband is head of the household, that is true all over Europe." However, Gina's spirited personality probably contradicts her statement that "an Italian woman likes to feel protected." The actress is one of the classic examples of the self-sufficient, independent woman who doesn't need the protection of a man to survive and she should be, and probably is, proud of it. The amazing thing is that even though Gina Lollobrigida has always been a leader, she knows how to maintain the essence of her womanliness in her private and social life.

Always dressed to kill in a Dior, Chanel or Balmain set off by exquisite jewelry, Gina was taken by surprise to see American women shopping with hairpins and curlers and wearing slacks, something you'd never see in European cities, at least in those days. Gina's point of view on American women's standards of dress were perhaps shared by most Latin women who wouldn't even venture out to the next door market as Gina described.

*\*\*\**

Absence makes the heart grow fonder, and even though Gina's popularity at home had decreased with her filming in Hollywood and the probable move to Canada, she was still recognized as a top actress. La "Gina nazionale's" truancy from Roman cameras didn't hinder the Società Caserta Ugoletti Ferrau, the Union of Cinema Trade Publications in Italy, from awarding the actress a gold medal for her praiseworthy contribution to motion pictures as "The Oustanding International Actress of the Year 1960." The award presentation took place on July 5, 1961 when Gina was in Rome to discuss *Imperial Venus*.

The week after Gina accepted the award, she left for the Soviet Union to attend the 1961 Moscow Film Festival. Much to Gina's displeasure, things didn't go smoothly upon her arrival at the Moscow airport; she was rushed to attend the festival opening at the Lenin Stadium without being given a chance to stop at her hotel to change and freshen up her make-up. "I looked like a gypsy," lamented Gina.

To make matters worse, once at the Lenin Stadium, Gina and all the participants had to listen to Soviet Minister Ekaterina Furtseva deliver a 45-minute speech praising Khrushchev and Communism with very few references to movies (although some 52 countries were showing films there) and none at all to Gina Lollobrigida. The star had been given a seat in the third row instead of on the platform with the Communist dignitaries. As for Khrushchev, he was in a very special box with First Deputy Premier Anastas Mikoyan and Communist party secretary Frol R. Koslov.

Gina patiently stayed throughout the formalities and suddenly, when the screening of Russian film *Saturday Night and Sunday Morning* began, she walked out in a huff in the company of other celebrities. Khrushchev and his comrades on the platform looked perplexed.

# 149–Imperial Gina

The day following the episode, the international press declared that Gina's behavior had been an insult to Nikita Khrushchev; nevertheless, there were columnists who spoke out in her defense. She had suffered through tiresome formalities and when the screening began, the English soundtrack of the picture was drowned out by the Russian commentary, thus making it impossible for non-Russians to understand and enjoy the film, a documentary on Soviet spaceman Yuri Gagarin.

"WE CAN'T BLAME HER" wrote the *Hollywood Citizen News*, elaborating that Gina had not been rude; the ones to blame were the "Soviet officials who had seized that opportunity to spread Communist propaganda. The occasion for which Gina and other film celebrities had gone to Moscow had to do with films, not with Communism," emphasized the paper. "If the Soviets continue to exploit the affair with their propaganda we hope that others walk out as Gina did," concluded the columnist.

After Gina's sudden departure from the Lenin Stadium, she was interviewed in her hotel room where she maintained that she wasn't angry, just upset. "I was very strained after a two-day trip to Moscow."

Gina's frustration stemmed partly from the fact that she had been rushed to the festivities with no time to go to the hotel to wash and change clothes. "At the festival Gina looked lovely," began the *L. A. Times*, "but her tall blue straw hat and two-piece blue travelling suit were scarcely the costume the glamorous actress would ordinarily have chosen for a major public appearance."

On the 15th of July, the Kremlin held a reception and for that, Gina took pains to see that she was properly dressed. The elegant St. George's Hall with its white marble walls and crystal chandeliers in the Grand Palace was about to witness a most bizarre event involving Gina and another famous movie star.

International film celebrities, producers and directors, Communist leaders, and Russian musicians, singers and dancers filled St. George's Hall. The reception was scheduled for 3:00 p.m. At 3:15, Minister of Culture Ekaterina Furtseva gave up waiting for a particularly tardy actress and delivered her official speech. In Moscow nobody is late at the Kremlin.

At the end of the hall stood Gina Lollobrigida, stunning in her new white, short, lace cocktail dress with a boat neckline and a wide, bell-shaped skirt. At 4:00 p.m. the dilatory guest entered the hall wearing precisely the same Dior! She walked along the red carpet under the crystal chandeliers and, upon reaching the rear of the hall, caught an eyeful of her Italian double, who welcomed Liz Taylor with an "Oh, how nice to see you."

The chances of two famous actresses appearing in identical dresses at the same film festival are probably one in a billion, but like the implausible collision of two heavenly bodies in the galaxy, it did happen. According to Eddie Fisher, who accompanied Liz, the star was infuriated, but when someone asked Gina what she thought of la Taylor's dress, she smilingly said: "Oh, it's very nice."

As if this fashion nightmare hadn't been enough, both actresses had the same hairdos. The twin sisters' accessories were, thankfully, quite different. Gina wore a red sash and Liz a blue one; Gina displayed a pearl necklace while Liz had white flowers in her hair. Eddie Fisher, however, describes the ladies' appearance somewhat differently from the *L. A. Mirror*. In the popular singer's words, Gina "was wearing blue with sapphires and Elizabeth was in red with rubies, but their dresses were identical."

The happening made headlines all over the world, and while in Paris, on their way back to America, Liz sent Eddie to Dior to find out why he had sold the same dress to the Italian actress. The Frenchman told Eddie that Gina's dressmaker had been over to see his collections and had probably copied the design, an explanation impossible to believe since Gina had several Dior gowns in her collection and was certainly wealthy enough to commission new designs; Gina had no need to send her dressmaker around to furtively copy Dior's ideas.

After the fashion disaster at the Kremlin, Gina only bought clothes from Paris couturiers especially made for her, or had her gowns made and designed in Italy. In an exclusive interview for *The New York Times*, Gina showed columnist Marylin Bender an array of Dior, Chanel and Balmain gowns, stressing that she preferred Dior for important events and Chanel for something more casual. Back in the Sixties, Gina used to buy some 25 outfits a year, favoring beaded ones because they didn't wrinkle, a plus for a frequent globetrotter.

The Lollobrigida-Taylor-Dior incident was probably recorded as one of the strangest clothing-related chapters in show business history; more bizarre is that it had happened seven years earlier at the Italian Film Festival in London. On that occasion Sophia Loren and Gina Lollobrigida wore the same costume, but in different colors. Both ladies were photographed smiling side-by-side!

# 151–Imperial Gina

\*\*\*

Nineteen sixty-two saw Gina working again for the Italian cinema to the delight of her compatriots. Gina's comeback indicated a vote of confidence from the actress, who agreed to work with a virtual unknown: Giancarlo Zagni. The 36-year-old director had been an assistant to Luchino Visconti in *senso* and now, after a nine year absence, debuted with *La bellezza di Ippolita* (The Beauty of Ippolita), released in America as *She Got What She Asked For*.

Playing Ippolita, however, didn't render Gina full satisfaction, for her dream role was "that of a woman harassed by problems of everyday living - a woman who faces the obligation of being true to her husband."

Gina's gas station attendant's coveralls in *Ippolita* are a far cry from the smashing gowns by Morton Haak in *Come September*, but she soon replaces the greasy outfit with skimpy spangles and feathers to return to the stage as a chorus girl when a former colleague beseeches her to come back in order to help a small touring company. On stage Gina's fans saw her tossing legs and hips in torrid dance numbers. To do *Ippolita*, Gina wore a very becoming shoulder-length flaxen wig over her famous raven locks. The new Lollo image reaffirmed King Vidor's comment about the actress: "She looks good in anything."

After seeing *Ippolita* at the Berlin Film Festival, French director Luc Moullet opined that Lollobrigida's performance in the film was second only to *The Wayward Wife*, which was certainly one of Gina's better films of the early Fifties.

Right after *Ippolita*, Gina took on the role of Paolina Borghese, the favorite sister of Napoleon. Considered one of the most beautiful women of her time, Paolina was tender and passionate, impulsive and restless; she was also fickle but faithful to Napoleon. Gina had chosen an excellent part, a role for an actress which successfully drew on her talent. Her performance in *Imperial Venus* rendered her the "Silver Ribbon" as the best Italian female protagonist of 1962.

Conceived in 1958, the film had a rocky history involving several lawsuits. Producers Henri Deutchmeister of Franco London Films and Angelo Rizzoli of Rizzoli Films had signed a contract with Gina for the lead in *Imperial Venus*. French actor Julien Bertheau had been cast opposite her as Napoleon; Pierre Aumont and Daniel G lin were assigned supporting roles. The film was to be directed by Renato Castellani and filmed in France. Gina had signed the contract in March 1957 for $160,000, half to be paid in Switzerland, the remainder in Italy. Work on the picture was about to begin in February 1958 when the papers announced that the actress had reneged on her contract.

The press registered that Gina wasn't satisfied with the cast and had asked for American leading men; furthermore, she wanted the picture to be made in English on location in Italy. Rizzoli pointed out that an American cast wouldn't fit the picture esthetically. But at this point, for reasons not stated, Castellani had been replaced by Christian-Jaque who had directed Gina in *Fanfan la Tulipe*. Also, Gina's option with Hughes was nearing its end, and rumors were rampant that Gina had her eye on Hollywood, eager to move to the Mecca of the cinema to catch up with Sophia Loren.

When Gina refused to do the picture, the producers threatened to sue the actress for return of prepayment of $65,000 plus damages of $250,000 for money already spent on the production. The National Union of Producers sided with Angelo Rizzoli when Gina sued him for $35,000 on grounds that, instead of the famous Hollywood actor the producer had promised as leading man, Lex Barker of *Tarzan* had been cast opposite her.

Lex Barker added to the confusion with his legal action against Gina's husband for telling reporters that if his wife hadn't put her foot down, the film would probably have ended up with the press, in inevitable irony, calling it *Imperial Tarzan*. Barker's lawyer, Giovanni Ozzo, declared that his client's libel suit against Milko wasn't because of the *Imperial Tarzan* crack, but in reference to a statement published in *Paese Sera* that the American star was a "déclassé" (outmoded) actor who came to Italy in search of fortune.

When *Imperial Venus* was finally made in 1962, it had undergone a complete face-lift with a script by Castellani and Delannoy directing it. The new cast featured France's Raymond Pellegrin as Napoleon and Irish actor Stephen Boyd (the villain Messala in *Ben-Hur*). The cast also included Micheline Presle, Massimo Girotti and Gabriele Ferzetti, a very credible Latin cast (with the exception of Boyd) for an original French-Italian story that took place between France and Italy.

The film was worth all the headaches it cost Gina, for the critics oohed and ahed. Lollobrigida's years of experience beneath the bright lights were continuing to pay off, contributing to the film's triumph.

This doesn't mean that Gina couldn't have rendered an outstanding performance had the picture been made four years earlier, but even fine wine improves with age.

Italian columnist Giovanni Grazzini, writing for *Corriere della Sera*, gushingly addressed himself to Gina's new film: "Burnished with beautiful color effects" (the picture was photographed in Technicolor), "crammed with sumptuous costumes, showcased in great cities and deluxe palaces, and interpreted by a star like la Lollobrigida, who is deservedly very dear to the public's heart, *Imperial Venus* has every chance of being considered the most elegant and exquisite of Italian films... In short, a vehicle upholding the high standards of the best Italian artistry."

Talking about high standards, Gina demanded that only the extremely necessary personnel remain on the set at Cinecittà for a risqué scene where Paolina Borghese poses nude from the waist up for sculpturer Antonio Canova (Gianni Santuccio). The scene lasts only 30 seconds but Lollobrigida's bust is NEVER revealed. The public only sees on screen the profile of the actress' torso as she poses reclined on a sofa. The lower part of her body is covered with a sheet, consistent with Gina's conservative screen attitude. In fact, Paolina posed for Canova at Villa Borghese, but instead of bringing her statue to the set, a replica of it with Gina's face was used instead.

To close the trilogy that brought la Bersagliera back to the Italian cinema, Castellani's *Mare matto* (The Wild Sea) provided the vehicle for the actress to deliver what she considered her best dramatic performance to date.

When Castellani thought of casting Gina as the plain old Margherita he feared she would refuse the part, so he first approached Milko, who felt the script wasn't good for his wife. The director then talked to the actress who, after hearing his interpretation of the role, said: "I'll do it." I'd like to clarify that Castellani didn't influence Gina to take the part; she accepted it of her own free will, convinced that it was worthy. No one yielded power over Gina's decisions; she had a mind of her own.

The film tells the story of an older woman who owns a boarding house for sailors on the Genoa waterfront. The unfortunate Margherita falls in love with a Livornese captain (Jean-Paul Belmondo), who depletes her savings and gives nothing in return.

The most difficult task involved in the characterization of Margherita was that of making Gina look older and plain looking: a beauty turned into a spinster. Glasses didn't seem to help because they gave her an intellectual air; the hair, no matter how twisted, appeared too lush. The transformation was finally achieved by whitening the eye sockets and the lips. Gina wore a loose sweater over an unflattering skirt, cotton socks and low heel shoes; the hair was drawn back. To complete the transformation Gina prepared herself for the role by walking around her villa mumbling that she was unattractive. This psychological exercise facilitated Gina's gradual understanding of what it meant to be undesirable. But the fact that she was supposed to look ugly didn't bother her and she emerged really glad to have had the experience.

Despite Castellani's efforts to present a Lollobrigida deprived of glamour, the director failed in his purpose. Probably the blame should fall on the make-up and wardrobe departments, which were unable to find the key to creating an unglamorous Lollo. Her skin, hair, hands and fingernails don't show traces of a woman who spends most of her time cooking and cleaning in a boarding house. Sophia Loren's transformation into a tired and good "fascist" mother of six is more convincing in Ettore Scola's *Una giornata particolare* (A Special Day, 1977). By that I don't mean that it was easier to ungloss the exotic actress; the make-up and wardrobe departments simply did a better job.

*Mare matto* had its merits though. The theme was taken from a new and unknown world cinematically exploring the humble people of the sea and their life. Castellani also gave more credibility to the dialogue by concentrating the language in the Livornese dialect. The photography by Toni Secchi was good and reviewers praised the cast.

\*\*\*

Because Gina was such a fine and popular actress, British director Jack Cardiff wanted her for his film *The Long Ships*. (Cardiff had been the color cinematographer responsible for the good photography in *Crossed Swords*.)

After an interview with the press, Cardiff angrily read in the papers that he had turned down Gina for his film. "I'm absolutely furious," he seethed at his London hotel. "An interview I gave through an interpreter has been misconstrued." The papers said the director was trying to substitute the Swiss star Ursula Andress, then 26, to play the part of a princess he had originally offered Gina. The truth is that from the very beginning Jack had Ursula in mind to play the 19 year old princess, but she wasn't available. The part Cardiff intended for Gina was that of a concubine, but upon reading the script, he realized that the part wasn't substantial enough for an actress of Gina's calibre. He told reporters he had never said "he didn't want just a pretty face" to star in his movie, as it was printed in the papers. "Who could say that of Gina? She is one of the world's greatest actresses. We are the greatest of friends," he beamed. Gina in Paris, told the press that Jack would never have said those things about her.

A Columbia picture, *The Long Ships*, starring Richard Widmark, Russ Tamblyn, Sidney Poitier and the Italian Rosanna Schiaffino, was definitely not a picture for Lollobrigida, as there were no really significant female roles. Had the movie been made in the late Forties the part of the concubine intended for Gina could have been appropriate, but the film was made in the early Sixties when playing a secondary role could have been a setback in Gina's career.

Another would-be Lollobrigida film in the early Sixties was the Spanish J. A. Bardem's *Les Pianos Mechaniques* based on the French novel by Henri-François Rye. The screenplay, "a kind of *Dolce vita* without the filthy language," said Gina, involves a group of intellectuals who are brought together by chance in a resort hotel. When the season is over and each one disappears his own way, the village returns to normal. The film wasn't made until 1965, when it starred Melina Mercouri and James Mason.

\*\*\*

Basil Dearden's *Woman of Straw* (1963) was Gina's first film made in England since the Anglo-American production of *A Tale of Five Women* back in 1951. Dearden's work unravels the story of a nurse, Maria Marcello (Gina), who is persuaded by Anthony Richmond (Sean Connery) to marry his unsympathetic uncle, Charles (Ralph Richardson), who is confined to a wheelchair and so, in due time, inherit and share with him the old man's exorbitant fortune. For a while, things go more or less as planned. The uncle grows fond of Maria, who by then has developed a genuine affection for the old man and accepts his proposal. However, when Charles dies prematurely, Maria is convicted of murder. The denouement soon becomes clear; Anthony murdered the uncle. With Maria in jail, he is eligible to inherit the fortune as next of kin. The tables turn on Anthony when one of the black butlers who has come to like Maria presents concrete evidence of the crime.

The critics received the picture with polarized opinions. An American columnist wrote: "*Woman of Straw* brings together three outstanding international stars in a suspenseful drama set against a plush Continental background... With Connery and Sir Ralph struggling to dominate the beautiful Gina, leading to a murderous climax... For Miss Lollobrigida, magnetic and beautiful Italian actress, the part of Maria in *Woman of Straw* is one of the most demanding and emotional roles of her career." Much less generous was the *Monthly Film Bulletin* "which approved of Connery, but wished greater inventiveness with the material." William Pepper in the *New York World-Telegram and Sun* concluded that Connery portrayed a "handsome but rather colourless figure" and that the actor was "much more fun as James Bond."

*The New York Times* was simply unfair to Gina. "Try as the script and camera may to convince us that Miss Lollobrigida is the most irresistible of females, she stubbornly remains her placid, matronly self." On the other hand, author Michael Feeney Callan in *Sean Connery: His Life and Films*, averred that "no matter what *The New York Times* says, la Lollo is sinful in slinky black satin, and the staging is good." Columnist Allen Eyles, writing for *Films and Filming*, defended the complete cast stating that the stars were adequate in their roles.

The Connery-Lollobrigida formula, however, didn't work off-screen. Despite Gina's gracious comment "I would accept another part opposite him [Connery] without even reading the script," the press reported that the two stars didn't get along well during the shooting of the picture.

For an actress of Gina's rank to say something flattering about her co-star was indeed generous, taking into consideration that Connery was practically an unknown, having just made his first 007 film, *Dr. No*, (1962). The actor should have felt flattered with the actress' comment, remembering her silver screen relationships with Anthony Quinn, Burt Lancaster, Yul Brynner and others. Moreover, it wasn't until 1965 that Connery became a box-office attraction in both America and Europe. Working with Gina Lollobrigida was Connery's first opportunity to co-star with a world famous actress, the most expensive in the cast of *Woman of Straw*.

# 157–Imperial Gina

When Lady Lollo and the "licensed to kill" actor met for the first time at the entrance of the Pinewood Studios restaurant, the encounter was anything but dramatic. "I'm your partner. My name is Sean Connery." "In that case, I don't need to tell you that I'm Gina Lollobrigida."

Connery didn't seem to have given much importance to the fact that he was going to play opposite one of the world's most famous actress; of all Gina's films he had seen only "*Fanfan la Tulipe*." Unlike Rock Hudson, he hadn't bothered to view one of her more recent pictures.

Making the film with Connery and "the short-tempered" Lollobrigida was no easy game. "The on-set mood was horrendous" wrote Michael F. Callan, "and technicians reported daily conferences, where director Darden cast oil on trouble waters." On one particular day Gina walked onto the set, huddled with Dearden, and then went into the scene with Connery. When the first take was over she walked to the far end of the stage and motioned to Dearden to follow her. She talked with him for a few minutes, returned for the second take, and consulted with Dearden again afterward. Connery, on the other hand, "was constantly suggesting script rewrites."

On location in Mallorca, their relationship worsened and the unhappy atmosphere prevailed until filming finished in December. Upon its completion Connery exclaimed: "I'll never work with that woman again." If his statement is true and not the work of some gossip columnist, it stands out amazingly with Gina's assertion that she'd accept another part opposite him without reading the script.

If there was a man who knew how and was happy to please Gina's demands, it was a representative of General Artists Corporation, Franco Reggiani, a dynamic and ambitious young man always ready to devote himself to Gina. Though the people at General Artists were happy to have the actress as one of their most prestigious clients, they didn't have direct contact with her, for all was taken care of by Reggiani.

When Gina arrived in London for *Woman of Straw*, he had everything under perfect control and was the first to be at the airport to receive her. The unbelievable young man had a Rolls-Royce at hand to take her to the Savoy where he himself inspected Gina's suite; he had also given instructions to the hotel management to have someone to greet her in Italian in the hotel lobby. (This wasn't really necessary since Gina spoke fluent English, but it was a thoughtful gesture.)

To smooth things at the airport, Reggiani had contacted Pinewood Studios and asked for someone to be there to help the actress to go through customs, and he visited the studio before her arrival and made arrangements to improve her dressing room. Undoubtedly, Gina was received like a queen; that was what she expected and that was what she got.

Because Gina was (and still is) a demanding and self-suficient woman, it certainly was difficult for her to compromise with anyone involved in filmmaking and in many ways, according to one critic, the actress was less flexible than Sophia Loren. A De Sica or perhaps a Castellani could in all probability make her bend, nonetheless her concessions would be minor ones. American or Italian agents couldn't influence la Bersagliera in her decisions. Her American agents had to work fast because once Gina made up her mind, chances were that no one had the power to make her change.

Right after the *Lady L* episode, Gina dismissed the Ashley Steiner Agency, which had been responsible for her Hollywood films. Even though the agency had top class clients such as Willian Holden and Yul Brynner, she opted for General Artists Corporation, whose list included celebrities such as Bette Davis, Cliff Robertson and Hugh O'Brian. While commenting on Gina, one of the directors from United Artists said that negotiating a contract with her was more strenuous than dealing with Marlon Brando, Cary Grant and Yul Brynner put together.

Extremely confident of herself, Lollobrigida usually got almost anything she asked for. Peer J. Oppensheimer, after visiting the actress in her dressing room on the set of Universal's *Strange Bedfellows*, wrote for *Family Weekly* that "Gina negotiated her first movie contract herself, and it is she who takes care of her own make-up, designs many of her clothes, touches up photographs submitted for her approval, and receives more publicity by her own efforts than most movie stars do with an entire studio press department!" As a matter of fact, her popularity in the early sixties was such that according to Ciné-Revue Gina received 20,000 letters in 1964, half of them being marriage proposals.

The desire to be an independent woman dates way back to her childhood and the war period. The second of four daughters, Gina soon established her pre-eminence by asking her parents to let her have a room of her own while the other sisters shared one bedroom. At first the Lollobrigidas didn't take the child's request seriously but Gina insisted. Many were the times when the girl wanted to have her meals alone, and when the family fled from Subiaco under dropping bombs it was Gina, then 17, that her parents turned to for advice.

This total self-reliance didn't always work to Gina's benefit, and the actress herself told the Italian magazine *Epoca* in early 1976 that she had been a bad actress in real life; too sincere and not very diplomatic. She understood she had made the mistake of going her way when sometimes it was necessary to yield to things as they happened. Despite this enlightment, Gina Lollobrigida has remained a woman of solid character who, according to her lifetime friend Rosina, never bent her head to anyone.

\*\*\*

It was Sophia Loren who once stated that the Skofics had been married for a long time and that people like them were married for good. Nevertheless, after 15 years of conjugal life, Milko and Gina were on the verge of separating. What could have gone wrong?

In a working environment such as show business a long lasting marriage is a praiseworthy accomplishment. Paul Newman and Joanne Woodward are a perfect example and so were the Skofics until rumors appeared that they were terminating their idyll. Sometime in 1962 Milko sought to still the stories of their supposed separation. Dr. Skofic then informed the *Citizen News* that he and his wife were "most happy and frankly speaking I enjoy being married to such a great star." His sense of humor prompted him to say that whenever he went to the Cannes Film Festival he didn't need a passport because he was accompanying Gina.

While Mrs. Skofic was in Mallorca in September 1963 for *Woman of Straw*, a staff correspondent for *The News* - Reynold Packar - mentioned that Gina had been on her own "for longer than ever before." On October 23, an Italian ladies' magazine, *Amica*, reported that when Gina, on her way from Barcelona to London, was asked if the rumors of her separation was true, the actress honestly replied: "Yes, we are separating." In Rome when asked to confirm or deny his wife's statement, Milko responded: "Why not ask Gina?" With the news of the Skofics' separation it was brought to light that the actress' husband, then 42, was very enthusiastically interested in the publication of an international encyclopedia on medicine for circulation in Europe and therefore had gradually lost interest in managing his wife's career.

While in London in the fall of 1963 Gina was staying in a hotel with her secretary and close friend Marta Descars, who denied insight into the reason for the Skofics' troubles. Miss Descars simply said that "they've been both drifting for some time." Meanwhile, a spokesman for United Artists was quoted as saying that Gina "has appeared to be under some sort of strain, but that of course is her business and none of ours. As an actress, she's been perfect."

Others touched the wound less gingerly. A friend of the actress related that Gina was "depressed and quite unhappy, but it isn't much of a marriage right now, and I wouldn't be surprised if it reached the breaking point fairly soon."

Until the Skofics were officially separated on October 24, 1966 there were no scandals involving the two parties and the couple managed the separation procedures as quietly as possible. Gina was proud of Milko for his efforts in the literary field and the physician was sure that his rich wife could take care of herself without him. Eight-year-old Milko Jr. was entrusted to Gina's care.

Amidst troubled waters, Gina did her best to cover up her unhappiness during a magnificent reception that the star held at her $1.5 million villa to honor movie czar Jack Valenti, who was on his first European tour as the new President of the Motion Picture Association of America.

After a fine cold buffet, the 80 guests, which included actresses Rosanna Schiaffino, Claudia Cardinale and Virna Lisi, producers Franco Cristaldi and Dino De Laurentiis, and actors Alberto Sordi and Walter Chiari, watched a performance by Spain's leading Flamenco dancer Antonio Gades and his troupe, which Gina had brought over from Madrid for the occasion. The actress herself exuded gypsy charm dancing with Gades.

In an interview given to *Oggi* almost a year after their separation, Dr. Skofic was quoted as saying that he hoped to obtain a divorce from Gina in Vienna in order to marry Austrian singer Ute von Aichbichler. Milko wasn't an Italian citizen and would find no barriers to taking new vows at the altar, but without an Italian divorce, Gina wouldn't be able to take the same step. Did she want to? The actress told the press she'd marry again when she was seventy. Gina had requested an annulment from the Vatican but Milko thought it would be impossible.

Early in 1967 Vittorio Gassman obtained such an annulment almost 16 years after separating from his first wife. There had been cases with a longer period and Gina was now on the list. Sophia Loren and Carlo Ponti solved the problem of Ponti's first marriage by both taking French citizenship and marrying in France. There were rumors that Gina was applying for Swiss citizenship, but the actress is as Italian now as when she was born.

After a legal separation of 18 months, Gina received the news that she had won a divorce from a Vienna court while she was in Catania (Sicily) filming *Un bellissimo novembre* (That Splendid November, 1968). However, under Italian law she was still Mrs. Skofic until the Vatican decided otherwise. The physician married his Austrian singer in Scotland sometime in 1969, although later the soprano won a divorce from him in Milan.

How did Signora Lollobrigida feel now that she was relatively speaking, a free woman? "I am happy since my divorce," quoted the *Citizen News* while the star was in the United States promoting "*Buona Sera Mrs. Campbell*" for United Artists. "Of course in Italy we don't have divorce," continued Gina, "but I feel free anyway."

Some eight years into her marriage, Gina realized that she had been working steadily at her career, staying home in the evenings and only infrequently going out. Probably with that awakening came the realization that she was bored with her married life and craved freedom. "Marriage is one thing. Love is another," she told reporters. "Love can last through life - marriage cannot. If I do not know how I shall feel or think tomorrow, how can I know what I shall feel about my husband in years to come?"

Gina finally became a completely free woman with the introduction of divorce in Italy in 1971. Gina had spent the first three months of that year in the United States and upon her return to Rome in April, she told *Gente* that she had heard the good news while overseas. Gina agreed that divorce was a necessary thing in Italy and opined that in any society it should be more difficult to marry and easier to divorce. Furthermore, like the ancient Etruscans, Lollobrigida felt that children should bear the mother's name since the birth of a child is entirely a mother's job.

Once Gina had obtained her Italian divorce she was quoted as saying: "I want to be free. Free to go out, to think, to dance, to do nothing if I like. I want independence - yes, that is the word. And freedom." Despite her yearning to slough off her marital shackles,

Lollobrigida's liberation was by no means a passport to lax morals; her reputation continued as that of a respectable woman.

Eleven years after their divorce, Gina said that she had never lived with another man after her marriage was dissolved. The actress elaborated on the topic saying that she'd rather go without love because it always brought her pain. Gina told the *Sunday Mirror* that she had married too young and "although the marriage lasted for many years it was never really happy." She felt something was wrong with it but she couldn't do much of anything about it. She was starting in her career and "working like a machine." Not knowing exactly what was wrong with her conjugal life, she just buried it. Thinking back on her marriage, Gina concluded that "the whole experience was a bad and hard one" and that she had been quite hurt by it. Moreover, Gina claimed that if either party had been at fault, it had been Dr. Skofic. "You meet a person and you think you know him. Then after 20 years you find he's another person."

Signora Lollobrigida could probably write a book about what really happened with her married life, but she doesn't want to talk about it. "Not now. Not ever."

\*\*\*

"You can rate an actress' popularity by the names of her co-stars," avowed UPI Hollywood reporter Vernon Scott in the early Sixties. "And using this measuring device," he expanded, "Gina Lollobrigida ranks among the top two or three." Scott may be just as biased as I, but Gina certainly starred with her share of top leading men. In the early-Sixties she had starred opposite Stephen Boyd, France's Jean-Paul Belmondo, and Rock Hudson, not to mention her long list of celebrated screen partners in the Fifties.

The triumph that Lollobrigida and Hudson achieved with *Come September* led Melvin Frank to reunite the two again in *Strange Bedfellows* (1964), filmed on the new European set in the back lot of Universal Studios.

In these two Hollywood comedies, as in the future *Buona Sera Mrs. Campbell*, Gina's part was that of a quarrelsome, unpredictable, and thoroughly intransigent Italian. *Strange Bedfellows* was a funny film that "looked good, and boasted a clutch of engaging comedy performances from Arthur Haynes, David King, Terry Thomas, Peggy

Rea, Nancy Kuop and Lucy Laundau." Actor Gig Young was good in the suporting role as Hudson's public relations man.

The picture tells the story of Carter (Hudson), an American oil executive stationed in London, and his beautiful but explosive Italian wife, Toni (Lollobrigida). The seven-year old marriage is on the rocks, jeopardizing Carter's promotion to the top. Richard Bramwel (Gig Young) is stuck with the difficult task of smoothing things over for his boss. The scheme to clean up "Carter's image seems to be working just fine when Toni decides to ride through Soho on a horse a la Lady Godiva. (Lollobrigida wore skin-colored tights.)

The oil executive arrives at the site as Toni and her group are about to begin the parade, too late to prevent her further damaging his career. Husband and wife are caught in their conjugal struggle by Carter's boss, who happens to be driving by. Ultimately, all problems are solved in court and merge into a Hollywood happy ending.

While Gina was in Hollywood for the picture, Milko limited his trips in order to spend more time with his six-year-old son. This was a difficult period for the Skofics for they were separating. In the Appia Antica the boy was always surrounded by the couple's staff; nevertheless, Gina and Milko spent as much time as possible with the boy.

Even though Milko Jr. visited his mother on many movie sets, seeing Gina in radically different clothes and make-up was a problem for him in earlier days; the child used to scream and cry every time he saw her in costume, and avoided her when he was brought over to the studios. The first time he noticed Gina in a long dress, he thought she was a nun.

Scared because of the ever present metamorphoses in his mother's physical appearance, the boy also screamed when she came into his room; but Milko Jr. was just a few years old then and his reaction was completely understandable. How could he tell whether his real mother was Gina Lollobrigida, Esmeralda or Sheba?

Gina adored her little boy; he was her cherubim and played a very important role in her life. If he couldn't be with her in California, they talked on the phone quite often. To help him have an idea of her career, Gina had shown him *Bread, Love, and Dreams*, and *The Hunchback of Notre Dame* but he still couldn't comprehend his mother's job.

In July 1964 Milketto, as the family called the boy, turned seven, and the first day he went to school he told the boys: "Do you know that my mother is Gina Lollobrigida?" He was proud of her. One day he came back from school with a black eye because he had fought with an older boy who had teased him about Gina. She was proud of him and rejoiced when Milketto was ranked 5th in his class.

Milko Jr. was a bright lad. As he began to grow and understand his mother's position, he also grasped his future. While riding with Roberto one day, the chauffeur asked him why he loved his mamma. The answer came with no hesitation: first because she loved him; second, because she was Gina, and third because she was a wealthy woman. When the family chauffeur told him that to become rich required much work, Milketto rebutted that, in his case, mamma was already a millionairess. Talk about being smart! At age 12 Milketto was very jealous of Gina and didn't like people paying her too much attention. Once when students in his school asked for her autograph, he became very angry. As years went by he began to mature and understand that his mother's profession required her to sign autographs.

***

Elegantly dressed all in white, Gina arrived at Tokyo's Haneda Airport on March 1, 1964 via Alitalia for the Italian Film Festival. It was the actress' first visit to Japan, where she had many fans and was best remembered as the gypsy Esmeralda. That spring the Japanese were about to add to their Lollo repertoire yet another film: *Imperial Venus*.

While in Tokyo, Gina stayed at the Akasaka Hilton Hotel where she was interviewed by the *Mainichi* newspaper. Gina, who had seen Kurosawa's *Rashomon* and *The Seven Samurai*, expressed her admiration for the Japanese filmmaker and told reporters that she would like to act under his direction one day.

Italian film stars Rosanna Schiafinno and Claudia Cardinale were also featured in the festival that lasted from the fourth to the eighth of that month.

After Gina's brief visit to Tokyo she returned to Italy for another film. Quite in contrast with the white outfit she wore for her arrival in the Japanese capital were the sexy black gowns she wore in *Le bambole* (The Dolls). Four highly regarded Italian directors - Mauro Bolognini, Dino Risi, Franco Rossi and Luigi Comencini - directed Lollobrigida, Virna Lisi, Monica Viti and Hollywood star Elke

Sommer, respectively, in four spicy episodes. The picture, originally entitled *The Vipers*, had been first idealized by director Mario Monicelli with la Lollo and la Mangano in the starrring roles, but the project fell through.

Two out of the four risqué sequences, *The Phone Call*, and *Monsignor Cupido*, were too spicy for an Ugo Rolfo, "a zealous public prosecutor" from Viterbo who filed charges against Lollobrigida and Virna Lisi, actors Nino Manfredi and Jean Sorel, directors Bolognini and Risi, and producer Giovanni Hecht.

Complaints fell most heavily against Bolognini's and Risi's sketches; Rossi's *The Soup*, and Comencini's *The Treatise on Eugenics* weren't mentioned in the case, so I suppose they weren't undully morally offensive to the Italian public at that time.

Actress Virna Lisi and her co-star Nino Manfredi were charged with participating in a particular scene in *The Phone Call* showing a husband trying to make his wife recline in bed; the prosecutor accused Gina of appearing "half-nude" in one scene of *Monsignor Cupido* with French actor Jean Sorel. Thus began a court case not destined to be resolved until 1967.

Bolognini's episode, an adaptation from a 14th century Boccacio story, depicts the adventures of the hotel keeper Beatrice (Lollobrigida), who seduces Vicenzo (Sorel), the nephew of Monsignor Arcudi (Akim Tamiroff).

The young man and his uncle arrive in Rome for the Ecumenical Council and lodge themselves in Beatrice's hotel. The gorgeous woman hides her beauty under black gowns to receive the priests and friars, and assumes an air of respectability, but falls head over heels for the handsome but serious Vicenzo, who ignores her approaches; ultimately, of course, he relents.

Prosecutor Ugo Rolfo charged that Bolognini's installment "culminates in an embrace between a youth and a woman who is shown on a bed with half her body completely nude." It's curious that the prosecutor took legal action after the government censor's approval of the picture as well as after its première in Northern Rome.

When Gina first appeared in court, she had to face a mob of some 50 paparazzi; the police had to form a barricade for the actress to get into the building and, although the court was officially closed to journalists, someone quoted the actress as flatly saying: "I wasn't nude. I had on flesh-colored tights." Gina told Judge Julio Franco that she'd be more than happy to offer him a copy of the original script to prove that the episode she had interpreted "wasn't obscene in any way." After a twenty-minute consultation, Judge Franco shook hands with Gina and went off to study the evidence of art imitating reality.

A blonde Lollobrigida was in Paris filming *Hotel Paradiso* for MGM in August 1965 when she told the press, referring to *The Dolls*, that she "didn't feel guilty at all." Gina was going to face the Roman court again in October and she was ready for it. On the day of the trial, the judge and other members of the court would be shown the uncut version of the picture which, after being seized, had been re-released with cuts.

On 7 April, 1967, Gina was cleared of charges by a five-judge tribunal which interrupted its hearing to go to a next-door theater for firsthand experience of the scene that had brought legal action upon the actress. Once back in their courtroom the judges took two hours to deliver the verdict. For them, Gina had committed a minor infraction, that of "offending public decency," but wasn't considered guilty of participating in "an obscene spectacle." Gina was granted amnesty. The verdict was also extended to Gina's co-star Jean Sorel, director Bolognini and the others involved in the case.

When Jane Russell starred in Hughes' *The Outlaw* the censors and the Catholic Church, forerunners of our Italian prosecutor friend from Viterbo, also raised hell because of a particular scene also involving "art imitating reality."

The script required Miss Russell to be filmed in bed with her co-star. When she started undressing, the screen went black; the next scene showed the supposedly nude actress under the sheets, but she was actually clothed; there was only the mystery of being naked involved. When the film, after a long battle with the pious ones, was finally released in 1943, "the Catholic Church was now excomunicating anyone who saw the picture and every pulpit sermonized the evils of the picture," as Miss Russell recalled.

Had the star appeared in the nude or wearing flesh-colored tights, she'd probably have been burned at the stake. What her tormentors ignored was that Jane Russell came from a very religious family and that the star herself wasn't the woman she portrayed on the screen; nor was Lollobrigida of *The Dolls* the real Gina that the world went gaga over.

# 167–Imperial Gina

During the whole period involving Gina's trial, she defended herself stating that her artistic and private lives were beyond reproach. Furthermore, the film was about "things that happen in life," said Gina. Then she added: "What do they want us to do - stick our heads in the sand and pretend the world is filled with saints?"

Speaking of "saints," it was rumored that Gina was going to play Mother Superior in a screen version of the Peruvian novel *Ivory Tower*. The actress had bought the rights herself and hoped to be rolling the film by early 1966. The story chronicled the fate of four nuns who were violated by rebels during the Chinese revolution. The picture was to have been filmed on location in Hong Kong, but the project was never realized.

\*\*\*

On 9 April, 1965, Gina Lollobrigida was in Beverly Hills to tape a TV show with Bob Hope. As if the trial involving her last film hadn't been enough, State Franchise agents took action against her for unpaid taxes between $13,000 and $14,000 on state claims dating from 1959. While Gina was staying at the Beverly Hills Hotel she discovered that she no longer had access to her own jewelry. A court order had sealed her safe deposit box at the hotel. Gina, naturally, was burning with anger over the incident, saying that it was "a silly, stupid misunderstanding."

Temporarily deprived of her regalia, Lollobrigida huffed that she felt naked without her jewels and claimed they were part of her wardrobe for the evening show. Even though Gina had the key to the box, she was forbidden to touch the gems until the tax men collected their share.

According to a spokesman for the star, that was the first time she ever knew about owing California taxes. Since she was constantly filming in different countries she had no time to worry about bureaucratic details which she usually left in the hands of lawyers. Doubtless the papers demanding payment of back taxes had been zigzagging between the desks of her many lawyers without her knowledge. Gina had always paid taxes in Switzerland, Italy and Canada; there was thus no reason for her to attempt evasion in the United States. And since Gina also had a business manager in Rome, she assumed that all bases were covered.

Signora Lollobrigida was shocked by the crude and unexpected manner in which the tax officials had dealt with her by confiscating jewels that were far more valuable than the amount they were meant to cover. "They didn't ask me. Not once. They would have had a check immediately if I had known about the taxes," Gina told the reporters.

On the day the jewels were confiscated, Lollobrigida made efforts to contact her banks in Europe but the difference in time (it was 3:00 a.m. in Switerland) foiled her attempt. She was scheduled to depart for Rome the following Monday morning, but she refused to leave the country without her stones. Happily, on Monday, Gina left for Rome on an early flight instead, her debt to the state paid and her treasure intact.

\*\*\*

The first half of the decade saw Gina's name linked with other motion pictures that, like *La dolce vita*, *Rocco and His Brothers*, and *The Long Ships*, ultimately finished without her. In *Return from the Ashes*, to be filmed in England, Gina was replaced by Swedish actress Ingrid Thulin playing opposite Maximillian Schell. Gina sued United Artists for $1 million for breach of contract. British director J. B. Thompson was surprised when he learned of the suit. "Although negotiations were started with her to play the part," he explained in London, "they were never completed because of our opposing concepts of the role." Gina addressed the world from Paris, declaring that it was "a most painful affair and very serious."

Meanwhile, back in Hollywood, United Artists tried to solve the case amicably by offering her two new pictures: *A Few Days in Madrid*, and a second one which wasn't specified. The only other Lollobrigida picture for the studio until the end of her career was *Buona Sera Mrs. Campbell*.

Gina was also suing Galatea Films of Rome for $145,000 for cancellation of *The Thaw*, to have been directed by Franco Rossi with the actress in the starring role.

The next occasion Lollobrigida made news wasn't a lawsuit, but her refusal to co-star in Robert Aldrich's *Four for Texas* - a "raucous and good-natured nonsense which made no demands on the intellect and pleased the fans." (The picture starred Ursula Andress and Anita Ekberg opposite Frank Sinatra and Dean Martin.)

# 169–Imperial Gina

In 1964 Paramount planned to put Daniel Defoe's *Moll Flanders* on celluloid, directed by Terence Young in London. The production debated whether to cast Sophia Loren and Warren Beatty or to star Gina Lollobrigida with Richard Harris. The final choices were Kim Novak and Richard Johnson. (The cast also included Vittorio De Sica, George Sanders and Lilli Palmer.)

\*\*\*

Fourteen years after Gina's enormous success in Blasetti's *Times Gone By* she was again reunited with him in *Io, io, io... e gli altri* (Me. Me. Me... and the Others, 1966), a study of selfishness in the human being. The picture, an Italian film industry's all-star tribute to Blasetti, included an exceptionally fine cast with Walter Chiari opposite Gina Lollobrigida, supported by Vittorio De Sica, Marcello Mastroianni, Silvana Mangano, Nino Manfredi and Silvia Koscina. The acclaimed film, Blasetti's official "arrivederci" to the cinema, was considered by an Italian critic as Lollobrigida's crème de la crème to date.

Gina's following movie, Delannoy's *L'amante italiana* from Christiane De Rivoyre's novel *Les sultans* (The Sultans), paired the actress for the first time with Louis Jourdan. Portraying Gina as an Italian photographer in Paris, the picture oddly foreshadowed Gina's second career, but failed to receive encouraging reviews.

To continue with her marathon film making, Gina was at the St. Maurice Studio outside of Paris to star in Glenville's *Hotel Paradiso* from George Feydeau's domestic farce *Hotel of Free Exchange*. The script presented Gina with a kingsized opportunity to give full rein to a form of comedy entertainment she had never before ventured on the screen. Co-starring with the celebrated Alec Guinness, Gina portrayed Marcelle Cot, a suburban housewife whose attempts at a one night stand with Benedict Boniface (Guinness), her next door neighbor, resulted in a terrible night of comic misfortunes at the "Paradiso," a hotel of ill repute.

The international cast responsible for the hilarious and confusing night of mistaken rooms and identities included Robert Morley as Mr. Cot, Peggy Mount as Boniface's wife, Derek Fowles, Ann Beach, Douglas Byng and guest stars Marie Bell and Akim Tamiroff.

In 1965, Glenville had successfully staged Feydeau's play in London and New York starring Alec Guinness. Together with

Jean-Claude Carriere, Glenville elaborated on the script and himself played the French playwright who throughout the movie observes the intrigues involving the two curious couples. The audience wonders why this good-looking chap seems to hang around the Bonifaces' and the Cots' taking such interest in the goings-on there. The film thus has excellent continuity culminating with the mysterious playwright's work unfolded on stage before the not-really-guilty Madame Cot and Monsieur Boniface.

Glenville, a theater man, incorporated asides and a high-toned, clear recitative speech into this MGM production, thus giving the impression that one is watching a play. "It's the most difficult thing I've ever done," admitted Gina. "It is just like theater." Gina's performance was outstanding, hinting at stage potential. Guinness, who began his career as a fine Dickensian actor, couldn't have been better in the role of Peggy Mount's henpecked husband. Monsieur Martin (Douglas Byng), the Bonifaces' dear old friend who stutters when it rains, was brilliant.

Gina, who enjoyed the interlude, presented the crew with an individual photograph of each member, taken by herself, when she left the studio.

After working with Glenville, Gina returned to Rome to do *Le piacevoli notti* (Pleasant Nights) for Fair Films. Of the three tales comprising the picture, critic Aldo Scagnetti considered Gina's the best. The other two episodes featured Vittorio Gassman and Ugo Tognazzi.

Under the direction of Armando Crispino and Luciano Lucignani, the picture transported the audience to the Middle Ages with the story of a painter, Bastiano di Sengallo, who embarks on a journey disguised as Pope Giulio II. The narrative concerning Lollobrigida is the second where Domicilla (Gina), wife of astrologer Bernadozzo (Adolfo Celi), begs the Pope's forgiveness for an illicit dream involving three soldiers.

Following this medieval adventure in Eastmancolor, Gina was in Spain to play Giulia Toffolo in Vincent Sherman's *Cervantes* based on Bruno Frank's novel on the life of the Spanish novelist and playwright. King Vidor took several months preparing the film, but it was Sherman who finally directed it and little of Vidor's effort was visible in the final product.

It's surprising that, until then, the adventurous and passionate life of the celebrated Spanish warrior-poet had never found its way to the screen. Bits of Cervantes' life appeared on Enrique del Campo's *El huésped del Sevillano* (The Sevillano's Guest, 1939), but the film was far from what Cervantes deserved.

Photographed in Supertotalvision 70 mm. Eastmancolor, Sherman's *Cervantes* presented moviegoers with entertaining biographic episodes of the poet's youth, while Arthur Hiller's *Man of La Mancha* (1972) starring Sophia Loren and Peter O'Toole, emphasized the adventures of the noble knight-errant of La Mancha, an adaptation of Dale Wasserman's popular musical based on *Don Quixote*. (Other versions of Cervantes' masterpiece were filmed in France in 1902, 1908 and 1911, Italy in 1910, USA in 1915, Britain in 1923, Denmark in 1926, Spain in 1927, USSR in 1957, and Britain again with the ballet version of Rudolf Nureyev in 1975. In the Fifties Orson Welles undertook an intriguing production of *Don Quixote* but the picture was never completed.)

Released in America as *The Young Rebel* (1966), the picture reconstructed, as faithfully as possible, the events that were closely related to the venturesome years of Cervantes' younger days. German actor Horst Buchholz starred opposite Lollobrigida as the young Don Miguel de Cervantes Saavedra. The cast also included Louis Jourdan as Cardinal Acquaviva, Best Actor Academy Award winner José Ferrer (*Cyrano de Bergerac*, 1950) as the Mussulman Hassam Bey, and a host of Spanish stars such as Francisco Rabal, Fernando Rey and Soledad Miranda. The cast rendered a brilliant performance; however, the Puerto Rican born José Ferrer, once a Princeton University student, speaks impeccable English and therefore the characterization of his role lacks credibility. Peter Ustinov, who can imitate any accent with perfection, would have been the ideal choice for the part; his matchless performance as an Arabian slave trader in *Ashanti* (1979) speaks for itself.

For all its luxurious decor, lavish costumes, and faithful exterior and interior reconstructions, *Cervantes* received mixed reviews. There were hurrahs for such scenes as: the Battle of Lepanto against the Turks (filmed in Cartagena), in which Cervantes was seriously wounded in the left hand, Giulia's (Lollobrigida) farewell to Cervantes, the imprisonment of the Spanish hero and his encounter with the Spanish King Phillip II.

\*\*\*

Of the world's festivals there's nothing that can be compared to the Rio Carnival. International tourists flock to this former Brazilian capital to enjoy the city's dazzling Samba parades. Dances at the most prestigious clubs and hotels defy description, displaying lavish costumes worth thousands of dollars.

Another attraction of the Rio Carnival are the celebrities invited by the Minister of Tourism. International V.I.P.s have danced at least in one, if not in several, of the most distinguished Rio clubs during Carnival. Gina was to have been the guest of honour in 1966, but because of her busy schedule she had to cancel the invitation, and the Minister of Tourism invited the Nobel prizewinning American physicist Richard P. Feynman instead. What a curious replacement!

The 1967 Rio Carnival welcomed Gina Lollobrigida as its main attraction. While in town, Gina, whose popularity in Brazil is enormous, stayed in the Copacabana Palace Hotel. A couple of days after her arrival, a press conference was called and hundreds of reporters, photographers and movie directors waited anxiously to question the actress in a luxurious salon of the Copacabana Palace. Unfortunately, the whole thing turned out to be a disaster.

Gina, who is an expert on Lollobrigida, told photographers not to direct their cameras on her inside the hotel. They didn't listen to her and as they raised their flashes above their heads, an angry Lollo walked out on them. The disappointed journalists and paparazzi didn't like the lesson and left the hotel.

When the particular event took place, the reporters of popular weekly *Manchete* decided to wait, for they knew that Gina would concede them the interview she had promised. After the storm was over, a calm and smiling Gina, dressed as Countess of Castiglione (a figure of the Italian great national revival of the mid-19th century), posed for the delighted photographers of the referred magazine.

An eternal shutterbug, Gina, wearing a gorgeous turn-of-the-century costume, later photographed parades and dances; she was completely overwhelmed with the decoration of the Copacabana Palace Ballroom where for three hours she joined the jury of the Costume Contest. Then, wearing one of her Paulina Bonaparte gowns from *Imperial Venus*, la Bersagliera danced until 2:30 a.m. at the Copa with rhythm, lights and fantasy.

At one particular club, however, it was rumored that Gina refused to do the samba and the media wasn't very courteous to her, saying that she was "too 'mature' to be a swinger." Gina was 39 then, and exuded youth and vitality. "I'm very vexed with the press," she protested. "If they think I'm old, they might at least leave out the adjectives for the sake of delicacy." Apart from this ill-natured journalist's comment, Gina was mostly celebrated in Rio; from her talent, beauty, and costumes to the short, blonde wig she wore at the Baile da Rosa de Ouro (The Golden Rose Ball) where more than 1,200 Brazilians and huge numbers of tourists danced.

Concerning her career in the Sixties, Gina informed the Director-Editor of *Manchete*, senhor Roberto Muggiati, that now she could choose screenplays that pleased her since she absolutely had no need to work anymore; she'd rather enjoy the present, go on trips around the world and know more about life and not think about work. Also, quality roles were becoming rare and Gina usually sent back poor scripts, explaining the dearth of Lollobrigida films in the new decade when compared to the glorious Fifties. There were also rumors that Gina's popularity had declined and that the better parts were offered to Sophia Loren instead. This wasn't really the case. It's true that Mrs. Ponti gave a brilliant performance in De Sica's *Two Women* (1961), which won her an Oscar, but "the early Sixties was the high point of her career; most of her films since then have been disappointing, leaning unfairly on her charm, warmth and resplendent poise."

***

Looking better than ever, on July 4th, 1967 Gina turned forty and she was proud of it. She had become more beautiful. "If this is what age does to me," she told Italian reporters, "let's have more of it. I simply photograph better. I am still all good angles." *Photoplay* writer, Ken Johns, commented that "at forty she looks even more beautiful, more serene, more enchanting and so much more radiant than when she was twenty." Gina agreed and elaborated on Johns' words. "When I was younger I had a roundish kind of face. Now I am a little thinner in the face. I don't look so babyish. My face now reflects greater serenity too. It has more expression than it used to have. So as a consequence it is more interesting than when I was younger."

Indeed, Gina was very happy with her looks as well as with her life, and growing old for her generated no fears. "I do not regret growing old if this is what age does to me. Even I prefer the way I look nowadays. Every year is more interesting for me, life gets longer and very much better. I have always lived very intensely and that is the only way for me." Also, adding to her happiness was the fact that she was working for pleasure. La Lollo loved to work and had always been very active. In the beginning of her career she worked hard to establish herself, to become famous, to be in demand. "Now that I have the possibility to choose my roles, it's somewhat different. Every time I do a film nowadays, it's because I like the role. I refuse to plan ahead; I change my mind so quickly. But as long as picture making gives me pleasure and satisfaction, I'll continue to go before the cameras."

As far as producing her own movies was concerned Gina once affirmed she had no interest in it. She felt she was a better actress than a business woman. However, years later, she got herself involved in business, adventurously founding The American Cosmetic Company, which went bankrupt, a finale not entirely her fault. Nevertheless, Gina's business sense couldn't be that bad, for her Photo Studio Lollobrigida and her career as a photojournalist flourished in the Seventies and Eighties.

*** 

Early in the summer of 1967 Gina received a phone call from Bob Hope asking if she'd accept a guest star role in Frank Tashlin's World War II comedy "*The Private Navy of Sgt. O'Farrell.*" Since Gina had pleasant memories of working with the acclaimed American comedian, she gladly accepted the invitation. Gina immediately called her agent and made plans for postponing two films she had signed to do in Italy in order to have time to work with Bob.

The picture was filmed in Puerto Rico, and Gina loved the warm island which isn't as hot as Rome in the summer because of the trade winds that always blow. Gina's part was small, giving her plenty of time to explore old San Juan, which came alive in the evenings. Gina also went to the theater almost every night.

Participating for the first time in a feature film with Bob Hope was an uplifting experience for Gina, who enjoyed working with him more than she had anticipated; Bob's sense of humor and easygoing personality put her at ease. "He's always telling funny jokes, so that we laughed before the scene and after, and sometimes during the scene, though director Frank Tashlin didn't find this as hilarious as we did. Bob gets one in a relaxed mood - very important when I'm still unsure of certain English words. He's a very nice man, gentle and friendly. And he's a wonderful actor, too."

After this Lollo-Hope friendly encounter, Gina was again in Rome with only one day off before she started working for Giulio Questi's *La morte ha fatto l'uovo* (Death Has Laid an Egg) with French Actor Jean-Louis Trintignant. The film, also quoted as *Chickens*, was released in America as *Plucked*.

Director Questi and his co-author Franco Arcalli tried to take to the screen a sort of cinema kitschy, and to make a popular film about chickens with Lollobrigida in the starring role was in itself quite an undertaking. Questi was very enthusiastic about the project and Gina herself thought the plot was interesting.

A psycho-sociological thriller, the film involves the lives of Marco (Jean-Louis Trintignant), a young intellectual who runs a modern chicken farm, and his wife Anna (Lollobrigida). Marco is carrying a on love-affair with Anna's cousin, Gabri (Ewa Aulin), who betrays Marco with her lover Mondaini (Jean Sobieski) with the intent of murdering the couple and inheriting the farm. When Anna's husband finds his wife's corpse he's afraid of being accused of uxoricide and plans to get rid of the body. While trying to throw it in a millstone he stumbles and falls, meeting his death. Gabri and Mondaini, unaware that Anna's corpse lies unburied, sing victory. Ultimately, the crime is discovered and both are arrested.

*Plucked* certainly wasn't one of Gina's top ten but it presented her with the opportunity of doing something unusual. Times were changing and it didn't hurt to try a new celluloid adventure. The film, however, was rather peculiar for those days and received lukewarm criticism.

***

An anonymous quote on friendship reads: "Fare thee well for I must leave thee/ Do not let this parting grieve thee/ And remember that the best of friends must part."

When the Lollobrigidas departed from Subiaco in 1944, the move was done rather hastily, and Gina and her best friend Rosina couldn't say goodbye. A couple of years after their arrival in Rome, Rosina went to the Italian capital one afternoon and by mere coincidence spotted Gina in the street. During the brief encounter filled with mixed emotions, they talked as they had in the old days, listening to each other's dreams. Gina told Rosina about her being approached to be in the movies and that she was also posing for a magazine.

There wasn't much time for the two friends to share their thoughts; Gina was on her way to Cinecittà and Rosina had to take the bus back to Subiaco. As they said goodbye the two promised to keep in touch. Even though they nourished their friendship in their hearts, communication wasn't the best despite their efforts to exchange letters. Once in a while, after Gina became a celebrity, Rosina received a post card from the star who was then filming either in Paris or Hollywood. Their lives had taken different roads.

Sometime in 1967, twenty years after the two friends met in the Eternal City, Rosina was taken completely by surprise when one afternoon Gina and Milko Jr. arrived unannounced at her house in Subiaco. Lollobrigida was elegantly dressed but that didn't embarrass Rosina, who was doing housework; as soon as the two met, Gina was again Ginetta - she put on no airs.

As they talked in the region's dialect and laughed like old friends, Rosina noticed that Gina's looks had changed drastically. She was more beautiful and refined, nevertheless deep in her heart she was the same as when the two knew each other in their childhood. The ocean that kept these friends apart - a film actress and a local director of education - hadn't drowned their friendship. Signora Rosina is today one of the few privileged to have Gina's private telephone number in the Appia Antica; and, as a dedicated friend, the teacher never missed one Lollobrigida film.

After this short informal visit to Subiaco that lasted for a few hours, Gina returned again to her hometown on an official visit in 1971. Until then, she kept herself busy working for different movie studios and planning her second career.

***

A superb comedy, *Buona Sera Mrs. Campbell*, awaited Gina in 1968. Funny and romantic, the film, under the direction of Melvin Frank for United Artists, presented Gina with a perfect role. "Mrs. Campbell is so much the Italian type," remarked a happy Lollobrigida. "It's like I'm a hundred percent her. It fits me like a glove. It was not an effort to do, I was just being me all the time." Undoubtedly, the characterization of Mrs. Campbell (for which Gina was awarded a

"David di Donatello") was the actress' most brilliant performance of the comedies she did in the Sixties.

Carla Campbell is somewhat reminiscent of *Anna di Brooklyn*, where Gina also played an Italian woman in her native setting with an American background story.   Mrs. Campbell is beautiful, free, outspoken and explosive as a volcano in moments of anger. She's also a loving mother, a woman who - despite her short temper - can't nourish hatred.   She does, however, pop in and out of moods as though she were trying and discarding pairs of gloves.   One moment she's tender to Vittorio (Philippe Leroy) - her employee and lover - and the next, she's calling him a "ridiculous, stupid ass."   She adores Gia (Janet Margolin), her daughter, but when she finds out the girl is in love with a married man in Paris, the walls tremble with Carla's rage.   Nonetheless, her fury soon dissipates.

*Buona Sera Mrs. Campbell*, supported by an excellent American cast, contributed to the film's popularity in the States, for it gave the audience something to identify with; each of the three World War II veterans (Telly Savalas, Peter Lawford and Phil Silvers) is self-assured that he's the father of Carla's 18-year-old daughter.   Their wives are actresses Lee Grant, Marian Moses and Shelley Winters who, together with their husbands, return to visit Carla's Italian village 20 years after the war.

One of my favorite scenes is the hospital sequence after Gia has crashed her car into a wall.   When the girl discovers that there was no Captain Campbell (Carla got the name from the American Campbell soup) and that she's the illegitimate daughter of one of the three former GI's, she jumps into the car and leaves to join her boyfriend in Paris.   To stop her, Carla calls the police and tells them Gia stole the car and that she should be put in jail.   By doing so, the girl would have time to calm down, and Carla could have a chance to explain to her what happened during the war.   When the daughter, completely safe and sound in a hospital bed, tells her mother that the police arrested her on charges of stealing the car, Carla responds: "We'll sue them."   Here, as throughout the picture, Carla molds into Gina, ever ready to sue.   Gina was being herself all the time in the picture.

From the upbeat tune *Buona Sera* as the credits are superimposed over Gina's drive through the countryside until the end of the show, Melvin Frank keeps the audience glued to the screen.   The script has no monotonous scenes, and the story develops smoothly with funny, colorful, and sometimes romantic dialogues.   The direction is outstanding and Gina's timing is unmatched. *Buona Sera Mrs. Campbell* and the entire cast enjoyed positive reviews in *Films and Filming* and *Sight and Sound*. The picture also achieved nearly the same success that *Bread, Love, and Dreams*, *Beautiful But Dangerous* and *Fast and Sexy* enjoyed in the Fifties. An Italian critic considered it Gina's most outstanding Hollywood movie. Its success lay in the fact that American reviewers and the public saw a Lollobrigida completely devoid of the glossiness that the Land of Unfulfilled Dreams had cast upon her. On the other hand, her part was that of the Italian female Americans in general imagine - attractive and temperamental.

*** 

From comedy Gina jumped again to a dramatic role. Four years after the censorship battle and the lawsuit case with Bolognini's *The Dolls*, Gina was paired again with the Italian director in a French-Italian production, *Un bellissimo novembre* (That Splendid November, 1968), a delicate script dealing with the love affair of a 17-year-old youth and his aunt. Despite its plot the film didn't raise any eyebrows.

Based on a novel by Ercole Patti, the story takes place in Catania (Sicily), where love affairs among family members seem to be a common casualty. In Patti's work the nephew, Nino (Paolo Turco), dies. In the screenplay, though, he weds his cousin Giulietta (Isabella Savona), "a marriage of convenience for the young man that lets surmise the continuation of the relation with his aunt, once face is saved." The aunt, Cetina (Lollobrigida), is married to Biagio (Gabriele Ferzetti).

For some particular reason, Bolognini didn't get on at all well with Gina; he wasn't pleased with the film and considered it "of secondary importance." He believed he hadn't been courageous enough to study the nephew-aunt relationship and that the film lacked an apex which he wasn't able to find. Nevertheless, the picture is honest in its portrayal of the Sicilian background and the haut bourgeois family involved in the plot.

*That Splendid November* was Lollobrigida's 55th film and the first in which her voice had been dubbed since *The Wayward Wife*. Since Gina had long ago specified in her contracts that she wouldn't be dubbed in Italian, French and English speaking movies, her fans were at loss to explain why the trend was abruptly reversed at this stage of her silver screen career.

A minor production, *Stuntman*, was Gina's last film of the decade. Her part was that of Evelyne, a beautiful gold-digger who finances a happy-go-lucky group of movie stuntman against a gang of thieves about to steal a priceless Indian statue. Her motivation to help the stuntman stem not only from her desire for justice, but also from her love for Johnny (Robert Viharo), one of the young men in the group.

Something that pleased Gina about *Stuntman* was the freedom she had to design her wardrobe, a right she had also been granted in several previous productions. The picture, however, directed by Marcello Baldi for Ultra Film (Italy) and Marianne Productions (France) received mixed criticism. While *Films and Filming* considered this Baldi project a mediocre Italian commercial production and an unsuccessful mixture of thriller and comedy, *Il Messaggero* praised Lollobrigida and her American co-star.

Even though *Stuntman* is documented in Ponzi's *The Films of Gina Lollobrigida* as the actress' only 1969 film, Ronald Bergan's *The United Artists Story* lists Vittorio Caprioli's comedy of sexual antics *Scusi, facciamo l'amore* (Listen, Let's Make Love) as another Lollobrigida feature for that year. Also starring Pierre Clementi and Beba Loncar, the movie was shown with English subtitles on the "art cinema" circuit in the USA.

Like many other foreign films, *Listen, Let's Make Love* was first shown in its country of origin (Italy) and then distributed in America by United Artists or its associate company Lopert Pictures Corporation. While Ponzi's work excludes the picture from Gina's filmography, Giani Rondolino's *Dizionario del cinema italiano 1945-1969* includes the work in Caprioli's entry but deletes it from Lollobrigida's. To further complicate the mystery the actress has remained silent in her interviews concerning the subject. Could it have been an unpleasant experience that Gina would rather forget?

\*\*\*

The latter part of January 1969 saw a happy Gina promoting *Buona Sera Mrs. Campbell* in New York, where she did some dancing and singing in the Dean Martin and Ed Sullivan shows. When Gina returned to Europe she had a face-to-face encounter with death on

Italy's Super Highway of the Sun, some sixty miles north of Rome, on Sunday, February 16.

The tragic event that almost cost Gina's life made headlines all over the world; the *Pravda*, a publication that usually stays clear of human interest reports, dedicated two columns to Gina. In the States, news was updated by the hour, while Gina, recuperating in her hospital room received flowers and telegrams from friends and admirers, including Italy's President Giuseppe Saragat who sent both twice.

On that fateful Sunday, Gina was driving director Franco Zeffirelli, photographer Thomas Newman and critic Gian Luigi Rondi to a soccer match in Florence when her Rolls-Royce hit a patch of ice on the highway; it skidded and went completely out of control. The car bounced off the guardrail and then back into the wall before coming to a stop. On the left side of the road there was a 50-foot cliff; it was either the wall or the big fall. It was a miracle they were alive. Gina had grasped the steering wheel with such power that she actually bent it. "When you are on the edge of death, your strength is like that of ten people," she told *Photoplay*.

The victims were hospitalized in the city of Orviedo. Gian Luigi suffered minor injuries and the photographer emerged unhurt. Gina and Zeffirelli received the full impact of the crash. The director suffered serious cuts on his face and contusions on his head, but the doctors fortunately found no traces of a skull fracture. Gina's face was injured and her left kneecap fractured in four places, requiring her to undergo surgery. That Sunday evening the Orviedo doctors permitted Gina to be transferred by ambulance to a Rome clinic with Rondi.

Soon major newspapers and tabloids carried headlines giving the impression that Gina would never walk again: CRASH LAMES ACTRESS; GINA INJURED IN AUTO CRASH. One particular headline tried to offset the tragedy with a touch of humor: BROKEN KNEECAP BUT Ooooo, LA LOLLO'S.

From her bed in the hospital, Gina phoned Milko Jr. at the Rose High-School near Geneva telling him not to worry, although she herself feared she'd never walk again. After surgery, however, her physician, Prof. Gabriele Crespi, informed UPI that she'd be walking within a month. "The injury will have absolutely no permanent aftereffect. She can return to work fairly soon." Mother Nature healed the star's facial injuries and Gina's silky skin was left perfectly unscarred.

The psychological repercussions she endured during the long months of recuperation after the operation were worse than the physical injuries. She was afraid of going out, and felt insecure about practically everything. It was probably the most difficult adjustment period of her life and she had to fight it; she was depressed to the point of refusing dinner invitations with friends.

Three months after her kneecap was operated on, RAI UNO (Radiotelevisione Italiana), Italy's state-run television network, invited the actress to do a TV show with an hour of her own. In the past Gina had turned down offers for appearing on Italian TV for she felt that television fees in her native land were absurdly low, and she rejected the latest offer as usual. (Gina's participation in one installment of *Il mattatore* in 1959 had been the only exception.) Her doctor, however, sensed that work would be her quickest road to mental well-being, and strongly recommended her to consider the offer. She finally did the show, which turned out to be a well-received venture and thus therapeutic.

*Stasera Gina Lollobrigida* (May 24, 1969) produced by Guido Sacerdoti and directed by Antonello Falqui, was at the time one of the most popular Saturday night TV shows featuring well-known celebrities. Of the series, Gina's proved to be the most colorful. It moved at fast tempo and it was funny, since the actress herself didn't mind making light of her driving and the fact that she was in her forties. The car crash was used for several jokes which the public greatly enjoyed.

The main production number, If I Had the Zip of..., presented Lollobrigida lavishly costumed as Cleopatra, Marie Walewska (intimate of Napoleon), Lucretia Borgia, and cosmonaut Valentina Tereshkova. La Lollo even went Flamenco! And the big finale had Gina wandering seductively through a studio filled with flowers as a chorus sang: "I Love You, Lollo."

Director Falqui enjoyed working with Gina and described her as being "very active, willing, disciplined and serious." The day following the Lollobrigida special, *Il Messaggero* published one of the most striking comments on Gina: "One hears a great deal about a wonder drug against old age, 'Gerovital.' Just a few drops or injections are sufficient to keep one young and fit. The sale of 'Gerovital' is forbidden in our country and people go to buy it in Switzerland. But what need is there of 'Gerovital' when here in Italy we have 'Lollovital'?"

Not all Italian critics, however, were in tune with *Il Messaggero*. Many of them seemed to resent that Gina insisted on continuing to act as if she were the Lollo of the early Fifties. The Communist Party newspaper L'Unità, for example, remarked that "in the past RAI has puritanically covered the necklines of lady announcers and of the actresses in their shows. Yet, the latest *Stasera* program revolved, one may say, on Gina's decolletage. From an aesthetic point of view it is, without doubt, progress; but if RAI, besides uncovering the female graces, could also discover some ideas, it would not be a bad thing."

Falqui rejected the criticism as "unjustified." Gina, used to comments of all sorts dismissed the bad reviews. "You know, Italians are very critical of their own people. It's not easy for them to be generous," said Gina who was now eager to do more TV, but in the States rather than in Italy. "They're better organized in American TV," she advised. "They work fast, but at least they give you time to eat and sleep. Also, the money is better."

To tape Gina's special took ten 13-hour work days. Gina complained that on the last day she was given 22 pages of dialogue at 1:00 p. m. to shoot an hour later. "Of course, they have a prompter you can read, but still, to be natural, you must at least see the lines a little before." And all that work for a fee that Gina refused to reveal. The total budget for the show was only $48,000.

Regardless of the problems, Gina had the program to thank for pulling her out of depressing convalescence and opening a new field; she was showered with more invitations for TV shows, including one from Buenos Aires. She had already appeared on some American TV shows before the accident, and would do several more in the future.

Gina's second kneecap operation was successfully performed after "*Stasera*." The doctors removed the metal ring that held the broken bones of the kneecap together and Gina returned to her normal activities. In April of 1971 she was the guest star of Engelbert Humperdinck's TV show in London. Gina, an admirer of Humperdinck and Tom Jones as well, keeps the former's photo in a special place with those of other celebrities in her Roman villa.

\*\*\*

Road accidents involving show business stars have occasionally cost them their lives. Probably the most remembered tragedy of this kind befell James Dean in 1955 when the young idol was about to shoot the last scenes of *Giant*. Another car crash victim was Jayne Mansfield, who was killed on her way to a TV show in New Orleans in 1967.

Like Lollobrigida, Rock Hudson and Montgomery Clift (Monty) were lucky to have emerged alive from near fatal wrecks. Of the three, Monty received the hardest blow since his handsome face was never the same after he smashed his car into a telephone pole on his way home from a party at Liz Taylor's in 1957. His face and lips had been badly cut, his two front teeth were knocked out, his jaw was broken in four parts, his nose was broken in two places and one cheekbone was completely cracked.

Gina believes she was saved by a mysterious Egyptian ring she has. Latins in general are superstitious and Gina doesn't consider herself an exception. She knocks on wood, doesn't cross under a ladder, sees bad luck in a black cat, and avoids crossed hand greetings.

The day the accident took place she was already in the car with Zeffirelli and the other two passengers when she decided to walk back to the house to pick up her mysterious Egyptian ring that dates back to 100 B.C. Gina treasures the ring. Zeffirelli, however, convinced that Gina's amulet was involved in their misfortune, usually went out of his way to avoid Gina whenever he saw her wearing it after the crash; but Gina still believes that had it not been for her Egyptian ring, the four of them would be dead today.

The frightening Sunday accident yielded an altered Lollobrigida; she had always been in love with life, but now she embraced it with a greater intensity than before. In the early Seventies she was at peace with the world. She had a rewarding career, a handsome son, was valued by friends and admired by millions. Gina was never bored, and her enthusiasm kept her young. And whenever cloudy thoughts started to creep into her mind, she only had to look at the smashed Rolls-Royce that decorated the green lawn of her villa, and immediately relief and gratitude flowed through her veins.

\*\*\*

George S. Kaufman, a wealthy Manhattan real estate executive, met Gina at a New York party in the fall of 1969. Kaufman had never seen Gina on the screen, but his love and admiration for her had grown since they began to see each other. The American had been divorced for the last three years and had two daughters, 14 and 12. Gina was 4l (as was Kaufman) and Milko Jr. was 12 and still studying in Switzerland.

Lollobrigida and Kaufman decided to get married a couple of months after they first met, and December 20 had been set for their wedding day. Not too long after the announcement about the forthcoming ceremony appeared in the papers, a close friend, speaking for Gina and her beau, said the nuptial rites were postponed till January.

Meanwhile, Gina was in St. Moritz to shoot *Snow Job* opposite Hugh O'Brian, playing the role of a "sort of absent-minded Mata Hari," explained Gina "who gets into lots of hot water." The shooting was delayed for various technical reasons and two years later, the film still had no starting date. Gina never did the picture.

When one day Gina and George were flying on board a Boeing 707 from Geneva to New York, a photographer tried to take a snap shot of the two in the first-class cabin while they were having lunch. They had faced some 200 paparazzi at the airport, and the last thing they needed was yet another lens-happy creature. At the moment the shutter clicked, Gina was holding a bottle of champagne, which she flung at the startled man. The photo fared better than the photographer; the former covered newspapers around the world, while champagne drenched the latter.

Once in New York, the wedding was again postponed until spring, and then the announcement came that it was permanently off "for personal reasons," as Gina explained. Could it have been because under Italian law she was still Mrs. Skofic? Would she have married the Manhattan executive had they met after divorce was introduced in Italy in 1971? The *L. A. Times* quoted Gina saying that she had always been against marriages. "I have said that hundreds of times in the past, but I thought things were different this time. I was confident things could turn out well. But I soon realized the situation was not for me. I talked to George and we cleared all problems."

Years later, Gina confided to *Gente* that it was difficult for her to think about marriage. She was a very active woman with engagements in different countries and finding the right man wasn't easy. Furthermore, she wasn't looking for one. Gina found a happy balance in her professional and private lives, and cherished her financial independence. Moreover, since her Italian divorce in 1971, Gina has declared she's "too complicated for a man. If you're independent, you don't need a man. It's a problem."

Other than Gina's brief and quiet relationship with Kaufman, her only well-publicized romance was a short-lived affair with Dr. Christian Barnard. The two notables met in Rome sometime after the South African surgeon had performed the world's first heart transplant operation in 1967. He was still married and for a while he and Gina exchanged letters, but when he ultimately proposed he assured the actress that he was thinking of divorcing his wife. Gina turned him down.

In February 1970, Lollobrigida was in the States to consider new movie projects, and during a trip to explore work possibilities at the Riviera Hotel in Vegas, she discovered that the doctor's wife planned to publish in her memoirs a billet-doux Gina had once sent her husband. The actress told the press she'd take legal action if any letters she wrote to Dr. Barnard were published. That same month the surgeon, then 46, married Barbara Zoellar, the 26-year-old daughter of a Johannesburg oilman. A few days before the event, Gina sued him and his ex-wife since one of her letters had indeed appeared in the woman's memoirs.

According to Lollobrigida, she wrote the letter in English; it was then translated into German by *Quick* magazine and finally put into Gina's native tongue by the Italian press. The nuance of the final product differed from what Gina had originally expressed in English. The *L. A. Herald-Examiner* recorded that Gina lost the case - probably one of the very few she has lost in her life.

Four years after the episode, a Lollo fan wrote a letter to the editor of the above-mentioned newspaper inquiring what had happened to the actress' relationship with the surgeon. "These things flame up in the papers and then are never mentioned again," claimed the reader. "Miss Lollobrigida is quite candid about her romance with the famous surgeon and just as candid that it didn't take," answered the editor. Years later, Gina was quoted as saying she had "no wish to see this man again." In her opinion Dr. Barnard was a "publicity seeker." More recently, (April, 1986) the surgeon claimed that the stories about his romance with the Italian star were exaggerated and that "it wasn't the intimate mad love affair the press made it out to be."

\*\*\*

The Seventies welcomed a new Lollobrigida emerging behind her several cameras as an expert photographer, still very much in the limelight herself as she photographed and interviewed international celebrities from different fields. During the first two years of the new decade the actress divided her time between photography and her final screen appearances.

Gina also started off the 1970's with criticism from animal lovers. La Lollo, who always had a passion for fur coats, arrived in London in early January with a wardrobe of five maxi-coats made from the skin of wild animals near extinction, including tiger and jaguar. The main criticism focused on a tiger coat that conservationists claimed took at least ten animals to make of a species numbering only 600 worldwide. Gina returned that the correct number of tigers required for the coat was three.

A full-size picture of Lollobrigida wearing a maxi-length combination jaguar and silver fox fur coat appeared in the papers. The *L. A. Herald-Examiner* did underscore the fact that if the actress hadn't bought the coats, somebody else would have. When I think of all the movie stars and their closets full of minks, I wonder why Lady Dowding of the Antikilling League in London chose Gina as the universal scapegoat. I'm very curious to know the animal lovers' reaction to the $200,000 lynx coat - a species near extinction - that Stefano Casiraghi presented his wife Caroline of Monaco on her thirtieth birthday on January 23, 1986.

* * *

On July 19, 1970, Milko Jr. - escorting a grieving Gina - appeared in public for his grandmother's funeral service. The death two days earlier of the 70-year-old signora Giuseppina Lollobrigida, victim of a heart ailment, was a shock to Gina. There were now only fond memories of the mamma who had held her four daughters while bombs fell in Subiaco during the War. The fact that Gina had become an international figure hadn't changed the love she had for her parents; her father used to say that his famous daughter had always been generous and kind to them.

Although Gina mourned the loss of her mother on that summer day, her philosophy that one has to live the present locked the unhappy experience in her heart and allowed her to get on with life.

# 187–Imperial Gina

Father Lollobrigida remained with his eldest daughter, Giuliana (then 46), despite Gina's constant reminder that he was welcome at her villa. He lived to be 80 and died of old age in 1977.

In the early Seventies, Gina's three sisters - Giuliana, Maria and Fernanda - were 47, 41 and 36, respectively. They had all been married for quite a while and their husbands had good positions. One was an accountant for Unitalia (a food company), another worked for the American Embassy, and the third was a physician. In their early days in Subiaco, mamma Lollobrigida used to say that her daughters ought to marry doctors so that when someone got sick in the family there would be no need to call one. Gina, however, presents a different version of her mother's wish for her four daughters. The caption of a photograph showing four nuns in *Italia Mia*, Gina's first successful photographic essay, reads: "It was my mother's dream: four girls, all nuns...!"

If the information I obtained in Subiaco is correct, Gina loved Fernanda the most. The youngest of the Lollobrigidas' children, Fernanda Vallauri, like Gina, was also involved in a highway accident, but she was luckier than her famous sister. She was guiding a group of tourists in Tunis when the bus she was riding on collided with a truck. Tourist guides usually sit up in the front next to the driver, but a few minutes before the accident, Fernanda had taken a back seat to talk with a passenger. It was a move that saved her life.

\*\*\*

*Bad Man's River*, Gina's first and only "spaghetti Western," was her sole picture in 1970. The genre had made a popular star of Clint Eastwood with Sergio Leone's films which combined gun-fighting and lots of explosives with humor. Eugenio (Gene) Martin's *Bad Man's River* starring Lee van Cleef and James Mason opposite Gina Lollobrigida belonged to that school. Like Eastwood, Lee van Cleef gained fame in Europe with the genre in the mid-Sixties; *For a Few Dollars More* and *The Good, the Bad and the Ugly* were his most memorable appearances.

Although Gina's part was rather short, it seemed not to have bothered her. "Usually the Western is just for men. But in this one the man is the weaker one. The woman is more important, even if it isn't a long role," declared the actress.

As King (van Cleef), one of the four most wanted man in Texas, travels on an eastbound train with his three thieving comrades, he meets the blond Alicia (Lollobrigida), who persuades him to marry her despite the fact that she's already wed to Montero (Mason).

Filmed in Madrid, Gene's work was classified as a minor commercial product and the critics were tough in their reviews. *"Bad Man's River* goes under wasting the talents of Gina Lollobrigida and James Mason,"* pronounced the *Guardian*. *Cinema TV Today* observed that the film "tries much too hard to be a riot of fun and succeeds only in being a shambles;" while the *Sunday Express* classified it as "a lighthearted Western." In Spain, columnist Pedro Crespo pointed out that the screenplay by Phillip Yordan was extremely poor, asserting that even the combined talents of Lee van Cleef, "the still beautiful Gina Lollobrigida," and the veteran James Mason, couldn't save the show. In Rome, *Il Messaggero* chose to praise Gene's direction and made favorable comments regarding the cast.

On August of that same year Gina received in Rome a script from Universal TV producer-director Barry Shear inviting her for a guest-star role in *Name of the Game* for NBC TV. The segment introducing Gina would be *A Sister from Napoli*. Anthony Franciosa, Gina's leading man from *Go Naked in the World*, had originally been signed for the male lead, but for some unknown reason Peter Falk got the part.

After reading the script, Gina felt it needed improvement, and decided to accept it only on those terms. She was promised a polished script by the time she arrived in New York; but to Gina's disappointment, nothing awaited her when she reached Manhattan. She phoned the studio and was told they'd have a new script for her within two days. When she read the newly written pages, Gina was frustrated to learn that they were worse than the original version. She picked up the phone and announced that if that was to be the final script, she'd have no part in it. The executives agreed with her that the script was in need of changes, and that they could make them. Again, a new script was promised in the next couple of days and the show was postponed.

To please Lollobrigida, Shear said they had hired an Italian writer she knew, Carlo Faillace, to cooperate with the writing. For three nights running, Falk, writer Peter Fields, and Shear burned the midnight oil to accommodate Gina's changes. Her version of the story, however, portrays Shear as less sympathetic. During a script conference when Faillace began to speak, Shear told him: "I tell you what to do - don't open your mouth." Meanwhile, Peter Falk had also requested more changes than Gina had asked and that made it impossible for the production to have a new script on the promised date. At that stage of seemingly endless rewriting, Gina said she was sorry but she wasn't going to be in a film without knowing what the story was about. Apparently, the writers weren't just improving the old plot, but were restructuring it completely.

Finally when Gina was called in to read what had already been done, she informed the producer that she'd read the script for the last time. She was flabbergasted. They had changed the two scenes that were previously rearranged in her presence, including those by signor Faillace as well. La Lollo walked out. She wouldn't even talk to them. Producer Dick Irving accepted Gina's absolute refusal to do the part. The film was to have gone into production on September 30 and on October 5, Geraldine Page signed to begin Gina's part in the next two days.

Later Gina denied Shear's allegations that she had quit the show several times. Shear claimed that the actress was probably apprehensive about TV work where crews sometimes shoot ten pages a day. But the pace didn't worry Gina, for she had once done twenty-two pages of script for Paramount in Italy. The producer-director further maintained that Gina had objected to playing a nun. Her objection, it seems, was concerning the characterization of the nun which was "completely unreal." In one scene, for example, she was supposed to throw a teapot at someone - in the face, to be exact - and in another she was to slap actor Falk. Shear also pointed out that Gina didn't want to play a nun but a nun's sister instead, and the character should have been someone from Brooklyn, not Italy.

Lollobrigida dismissed his claims as "unfair and ridiculous" and labeled them "cheap publicity," adding that her "reputation as an actress after twenty years of a very successful career makes it unnecessary for me to answer such false statements."

With *Name of the Game* out of her way, Gina announced in December that she was going to publish a book with *Life* and the Graphic Society. Her photographic essay then had the tentative title *From Italy With Love*, which ultimately was published as *Italia Mia*. When Gina told an American columnist about the book to be published he asked: "Any nude pictures?" Yes, the work does include a beautiful artistic nude, but the model is DEFINITELY NOT the photographer.

\*\*\*

The Roman paparazzi rejoiced in the return of their "Gina nazionale" to Italy in the spring of 1971 after her three-month stay in America. Italian photographers were delighted to use their flashbulbs again after several weeks' dearth of celebrities along the Tiber.

The Lollobrigida they saw was a new one and her Roman friends thought she looked great. An Italian columnist described her as slender, her skin fresh and smooth as that of a teenager, and her eyes bright and alive. Those months in America had worked wonders for Gina. There she felt she could really enjoy herself like a normal person: both in New York and Los Angeles she accepted dates for dinner like anybody else without being disturbed. There she wasn't considered a national monument and therefore her private life was respected; Americans let her live in peace.

While in L.A. Gina appeared in three TV shows; and after exciting New York, she was invited to stay with John and Joland Kluge, owners of both a TV station and a large factory in Virginia. Gina visited with the Kluges and then flew back to New York in their private plane in time to attend a charity party for *Boys' Town of Italy*. She also appeared on a show for the "Italo-American Antidefamation League," featuring the "charismatic performer" and "shrewd businessman," Frank Sinatra.

In New York, the ever busy Lollobrigida took the opportunity to choose a couple of songs for a 45 she was going to cut for RCA: *Nel mio orto* by Floyd Huddleston and *Prendimi tu* by Richard Carpenter. Further engagements for the year included an exciting photographic project and an Italian film, *Le avventure di Pinocchio*. Gina's golden 1971 legally clarified her divorce situation with Dr. Skofic. Milko was now for Gina a figure of the past even though he phoned sometimes to see their 14-year-old Milketto. The Skofics had obtained a Vienna divorce in 1968, but the Italian law required a minimum five years separation before divorce could be granted. In Gina's case, the official separation was dated April 1966, but the couple had actually split in 1962; therefore, the actress was positive that with the introduction of divorce in Italy that year she'd obtain hers. Furthermore, Dr. Skofic had already remarried and that was a move in her favor. So in April of that year, according to plan, Gina Lollobrigida ceased to be Mrs. Skofic in the eyes of the Italian law.

\*\*\*

A movie critic once said that Luigi Comencini had created the two most beautiful roles of Lollobrigida's film career: la Bersagliera in *Bread, Love, and Dreams*, and that of the Fata Turchina, the fairy godmother with blue hair and blue eyes in *Le avventure di Pinocchio.* "Which fable is more Italian than 'Pinocchio'? And which Italian beauty could be fairer than Lollo to play the Fairy?" asked author Maurizio Ponzi.

Comencini's *Pinocchio*, a free adaptation from Carlo Collodi's novel, was filmed for RAI and broadcast in five installments. Due to its enormous success on the little "tube," it was transferred to the large screen by MGM in 1972 and replayed in 1975 and 1981.

As if Comencini had foreshadowed la Lollo's "addio" to show business, he included Vittorio De Sica in the cast as the judge. Nineteen years earlier, Blasetti had brought the two together for the first time with *Times Gone By*, Gina's first memorable Italian movie. Nino Manfredi, who had appeared in *The Phone Call* episode of *The Dolls* and in Blasetti's *Me, Me, Me... and the Others*, played Pinocchio's father, Geppetto. Thus Comencini reunited three substantial celebrities in Gina's last Italian film.

Gina was very pleased with the part. "While shooting I had a magic power over children who stared at me with admiration and respect," she told *Paese Sera*. "The modern version of the character," she elaborated, "lies in the fact that in the film I am no longer a fairy, but a mother. A mother like many others who worry about an undisciplined son. Also, in order to render a more current character, my wardrobe is extremely simple. The only rich and peculiar touch is the splendid blue wig."

Notwithstanding, Gina's spell didn't work on the seven-year-old Pinocchio (Andrea Balestri). Actor Franco Franchi who played the cat said the little chap was "precocious and fussy;" it was necessary to spoil him to get results on the set. There were days when shooting continued until late at night and on those occasions the boy got tired and irritable, demanding vast amounts of patience from the cast and the crew as well.

The Fairy-Pinocchio relationship on the set was anything but sweet. One of the scenes required the boy to kiss Gina, which he refused to because he was repelled by her make-up. The same thing happened one day when he had to kiss the Fairy's photograph; it took a day to shoot the scene.

Gina considered the boy a "peste" (pest). On the last day of filming, he was causing trouble while the cast was trying to pose for a photograph. Gina lost her patience and grabbed the little actor by the hand, saying: "Very well, let's finish with it." It was no fairy tale; the boy kicked Gina and got loose. She ran after him and, during the chase, fell to the ground when little Andrea threw a rock at her. Neither the fall nor the rock caused Gina any injury, but she probably never felt quite the same about "*Pinocchio*" again. From what I gather, Comencini, a loving man, was the only person on the set who successfully exercised control over the boy. He actually cared for the little fellow and demonstrated great patience with him.

\*\*\*

The Piazza San Andrea in front of the Cathedral was packed on the morning of May 24, 1971; the people of Subiaco impatiently awaited the arrival of Gina Lollobrigida. It was the occasion of their "Gina nazionale's" first official visit to Subiaco. There had been invitations before, but for one reason or another, they had all been postponed.

Lovely and appropriately dressed for the event, a sunny Gina arrived in a Rolls-Royce. "Viva Gina!" "We love you Gina!" and "Gina, you're always beautiful!" echoed the applauding crowd.

The festivities continued in a more formal manner in the City Council where Subiaco's Mayor, Giuseppe Cicolini, welcomed the actress. There, Gina received a bouquet of roses - her favorite flower - from the hands of Daniela Palmieri, an elementary school girl, who also read a short letter in the name of the school children. Mayor Cicolini offered a simple but warm speech. Gina, who had spent 17 years of her life in Subiaco until her departure in 1944, was filled with emotion. This symbolic embrace with her people flooded the actress with old memories as she shook hands with childhood friends.

When the formalities in the City Council were over, Gina left for the Rocca Abbaziale (Fortified Abbey), which in past centuries had served as a fortress, a luxurious palace and the home of popes. The rain that began to fall didn't lessen the size of the crowd, which continued showering their good wishes upon Gina.

From the Rocca Abbaziale, Gina was taken to the magnificent Hotel Livata di Tozzi on Monte Livata, painted green in the summer and mantled in snow in winter. At the Hotel, surrounded by dear friends and town hall officials, Gina had lunch and then left for San Lorenzo, Subiaco's stadium, where she attended a soccer match held in her honor.

It was on this occasion at the San Lorenzo stadium that signor Giuseppe Cicolini, the town's priest, and nearly three thousand people posed for Gina's super lens in a photograph that covers the first two plates of *Italia Mia*.

After the picture was taken, Gina went to the Narzio Theater where *Buona Sera Mrs. Campbell* was shown, drawing to a close the meaningful event.

Exactly 20 days before Gina was received like a queen by her countrymen, an Italian weekly magazine published a rather lengthy piece giving a distorted image of the relationship between the actress and the townsfolk in the past. The article, *They Received Gina with Eggs on Her Face* by Sandro Mayer for *Oggi* was based, according to the author, on interviews he collected from people in Subiaco. The defamatory story naturally upset Gina.

One of the interviewees, signor Orlando Orlandi, declared that the Lollobrigidas had left town with the Germans as the Allied forces marched in, thus raising the townspeople's hostility towards Gina and the family. With their house destroyed, signor Lollobrigida decided to leave Subiaco with his family, a fact that Gina pointed out in several interviews at the beginning of her stardom and in subsequent years.

The dwelling where Gina was born, Palazzo Romano on Via Papa Braschi II, survived the bombs that destroyed 70 percent of the houses. At the time of the bombing, though, the Lollobrigidas had already moved from the Palazzo Romano to a more spacious house on Valley Principe Umberto, and this was the house that was destroyed.

While the Germans occupied Subiaco, the town had become a strategic military target since a garrison and a resistance line were there in an attempt to stop the Allied advance coming from Cassino. It was the bombing of 1944 that forced the Lollobrigidas to search for a safer place.

Another anecdote in the slanderous piece that ruffled the actress' feathers dated back to 1948 when Gina, then already in the movies, was filming Mario Costa's *I pagliacci* not too far from Subiaco. The story, as told by signor Orlandi, suggests that when Gina was shooting Costa's film she was visited by many of her countrymen who threw eggs and tomatoes at her. Gina declared the story to be false. "I can't recall ever having a hostile manifestation from my countrymen." According to Mayor Cicolini, the news item had no principle and was probably a product of sensationalistic journalism.

A lawsuit for defamation followed at the Milan Court of Justice. The municipality of Subiaco, under Mayor Cicolini, prepared a large mural inscription plus numerous articles for Lollobrigida's defense. Gina won the case. *Oggi* published a retraction and the actress received a nominal sum for damages which afterwards she donated to a charitable institution. "Sometimes you have to sue papers because in the next article they will say you killed your mother," Gina told an American reporter. "When they are too nasty, you have to stop them," she concluded.

In September 1972, Gina returned to her hometown for a local festival; together with her were the Italian lyric singer Mario Del Monaco and Luigi Carnacina, gastronome of international fame. At the time of the visit, some Italian papers discussed Gina's "reconciliation" with Subiaco vis-à-vis the *Oggi* publication in the spring of the previous year. The term "reconciliation" was inaccurate, "seeing that no true discord had happened and that the whole story had been written with scandalous purposes," stated former Mayor Cicolini in response to one of my letters.

Busy mamma Lollobrigida also found time to share with Milketto who was spending his 1972 winter vacation in the Appia Antica. The 14-year-old boy was more mature and serious than other boys his age. Milketto was still attending school in Geneva where he met people with names more important than his own: the nephew of Aga Khan and the Rothschild children, for example. Milko Jr. was no longer the egocentric and spoiled child of years before adjusting to being the son of Gina Lollobrigida. Now he was interested in her career and was very curious to know how she had started in the movies. Moreover, he wanted to know the secret of how to be a successful man.

Vacation at the villa was also time for playing the guitar and the drums. The boy loved music. He usually returned from England, Germany or Switzerland with several records, sometimes the same ones Gina had herself bought. During his vacation of 1972, he also spent time practicing shooting with princess Lalla Aicha, sister of the King of Morocco, a friend of the family.

Gina naturally loved having her son around. She had finished filming Jerzy Skolimowski's *King, Queen, Knave* in Germany and planned to continue working on her Italian photographic essay until another script came in the mail... another suitable script that is. Gina wasn't impressed with most film offers, while photography gave her increasing satisfaction. Gina had turned down a million dollar film, which clearly indicated that she was losing interest in most movie projects. Gina also rarely bothered to go to movies. When she was taken to see *Hair*, she rated it "obscene," and she left the theater in the middle of *Oh, Calcutta!* The actress wasn't fond of what she considered pornographic productions. "It's disgusting. It's not professionalism. My previous films were made for nuns and babies compared with what they're doing now."

\*\*\*

Skolimowski's *King, Queen, Knave* - based on a novel by Vladimir Nabokov - presented Gina in probably the most risqué scenes and wardrobe of her entire career, but they were far from being obscene and were maintained in the artistic realm.

In the film, Gina plays Martha, the spoiled wife of wealthy Charles Dreyer (David Niven). Out of boredom, she seduces Charles' 18-year-old nephew, Frank (John Moulder Brown). But what starts as a simple caprice slowly but steadily turns into a relationship leading to a tragic end, Martha's death. The story is set in contemporary Munich with shooting in Cap-Ferat and Monaco di Baviera.

Every film is a potentially exciting or frustrating experience for stars since a fresh production brings a new combination of crew members and cast. A new formula doesn't work sometimes due to stars' idiosyncrasies, but that wasn't the case pairing the Italian actress with David Niven. Gina described her leading man as a marvelous and pleasant actor, very British with an enormous sense of humor.

Working with an avant-garde group was a new experience for both movie veterans, Niven and Lollobrigida. They were perplexed by the techniques of young Charly Steinberger, who utilized little lighting on exterior and interior sets. Gina and David, on the other hand, were used to the traditional filming methods and were very surprised to see the excellent results Steinberger's photography achieved on the screen.

Filming took seven weeks and Gina considered it a very demanding and tiresome affair. Although making pictures in English presented no difficulty for the actress, several scenes were shot directly with sound, an exhausting procedure when one is working in a foreign language. Also, the picture required Gina to wear some forty costumes - some of them quite sexy. Changing from one to the next was in itself enough to keep the actress busy. Frank, the nephew (in the film), dreams a series of erotic fantasies involving his aunt and in them she appears wearing seductive outfits; in a flash of seconds, Gina is screened wearing two or three different dresses. It wasn't like in *Bread, Love, and Dreams* when just a couple of tattered gowns served as the star's complete wardrobe.

The shooting of *King, Queen, Knave* presented no drastic problems and when filming was finished, they celebrated it with a spaghetti party. The happy mood didn't last long, for the film reviews weren't that hot. Niven wasn't surprised. When his agent sent him the script, he thought the screenplay wasn't very impressive. There was no doubt that Nabokov was a celebrated novelist, probably best known for *Lolita*; nevertheless, for the actor, the story seemed rather elementary. "In an easier time he might have turned it down," wrote Charles Francisco in *David Niven: Endearing Rascal*; Niven had been writing *The Moon's a Balloon* and hadn't made a film in more than a year, and so he accepted producer David L. Wolper's script.

The picture was shown in advance at the Cannes Film Festival, and the result was negative. "The unmerciful panning it received there prompted Wolper to pull it out of general distribution," recorded Niven's biographer. (The film was never released in the United States.) Niven showed little interest in the reaction to the film. *The Moon's a Balloon* had been published in England before the shooting of the final scenes of the film, and British literary critics were raving over Niven's book. Lollobrigida perhaps reacted likewise since she had her thoughts on *Italia Mia*.

Polish director Skolimowski felt involvement with the film had been a completely negative experience. "It's a horrible film" he admitted to Michel Ciment of *Positif*. Lollobrigida herself spoke of it with regret while *Sight and Sounds* came to its rescue praising Skolimowski and the cast.

\*\*\*

# 197–Imperial Gina

When Gina was invited to appear in the Italian TV program *Canzonissima*, she decided to wear a party outfit that had been designed for a scene in *King, Queen, Knave*. The costume, however, wasn't censored from the picture but by the Italian TV.

The sleeveless miniskirt dress made of thin golden metal plates dips in an exquisite décolletage. It opens again a few inches below the bust, revealing the navel; beneath it there are several strings of metallic chains from left to right, forming several semi-circles. The ensemble is capped with a gorgeous short blond wig (one of the many Gina wears in the movie), earrings and knee-length golden boots.

For the appearance in *Canzonissima*, Gina had already considered reducing the décolletage and eliminating the opening around the belly; however, she wished she could show her navel on TV like Italian popular singer Raffaella Carrà. The TV people told Gina that la Carrà could show her navel because it didn't cause tidal waves, but Gina's was too sexy. It was suggested that she wear tights. Gina agreed to wear skin colored tights, but the studio was afraid that the audience might think she was really showing la Lollo flesh. So, if Gina didn't want to give up the metallic dress for the show she'd probably have to wear black tights. Finally they agreed upon red ones. After so "much ado about nothing," Gina appeared before the cameras and sang *Nel mio orto*.

\*\*\*

The Spanish/French/Italian production *No encontré rosas para mi madre* (1972), released in America as *The Lonely Woman*, marked the end (at least for the time being) of Gina's 26-year silver screen career.

Directed by the Spaniard Francisco Rovira-Beleta, the film was a poor commercial effort introducing an international cast including French stars Renaud Verley and Danielle Darrieux, Britain's Susan Hampshire, Spanish actress Conchita Velasco and Gina Lollobrigida as special guest star.

Spanish critics considered Beleta's film inferior to other works he had previously directed such as *Los Tarantos*, based on a free version of *Romeo and Juliet* by playwright Alfredo Mañas, set among the gypsies in Barcelona.

It was unfortunate for an actress of Lollobrigida's calibre to have marked the end of a brilliant career with poor films. Had she walked away from show business with *Buona Sera Mrs. Campbell* or *Pinocchio*, she'd have had a glorious finale.

Some sources quote the Italian film *Là dove volano le pallottole* (Where the Bullets Fly) with Lionel Stander as another Lollobrigida film made in Spain in 1972. Ponzi's *The Films of Gina Lollobrigida* excludes it as well as a couple of minor pictures the actress perhaps did at the beginning of her career. Ponzi's work thus numbers Gina's film at 60, while Ediciones Urbion's *Las Estrellas* suggests she made 63. Since I haven't found any substantial references to these three films I accept Ponzi's filmography of the actress as the official one.

Regarding Gina's most memorable movies, author Ken Wlaschin lists the following in the order they were made: *Fanfan la Tulipe*, *Beauties of the Night*, *Beat the Devil*, *Bread, Love, and Dreams*, *Woman of Rome*, *Bread, Love, and Jealousy*, *The World's Most Beautiful Woman*, *Trapeze*, *Come September*," and *Buona Sera Mrs. Campbell*. (*The Illustrated Encyclopedia of the World's Great Movie Stars and Their Films*). Although the selection seems accurate, I feel that *Time Gone By*, *Anna di Brooklyn*, and *Solomon and Sheba* should also be considered as some of Gina's celebrated works, for they brought her enormous popularity. On the other hand, *Imperial Venus*, *Mare matto*, and *Woman of Straw*, are noteworthy for her dramatic performances.

For one reason or another, Gina Lollobrigida has always felt that she could have given more of herself as an actress; she thinks she owes herself a film superior to what she had done before. "If I ever did another film, I would want a role in which I could express myself fully. Something really good... something better than I did up until now," pronounced Gina at the end of her film career. I quite don't understand Lollobrigida's sentiment, for wasn't *Mrs. Campbell* a perfect role for her? Didn't Gina herself consider Castellani's *Mare matto* her best dramatic performance?

\*\*\*

After Gina Lollobrigida left the screen, no other movie actress came into my life; and as the stars of the Fifties and Sixties began to disappear from show business, my interest in movie celebrities waned, and from the early Seventies I began to see movies only if I was interested in the plot, regardless of the cast. Modern day stars don't have the glamour of a Liz Taylor or a Joan Collins, much less that of a Gina Lollobrigida.

In 1987, a poll by *People Weekly* on the occasion of Hollywood's one hundredth anniversary, the following was revealed when comparing past and present day movie stars: 65% of all voters said that stars 40 years ago were better looking, 53% considered them to have been smarter, 80% indicated they dressed better, 84% agreed that actresses of the "good-old-days" had bigger egos, and 87% were sure that "today's stars have more plastic surgery." When asked the main reason why they went to the movies only 20% cited the star. What we have now on the screen is no doubt technically better presented, but the cinema today is much deprived of good scripts - the stuff movie fans loved.

While sharing thoughts about the cinema with *Semana* in Barcelona sometime in October 1986, Gina anticipated and confirmed the results of the poll conducted by *People Weekly*. From her point of view, the cinema of her day was better and actresses had a glamour which doesn't surround today's stars. Gina blamed the TV for this lost quality because it projects the stars to a height the cinema cannot achieve. And while referring to the show business in its glorious period, Gina told *Variety* that "the industry was more solid then," and further pointed out that "the story that producers were putting on the screen was geared toward satisfaction of the public. Today they want to shock instead."

Gina was definitely not interested in the new trends; she would neither undress to do erotic pictures nor appear in horror movies with mutilated corpses floating in pools of blood - she has too much talent for that kind of stuff.

Back in the early Fifties at the beginning of her stardom, Gina declared that while people liked her she'd continue to act, but when they got tired of her she'd quit and grow artichokes. After four decades (1946-1989) of public appearances in front of and behind cameras, Gina still cannot grow artichokes, for her admirers have not tired of la Lollo.

After Gina started successfully working with photography in the Seventies, her photo exhibits took her from Paris to Tokyo and many of the world's important capitals. Her interviews - given and hosted - from New Delhi to Rio, her appearances on American and Italian TV in the mid-Eighties, Gina's requested participation in international film festivals in various European cities, and the 1988 remake of *La romana* indicate that while the legendary Lollobrigida may eat artichokes, she'll never plant them.

As Mrs. Campbell in *Buona Sera Mrs. Campbell* (1968). Courtesy Orion Press.

With Rock Hudson and Edward Judd (behind Hudson) in *Strange Bedfellows*. Universal Pictures, a Division

With her husband Dr. Milko Skofic and Milketto (early Sixties). Courtesy *Il Messaggero* (author's collection).

# Chapter 6

## Lollobrigida The Photographer

Gina Speaks About Photography:

"In films I am not my own boss. With photographs I can say what I want."

"For too long I had been in front of the camera. I wanted to see what life looks from the other side. To see the world, the people and their souls."

"I left school and went into films after the war, but I found myself as no more than an object in the hands of the directors. My art depended on them, whereas painters, writers and photographers can be masters of their art. They can be themselves and approach their work in a personal way without collaborating with, or being manipulated by, others."

"My work behind the camera has made me more of a woman. It has given me understanding of people. It took me away from eyes that were always focused on me, me... me, and I find the world a fascinating place. When I look through my camera, it is as if I see everything twice from a different perspective."

"But I have a great sense of humor even in bad situations when it is necessary to laugh and put things in their place. I am also sincere and generous... too generous at times. I need to give like I need to breathe and I hope people will see how much of my heart goes into photography."

In the first years of the Seventies, and from then on, Gina was more concerned with photography than with her film career. The new decade - Lollobrigida's third under the world's spotlight - was about to witness the girl from Subiaco as an international photographer of merit, winner of the "Nadar Award". Her private life had been enriched by her sculpturing and painting, and she had demonstrated through some of her best movies that she was a dancer, a singer and a fine actress. Now with photography her name was mentioned along with that of Henri Cartier-Bresson.

During the several weeks of convalescence that Gina spent in hospitals and wheelchairs after her car crash in February 1969, she had time to think, and she recognized a hidden longing to create something new that would express her taste and talent, something independent of assistance. And as Gina began to learn to walk again, she also took her first steps as a professional photographer.

It didn't matter which side of a lens she adorned; she was usually a winner. In the mid-Sixties Gina won a prize when she competed against more than 300 cameramen in a photo contest in Milan. For the event she had on display snapshots of her son, Audrey Hepburn, former Italian president Antonio Segni, and Indonesia's Sukarno, who for Lollobrigida were "all very interesting human subject matter."

When Time-Life Books requested Gina to do a photographic essay on Italy, she took the assignment as seriously as her former movie roles. At the time *La mia Italia con amore* (My Italy With Love) was being put together, between 1971 and 1972, Lollobrigida saw the need to change its title because Sophia Loren's *In cucina con amore* (In the Kitchen With Love) was about to be published and, even though the title for Gina's work had been carefully chosen much earlier, the book couldn't appear with the same *con amore* phrase. For that reason, and to avoid being fresh meat for the media wolves always eager to stir up a feud between the two actresses, *Italia Mia* was chosen instead.

Equipped with a 35mm. Nikon, a variety of lenses from wide angle to telephoto, a 6x6 camera, tripods, filters and electronic flashes, Lollobrigida and her assistant photographer Roberto Biciocchi, left Rome on numerous occasions to capture the Calabrese fishermen, peasants in the Abruzzi Mountains, Neapolitan beggars, Florentine nobility, Milanese merchants, market wives, children, cities and some of the actress' famous friends.

The two-and-a-half-year project consumed two thousand rolls of film, and out of 20,000 photographs taken, only 191 were selected for the album. The difficult final moments kept Gina working late on New Year's Eve of 1972 when no friends were invited over to the Appian Way and Gina refused party invitations. One of her exhausting tasks was to choose only three photographs of Venice were she used 78 rolls of film with 38 shots on each.

Photographing people and places without being recognized was a challenge. Once she was almost trampled by fans during a soccer match. A disguise was necessary in order to pass unnoticed. Sixteen years earlier Gina had fooled everybody on the set of *Trapeze* in a clown costume, and she was counting on the trick again. The wardrobe for Gina's new role consisted of a tousled hippie wig, rumpled blue-jeans, a baggy blouse and very large glasses. To change her face lines she stuffed prune pits in her mouth, which helped to puff-out the nose, probably her most recognizable feature. When the fruit pits began to give her a sore mouth she substituted buttons. La Lollo incognito, however, was a good-looking hippie and, despite the camouflage, her biggest challenge was to convince the people in one town that she was an old hag with a camera; everywhere else, people fell for her disguise hook, line and sinker. The disguise was so far out that her assistant said: "Signora, I'm ashamed to go out with you like that." Nevertheless, he steeled himself and provided the book with several amusing shots of hippie Lollo.

To give credibility to her part, Gina had her chauffeur made up and used a Fiat; she also stayed in small pensions and inexpensive hotels, forsaking her usual red carpet treatment. When her work was compared with that of Cartier-Bresson, Gina pointed out that the renowned photographer could work without being recognized, while peaceful outdoor photography for her was practically impossible.

In the spring of 1985, I was at the Orion Press head office in Tokyo doing research for my book and for the first time had a chance to actually examine *Italia Mia*. The company's book department had imported 1,000 copies of the album from SEDIFO (Switzerland), which held the 1973 edition global copyright, to be sold at Gina's 1974 photo exhibition in Tokyo sponsored by Orion Press. At that time, Orion Books had the right to import and sell Gina's photographic essay in Japan, but they didn't hold any photo copyrights. Since the

1,000 volumes had sold out at the exhibit, it was natural that President Jintaro Takano, whose copy I held in my hands, didn't want to part with his sole remaining album.

I happened to see the coveted work again, autographed by Lollobrigida, at the studio of the Japanese photographer Eikoh Hosoe, who had met Gina at the Second International Congress of Photography held in Barcelona in the winter of 1977. But despite the desire to have my own *Italia Mia*, I returned to Kyoto without it. I knew I couldn't write about Gina's photography without a copy of the book by my typewriter, and the search for this El Dorado continued during my trip to Europe that summer. I was sure the book was waiting for me somewhere in a Parisian bookstore, but I left yet another capital with empty hands. Torino, Firenze and Roma weren't any more helpful.

Once back in Japan, I sent a couple of letters to possible American distributors and to Time-Life Books as well, but my search for *Italia Mia* continued to dead end.

On a rainy evening in April 1986 while visiting an avant-garde bookstore in Kyoto, I happened to mention to the clerk, an acquaintance of mine, that I was working on a manuscript about Gina Lollobrigida. The thought of asking him if he had ever heard of *Italia Mia* never crossed my mind. Since Tokyo, Paris and Rome had failed me, I judged that Japan's ancient capital would be of no help.

Eager to assist me, the young man said he had a book related to Gina but that it had no connection with her films. I was astonished when he brought me the store's only copy of *Italia Mia*. I had finally found the treasure and, back out in the rain, I carried Gina and Italy under my arm.

As one opens the album, the first double page shows Subiaco in the background with nearly three thousand people who gathered for the shot taken during the actress' 1971 official homecoming. In the center stands former Mayor Cicolini with other members of the Town's Council, the town's priest, friends of the actress, children, and young and old folks. Gina called the photograph "A Family Portrait."

The 175 black and white and 16 color plates that constitute the album emphasize the humorous and the serious in life: a young lady riding a scooter with two tires around her waist and another around her neck, which Gina captioned as "... Life Belts?" Or poor boys behind a fence, the director of the Bank of Italy posing in front of an empty safe, a fat man diving into the Tiber, a Neapolitan kneeling down as a hearse drives by, and a group of men by the Spanish Steps looking lustfully at a woman walking by them.

These, and other authentic pictures of life, were snatched by the camera to create a more personal, genuine and humane Italy. The album is a philanthropic symphony; it isn't the Italy of the right or the left, but Lollobrigida's. In the foreword by Alberto Moravia, the novelist describes the book as one "of real people, of humble artisans, of habitual devotion, of simple pleasures, of family feelings, tourist landscapes, of monuments so famous that now they have become almost invisible."

To lay stress on the contrast between the sacred and profane, the rich and the poor, Gina set some of the plates opposite each other. Photograph 8, for instance, depicts a snowy day in front of the Vatican where young priests play in the snow, while number 9, another face of Roman winter, shows ladies of the night in hot pants and black boots trying to keep themselves warm by a Lilliputian bonfire in the street.

Both Lollobrigida and Cartier-Bresson seem to have been governed by spontaneity; their photographs reveal reality, the comic and the tragic in peoples' lives, the stuff that *Italia Mia* is all about. The two artist-shutterbugs also photographed famous and common people alike. While the French master seized the image of Beckett, Capote, Renois, Camus and Picasso in an extensive record of internationally well-known figures, Gina focused on Steinbeck, Dali, Gagarin, Gandhi, la Cardinale, and a myriad of other familiar faces. Like France's most prestigious photographer, Gina also loves to photograph friends and *Italia Mia* has a good selection of them: Fellini, De Sica, Audrey Hepburn and Italian designer Sergio Soldano who perfectly dyed some of Gina's mink coats - free of charge. Lollobrigida, however, regrets never having photographed Anna Magnani.

In August of 1973, Gina was at a party in Los Angeles proudly showing her book to Italian Consul General Vittorio Farinelli and wife, and the David Rockwell Cudlips, who between them had the only two copies of the book in town.

While showing her photographic essay to the partygoers, Gina informed her friends and admirers that in those plates she had tried to capture the soul of Italy and hadn't just thrown a bunch of pictures together. Pointing as she talked, Gina explained her subjects: "That is my hometown, Subiaco, and these are many of the people I grew up with... I took this picture of people in Rome through the window of my parked car... Here is my son who's 16, standing next to his portrait, which I painted." Among the guests who also saw Italia Mia were her old friend Vincent Minelli, L.A. Country Museum Director Kenneth Donahue, Filmex Associaté Director Gary Abrahams and who knows who else on the party's V.I.P. list. During Gina's visit to Los Angeles to introduce the book to her friends, columnists referred to the actress in terms not different from those of the days of *Solomon and Sheba*. Ray Loynd, the entertainment editor for the *L. A. Herald-Examiner*, proclaimed that "she looked great, stunning, in fact," wearing a very exotic dress made of a 100-year-old shawl. And as Gina graciously moved among the guests, "her immense eyes illuminated the spaces about her."

*Italia Mia* was published by a Time-Life Books affiliate in Japan, but it was never distributed in the United States. My English edition of Gina's pictorial love letter to Italy was printed at Sagep S.p.A. Officina Grafica, Genova in 1972. (The album was also published by Salani Editors (1972), directed by Milko Skofic, and Editions Flammarion, Paris, in 1973.)

***

Following her positive experience with *Italia Mia* Gina worked on a series of photo projects and held exhibitions in Amsterdam, Copenhagen, New York, Paris, Madrid, Tokyo and other major capitals.

Gina's first assignment as a photojournalist was for the *Ladies' Home Journal* featuring the Secretary of State, Henry Kissinger. The magazine editors considered Gina's photography good enough and believed she could contribute well to the *Journal*.

Sometime in March of 1974 Gina was in Australia promoting *Italia Mia* and photographing kangaroos when she received a phone call asking her to come immediately to Washington, for Kissinger had changed his plans and the name "Lollobrigida" had been written in the Secretary's calendar for the following day. Within 24 hours, Gina was seated in Kissinger's office. The two V.I.P.s had never met before. Once when Gina was filming in Hollywood, the Secretary was a guest at one of Kirk and Anne Douglas' parties, but Gina had declined to attend. On another occasion he was staying with President Nixon at the Waldorf while she was at the same hotel, but their paths never crossed.

# 209–Imperial Gina

At the first Lollobrigida-Kissinger encounter both were nervous. There were no photographs taken on that day; they chatted and tried to get to know each other so that the photography session the following day would go smoothly. Kissinger was pleased to pose for the actress but he soon told her he wasn't photogenic. Gina explained that it didn't matter since "it's the personality I want to capture on film - not just looks."

Moscow was next on Kissinger's itinerary after which he'd be in Acapulco for a vacation and asked if Gina would like to photograph him there. "Can I bring my son?" she asked. Whether or not the Secretary made it to Mexico I don't know, but if he did, it was without the actress, for she had other commitments in the Orient. *The World's Most Interesting Men* was meant to be a series of articles of which only the first was printed in the July 1974 issue of the *Ladies' Home Journal*. Eventually, Gina did interview some of "the world's most interesting men," but the series didn't appear as planned.

The cherry blossoms in Japan usually are gone in early April and the traditional Japanese enthusiasm for flower viewing also dies. April 1974 was an unusually colorful year in Tokyo, for after the pink cherries had disappeared, Gina Lollobrigida, referred to as a Mediterranean flower by the Japanese press, arrived at Haneda Airport. Ten years earlier she had been in the Japanese capital for the Italian Film Festival with *Imperial Venus* and now she was returning for a photo exhibition of *Italia Mia* at Shibuya Seibu Department Store sponsored by Orion Press. An average of 8,000 visitors a day saw her work and Gina was always present at the show. (I missed the chance of my life to meet Gina Lollobrigida in a situation that didn't require preceding formalities; unfortunately I arrived in Tokyo in April of the following year.)

During Gina's brief stay in Japan she was guest of honor at the Foreign Correspondents Club where President Samuel W. Jameson offered her an honorary membership card. The actress, introduced as Italy's living Mona Lisa, spoke to a capacity of 322.

Talking about her photographic essay, Gina said she regarded it as her second baby. Topics like divorce, photography and film-making were, as one would expect, brought up in the interview she granted the Club. "If one found the marriage a mistake, he or she should immediately get a divorce," was one of Gina's messages. The actress, who appreciates her independence, voiced the same opinion in a press conference at the 1975 New Delhi Film Festival concluding that "the best age for marriage is 80. Then you cannot make a mistake. I had a husband once but for too many years."

Probably even more exciting than Gina's second Orient adventure was her 1974 visit to Cuba where she found herself riding in a jeep through tobacco fields with el generalissimo Fidel Castro. The visit came about from a protocol-skirting letter (that Gina herself addressed to the Cuban leader) to accompany a copy of her *Italia Mia*. Within days she received a formal invitation to visit Havana from Castro himself.

During the ten-day visit with El Máximo Líder, Gina directed an hour-long documentary entitled *Portrait of Fidel Castro*. Gina, who had already photographed statesman Henry Kissinger, astronaut Neil Armstrong, artist Salvador Dali, poet Yevgeny Yevtushenko and shipowner Aristotle Onassis, described her bearded friend as "without doubt, the most interesting man I have met." She elaborated "he has a personality that appeals to people, a magnetic power of attraction." The Cuban leader displayed much gentleness with the actress. Castro's magnanimity towards Gina was demonstrated when the sound system faulted during the interview and he volunteered to repeat the whole session.

Castro also proved to be a man gifted with a good sense of humor. In the course of Gina's stay in Havana, she went to visit a ranch with him. There he pointed out some of the country's techno-logical progress and explained that cattle breeding was accomplished by artificial insemination. "That's very sad for the cows," said Gina plaintively. "That's all right," retorted Castro, "for people we do it the old way."

When Gina left la Habana she was very impressed with the Communist leader. "Those eyes of his! He still is a mysterious man." For Gina, one of Castro's most striking personal traits was that he (unlike other men she had met before) didn't try to jump on her. There had been reports of a torrid affair with the rugged Castro but the two weren't intimate. Gina dismissed the rumors as "a lot of fantasy. Somebody else's fantasy." The only intimate exchange they had came just before her departure, when he insisted that she keep his Japanese Seiko and he remembered her with her diamond-studded Swiss Piaget. His was engraved "To Gina, with admiration - Fidel Castro." Gina concluded that with Castro, "it was a meeting of the minds..."; the *L. A. Times* quipped, "and a swapping of the watches..."

# 211–Imperial Gina

\*\*\*

"Live and let live" was Lollobrigida's message at the two-week Delhi Film Festival in March 1975, where she was the main attraction. Indeed, had it not been for Gina's presence, the festival would have been doomed a disaster due to the lack of first-class films.

Wearing a sari and a vermillion mark on her forehead, Gina presented Prime Minister Indira Gandhi with a copy of *Italia Mia*. Actually, the actress was planning a book on India, and by the time she returned to the country two years later, she had already taken some 4,000 shots. On this second visit she was in Bombay in connection with the inaugural shooting of Krishna Shah's Indo-American co-production *Shalimar*.

Hopscotching around the world with her cameras at a rather fast tempo, tireless Gina was seen next on a Chicago TV talk show to promote Italian tourism. As 1975 was a Holy Year, a visit to the Vatican would be very appropriate suggested Gina before a commercial. During the break she placed a hand on host John Coleman's thigh and said: "John, now don't get too wrapped up in this Holy Year thing. Come to Italy. Go to the Vatican first, then get out in the beautiful countryside." And what to do once there? *People Weekly* recommended its readers to look for the answer in Boccaccio's *The Decameron*.

The 1975 Berlin Film Festival was screening Lollobrigida's *Portrait of Fidel Castro* while she introduced a display of photographs in town. In between photo sessions (both in front and behind the camera), interviews, and screenings, la Lollo revealed she was putting together a series of documentaries tentatively called *Around the World with Gina*, with locations in India, USA, South Africa, the Soviet Union and Japan. Much of the material had already been prepared and was similar to her documentary about the Cuban leader. Indira Gandhi and Paul Newman were two of her subjects. In fact, she had interviewed and photographed the actor in his Connecticut house that year. Newman had just turned 50 then.

After Berlin, Gina flew to Moscow with bags full of photos. The Russians were interested in publishing her *Italia Mia* and seeing the Castro documentary at a film festival. The album was eventually published in the Soviet Union, but for unrevealed reasons the photographer never received a ruble in royalties; her friend Fidel Castro considered this unfair to Gina.

Sometime in 1975, Gina, who was used to photographing V.I.P.s and exotic places, received a very peculiar request for a photo compilation on the wild boar. A friend of hers was writing a book about this non-photogenic animal and asked her cooperation. When the news appeared in the papers Lollobrigida was quoted as saying that "when you've been an actress as long as I have you get to know a great deal about pigs." Fulfilling her professional calling as a photographer Gina went several times to the swampy region of Maremma in central Italy to stalk the wild pigs from birth through the subsequent stages of their growth. They weren't dangerous unless they were hurt.

In the midst of all these diversified photographic ventures Gina had little time to think about her film career. Nevertheless, the actress was tempted by a script based on a story from an 18th century Soviet writer. "It will be a deep and strong film about a Russian Lady Macbeth who lived in a Siberian village," commented Gina. Under the direction of Nikita Mikhalkov, the picture was supposed to be an Italo-Canadian production called *A Brief Season of Love*, but never materialized. Years later there were rumors that Gina would return to the screen in a light comedy to be filmed in Rome, but records indicate that she never returned to the big screen after her last picture in 1972.

\*\*\*

Gina's popularity surged with the quality of her photo journalism, and she took on new projects at a tempo reminiscent of her Fifties film pace. In 1976 she was immersed in her India project and a similar one on Iran when she began to receive letters from Imelda Marcos commissioning her to do two photo albums and a documentary on the Philippines. The First Lady had heard of Gina's fame and thought that with the actress behind the camera she could promote tourism more effectively in the islands.

At first, mainly because of the pressure of her busy schedule, Gina wasn't much inclined to accept the request, but Imelda kept insisting and Gina finally had no alternative but pack again and embark on another adventure. A delegation representing the International Monetary Fund was to hold a conference in Manila in the fall of that year and the documentary Gina was supposed to make would be shown then.

# 213--Imperial Gina

For the two books and the documentary that were to emphasize the best of the Philippines, the international press announced that Gina would be paid an advance of $250,000 and an additional $750,000 when the job was completed. Gina hired Roman cameraman Alfredo Gorbi to work with her and forwarded him money, plane tickets and production plans.

When Gorbi left Rome with his crew, he took with him a film he had previously made in Manila for the Italian TV and screened it for Gina and her Filipino bodyguards. Gorbi's *Nothing New in Manila*, a "truthful picture highlighting the poverty, corruption, filth, hunger and rebellion" in the country, surprised Lollobrigida. Word traveled fast. The Roman cameraman and his crew were invited to leave the country. Understanding that Gina had nothing to do with Gorbi's film, Marcos and Imelda, "The Iron Butterfly," gave her a second chance. The actress, operating from a business and professional point of view, carried on with her plans with the help of a new crew.

Photographing the Philippines wasn't as inviting as taking on her own country as a hippie. The job required a few shots of "a unique stone age people living in the deep rain forests where the climate only permits one to fly in for 28 days a year," said Gina. For her to work there it was necessary to build a platform above the trees so that a helicopter could land.

When her job was concluded Gina had the albums printed and delivered at her own expense. But she had yet to receive the remaining $750,000.

When Marcos' dictatorship saw its end in 1986, the Gina-Imelda episode was rehashed in the papers, focusing on the huge fee the actress was supposed to have received. Gina countered that although she had taken thousands of photographs and had completed the work as promised, her client was unwilling to hand over a check for the amount due. Gina had tried to see Mrs. Marcos at least a dozen times but had been refused a visit. An indignant signora Lollobrigida finally cornered Imelda at an international airport. Gina was accompanied by an Italian ambassador and the Filipina had no choice but to play the part of a good friend. The charade featured hugs and kisses but - unfortunately - no payment.

Gina sued and put the case in the hands of her American lawyer, Roy Cohen. The attorney representing Imelda suggested the case be solved in private and Gina received a small portion of what she was entitled. Fed up with the whole thing, Gina took Cohen's advice to drop the matter.

Months before their relationship soured in 1977, Imelda and Gina created a happy splash in the Philippines. The First Lady received Gina as protocol commanded. The official Philippine News Agency reported that in May of 1976 Gina Lollobrigida had been crowned an honorary Moslem queen in the Southern Philippines, and received a gold-plated likeness of a mythical bird for Gina's beauty and royal prominence. Notwithstanding, when she asked for the final payment gossip columnists affirmed that there was a female war between Imelda and Gina. "The Iron Butterfly" alluded that the actress had not carried out the terms of the contract.

When the government of President Corazón Aquino took over the country, one of the auditors responsible for updating the accounts of the former administration declared that Gina had not completed the job commissioned by Imelda.

If it's to be the word of the former First Lady against that of Gina Lollobrigida, my choice is obvious. Those who require more convincing evidence may wish to reflect upon the dishonest practices of Ferdinand and Imelda Marcos which were openly exposed to the world in 1986. Gina's mini-biography in the first pages of *The Films of Gina Lollobrigida* lists *Manila* and *The Philippines* as Gina's next two completed albums after *Italia Mia*. Furthermore, the actress' past life can speak for itself. Signora Lollobrigida was and is well-known for being a trustworthy person and dedicated to her careers; the lady would never have demanded payment for a job she hadn't satisfactorily finished, for she's a perfectionist. If the amount the former Philippine government had promised her for the two albums and the documentary *The Philippines* was as exorbitant as one Italian newspaper recently suggested, one has to keep in mind that the sum was what the actress agreed upon in the contract, not what she acknowledged receiving.

Although Lollobrigida had been seen with and photographed in the company of the Filipino autocrat and wife on several occasions in the mid-Seventies, Gina maintains that she never had close friendship with the couple. As a matter of fact, when President Aquino replaced the dictator Gina sent the new chief of state a telegram of best wishes.

\*\*\*

# 215--Imperial Gina

Photo Studio Lollobrigida (located in the large basement of Gina's villa) kept her busy, for the actress-photographer did her own developing and blow-ups of pictures.

The elaborate studio and darkroom contains a very efficient setup which includes a mammoth enlarger, filing cases, drawers, closets, and a refrigerator which - at the end of 1980 - already housed 150,000 negatives. By 1984, the studio was responsible for publicity art work requested from America and France under the direction of Antonio Quindi and Gina Lollobrigida.

Everything was running smoothly with Gina behind the camera when a film offer persuaded her to shift gears. The man responsible for enticing Gina out of her darkroom was the Spanish-American, Tony Navarro, an aspiring producer, director and script writer.

The son of a diplomat, Navarro had his start in Hollywood as a public relations man for Warner Brothers and was about to produce his first film, *Widows' Nest*, in the fall of 1977. It was a picture he considered worthy of an Oscar. The film, to be shot in Mexico, presented a fine cast starring Gina in the part of a Spanish woman with John Gavin as her leading man. Other parts were accepted by Yvonne Mitchell, Joseph Cotten, Patricia Neal and Valentina Cortese.

It all started when signora Cortese, Gina's friend, phoned her from Hollywood asking if she'd consider a script from the neophyte director who had managed to get major studio backing. The references were good and Gina saw no reason to turn down the offer. A very elaborate letter from Mr. Navarro contributed to Gina's enthusiasm to act again for a change of pace. The thought of spending some time south of the border conjured up appealing vacation images for Gina, who probably needed them; she also happily anticipated her new role. But despite a promising script and a fine cast, problems began popping up one after another.

The actress' first disappointment was that the location had been transferred from Mexico to Spain. Then, when Gina arrived in Madrid in August of that year, she learned that Navarro Productions, Inc. hadn't honored its commitment to deposit $75,000 into her bank account. To make matters worse, the 44-year-old producer informed Gina upon her arrival at the airport that he was out of money. Navarro's solution was for Gina to work first and be paid later when the film was in the can. Had he been a Mike Todd, Gina would probably have accepted the deal, but Tony Navarro was an unknown quantity. She refused. Tony insisted, protesting that the rest of the cast had taken his word and that Gina was making a mistake by passing up the opportunity to appear in an Oscar quality film.

The fact that la Cortese and other members of the cast had agreed to the risk in no way would oblige Lollobrigida to follow suit. Actually, Gina soon learned that John Gavin, Joseph Cotten and several crew members had left the production. Only Valentina Cortese, Yvonne Mitchell and a Polish actress remained.

Meanwhile, Gina returned to Rome. Then, for fellowship's sake, she decided to fly back to Madrid to be with signora Cortese and, at the same time, reconsider Navarro's situation. By the time Gina arrived in Madrid the project was off. Tony blamed it on la Lollo, saying that her absence from the cast had forced him to cancel the production; he added that Gina "wasn't Latin enough" for the role. She promptly filed a $75,000 lawsuit against Navarro Productions for breach of contract.

It was unfortunate that Gina's planned return to show business was so unpleasant, but the actress characteristically brushed off the dust from her shoes and was soon clicking away again with her cameras.

Back in Rome, Gina seemed to have already forgotten that Navarro Productions had ever existed. Nineteen-year-old Milketto was staying with her and that in itself brought the actress great satisfaction. But soon mother and son were again separated. The young man had to return to Switzerland to continue his studies in economics; he had spent the previous year studying at the College of Commercial Science in Amherst, Connecticut, and after a visit at the villa, was on his way to Switzerland.

While Milketto was studying in the Alps, his brave Mamma was photographing models on Roman roofs for none other than the prestigious French *Vogue*. After working with models on buildings not far from the Vatican, Gina switched to her villa for a change of decor. The model was signorina Vittoria Amati, duchess Boni Gaetani d'Aragona, wearing exotic outfits designed by famous couturiers. Gina's Roman collection appeared in the March 1978 of *Vogue*.

A new set of Lollobrigida photographs was chosen for the September issue of the same year featuring Givenchy, Yves Saint Laurent, Dior, Cardin, Lapidus, Jean-Louis Scherrer, Paco Rabanne and Hanae Mori collections in Paris.

# 217--Imperial Gina

*Vogue* considered Lollobrigida's photography spontaneous, clear, and a bit overwhelming because Gina didn't work with a flash. The photos were authentic and beautiful.

Since Gina obviously couldn't wear her hippie disguise to elegant fashion shows, there were times when one wasn't sure who the real focus of attention was - the mannequin sporting a Dior, or the fashionable photographer.

While *Vogue* readers feasted on her photographic work, Italian gossip lovers, never completely pleased with Gina's scandal-free life, were rejoicing in brand new rumors. The grapevine whispered of budding love between Gina and her Genoese furrier, Sergio Soldano, who was supposedly leaving his wife because of la Bersagliera. The Soldanos immediately called a press conference and denied the false reports. Gina, who was travelling in Chile accompanied by her faithful cameras, took no notice of the stories. It's true that she loved furs, but her relationship with the fur designer was merely based on friendship. Indiscreet voices, however, had found another candidate for the actress, saying that her eyes were resting upon the blonde, young German baron, Johannes von Lille.

Towards the end of 1978, Gina was in New York to shoot a spread for the international magazine *Mode*. One day while having lunch at Orsini's restaurant, Dustin Hoffman was taken completely by surprise when he noticed Gina sitting at the next table. The actress was accompanied by a friend, Ms. Cheri Royce, and the enthralled 41-one-year-old actor invited both of them to join him on the set of *Kramer vs Kramer*. Had Gina had her cameras ready during lunch, she'd have had the picture of the year capturing the actor modelling her pink mink coat for the crowd at the restaurant. Was Hoffman unconsciously rehearsing for *Tootsie*? Dustin's fun was just as spontaneous as Lollobrigida's *Vogue* photography, for the two had never met before.

*** 

Another decade was reaching its end and Gina Lollobrigida had lived every minute of it to its fullest. Without adhering to the paparazzi clan, she made a name for herself in her new profession without exploiting situations in poor taste, for she regarded sensationalists as literary parasites.

In the early fall of 1979, Gina appeared as the chief judge at the closing night gala of the Montreal Film Festival, and was again in the Canadian city in the summer of 1981 in the same capacity for the fifth annual World Film Festival. Film critics Les Wedman and Rex Reed, directors Garcia Berlanga and Gilles Carle joined Lollobrigida on the judges' panel.

On the occasion of her second visit to Montreal, Gina said that "being the president of the jury can be an interesting experience. It requires many diplomatic skills, which I hope to be able to utilize at the opportune moment." Gina's straight forward character made it difficult for her to adapt diplomatic skills in her life. A traditionalist in film making, Gina thinks that "new directors don't care if they please the public, nor do they care about telling a story." Expanding the thought, the actress believes that "the fashion today is to shock the public," which was the prevailing strategy of the 1981 Montreal Film Festival. Her dissatisfaction with present day cinema again emerged when she presided over the 1986 Berlin Film Festival.

The actress-photographer - courtesy *Il Messaggero* (author's collection).

# Chapter 7

## Four Decades in the Limelight

When Lollobrigida signed to star as Jane Wyman's Italian sister in five episodes of *Falcon Crest* for CBS towards the end of 1984, columnist Nicholas Leahy wrote that after the actress had retired from acting some 14 years earlier she had "been living alone in magnificent seclusion in her villa in Rome." The term "seclusion," however, isn't appropriate. Gina had temporarily withdrawn herself from show business but not from the public in general. The previous decade had probably seen signora Lollobrigida at more international airports loaded with photographic equipment than when she was making four or five films a year in the Fifties. In the last ten years Gina had surely spent more time away from her villa than in any other period of her life.

Gina Lollobrigida entered the Eighties taking Paris by storm as she had done exactly thirty years earlier as the gypsy Aline in *Fanfan la Tulipe*. Gina was in town for her big Paris première as a photographer in the prestigious Musée Carnavalet, and once again she had Paris at her feet.

To commemorate the month of photography, Gina's work was exhibited from October 22 through November 15, 1980. This was her first one-woman show in the French capital and she was naturally apprehensive, for she knew she had to please a difficult public; Parisians' taste in black and white photography had, to a very large extent, been shaped by Henri Cartier-Bresson. Gina needn't have worried. Her previous exhibitions around the world and the triumph of *Italia Mia* should have allayed her fears. Nevertheless, the director of the museum, anticipating a fiasco, "disappeared after the opening - only to show up again when he saw it was going well," remarked Gina.

The only obstacle Lollobrigida encountered was space, and she almost broke down in tears when she discovered that there was only room for 160 photos. The selection had to be the best, and she chose carefully.

"Her pictures depict intimate moments between people," described a French critic, "the ordinary human beings of this world caught in their moods of pathos and humour." And it was Gina's compassionate eye which unveiled her heart in this exhibition. Probably one of her best colored portraits on display was that of an Indian that she took late at night in Benares. "The man was so surprised to see a woman with a camera," explained Gina, "that he looked at me with an expression of hate mixed with desire." The original photograph decorates her Swiss home and "is usually mistaken for a painting" which, according to experts, resembles a Rembrandt.

At the post-vernissage held at Paris' posh night spot, Club 78, a bedecked and bejeweled Gina was once again the main attraction. At the party she had energy for a few dances and found time to introduce Milko Skofic Jr. to Parisian high society. Gina was escorted by Duc de Sabran-Ponteves. Tongues wagged. Would signora Lollobrigida become a Duchess? She never intended to. Her photography and her freedom were more precious to her than noble titles.

With her photo exhibition at Musée Carnavalet, Lollobrigida had achieved another success with the French. She was awarded the Vermeil Medal, an outstanding prize that had also been bestowed upon Chaplin.

During this Lollobrigida photo exhibition, *Le Monde* carried an article by French writer Hervé Guibert where Lollobrigida herself talked at length about her photography. In his second introductory paragraph on the actress' photographs, Monsieur Guibert wrote: "Gina Lollobrigida unleashes upon the small Parisian photographic world, with devastating energy and talent, bewildering photos and kitsch postcards, without distinction, ideas deviating from the normal, an incurable liking for life, people and perfection." He concluded that Gina was "a photographer who may have the eye of a Cartier-Bresson, but who refuses to allow herself to be restricted by normal standards. Despite the manufacturers of clichés who passively accept myths without calling them into question, Gina Lollobrigida is a true artist."

Even though the French writer refers to Gina as "a true artist" his feelings about her are actually more complex. Two years after his article appeared in *Le Monde*, he published a short story depicting a

# 221–Imperial Gina

Gina deprived of artistic taste. What could have gone wrong for the author to turn completely against the actress-photographer? The juxtaposition of his newspaper piece and his short story, *Le désir d'imitation* (The Desire of Imitation) confuse me. While in the first he praises (and to a certain extent criticizes) Gina's photography, hatred for the actress abounds in the second.

I wrote to Monsieur Guibert inquiring about the nature of his feelings towards Gina; he was considerate to answer my letter, but declined to elaborate on the topic. I wrote to him a second time, but I never heard from the author again.

Monsieur Guibert may argue that the woman in question in his work of fiction isn't Gina Lollobrigida, but another star, since Gina's name isn't revealed in the story. Nevertheless, the perfect description he gives to the protagonist's villa (without mentioning its whereabouts) and numerous thinly veiled references to the actress' life and films cannot fool anyone who knows signora Lollobrigida well either in person or through an extensive study, as in my case.

As a piece of literary fiction *Le désir d'imitation* is good indeed, but portraying Gina Lollobrigida as if she were an unsavory character is simply unfair.

Before I read the story for a second and a third time, I turned to my colleague, writer James Kirkup for help (since he is quite familiar with literary figures in most European countries), with the hope that he could shed some light on that particular French writer, for it was Kirkup himself who presented me with a copy of the work.

An avant-guarde novelist and playwright with works published by Editions de Minuit and Gallimard, Hervé Guibert is the friend of another Parisian writer, René de Ceccatty, who in turn knows James Kirkup, completing this double French, British-Brazilian connection. According to Kirkup, Monsieur Guibert "is rather antifeminist, which perhaps explains his sarcastic and bitter treatment of Gina" in the story.

The plot begins with a man - we learn he's French later in the narrative - leaving from L. station the day after Christmas in 19..., with R. as his destination. Even though the writer avoids dates and names, I deduce that L. refers to Lyon, where the author boards a train to Rome.

When he arrives at the Italian capital the lady's chauffeur and a Mercedes are waiting to whisk him away to a villa which could be none other than Gina's in the Appia Antica. The author later in the story also mentions the same bus ride I took to the actress' villa in August of 1985; the green gate with the interphone is also unmistakable.

After his arrival at the villa the narrative becomes increasingly absurd. One pictures an old castle with gloomy rooms. Guibert presents the main hall as a horrid canvas of Spanish, Chinese, Baroque and Classic styles. The room, he suggests, is highly overdecorated and devoid of artistic good taste.

During the tour through the villa's gardens he mentions the three German shepherd dogs that the actress keeps on the grounds. Since the dogs were trained by German police she talks to them in German: "sitz! platz! auf!" and they follow her instructions. Lollobrigida's torturer sneers that those three words are the extent of the woman's Deutsch, with the exception of two poems by Goethe that she recites "mechanically without understanding [their] meaning." The cruel visitor is on a scavenger hunt for excuses to ridicule his hostess.

The author then writes that his father used to tell him that this actress had been considered the most beautiful woman in the world. He quotes an episode in Hollywood related to a movie czar that could be no other than Howard Hughes in relationship to Gina in the Fifties. The actress' refusal to undress in any film, also mentioned in the story, sounds precisely like Lollobrigida, whom he wrongly describes as an empty woman relying on wigs and gowns to look beautiful.

If the author's intention was to disguise the identity of the woman about whom he was writing, his efforts fell short of the mark. As if events and places weren't enough of a giveaway, he threw in a few film titles to confirm the reader's guess.

While visiting with the actress, she first screens two films for him which he calls *Nuits de Chine* (Nights of China) and *Le grand Saba* (The Great Sheba); obviously the latter is *Solomon and Sheba*, and the former is *Beauties of the Night*. Later, as the plot develops, the visitor asks to see her *Les Nuits de Bagdad* (Nights of Bagdad) which I suppose is *Wife for a Night* and *Le Cirque rouge* (The Red Circus) which is without the shadow of a doubt *Trapeze*, for he also says that in the film she played the role of an acrobat loved by two men whom he sarcastically calls "dompteurs" (horse-breakers). In the film they were two rival aerialists, Tony Curtis and Burt Lancaster.

The absurdity of the plot is enlarged with the visitor's plan to kill the actress. In one episode, for example, he imagines the woman trying to embrace him and he avoids her with a violent movement; she falls and hits her head on an aquarium she has in the room. He tries to strangle her but holds back his hands. Blood trickles from her mouth. The scene is sadistic and clearly shows how much this man hates the actress whose voice he can't stand any longer.

After the Frenchman's complicated visit to the woman, we learn that he met her again in New York a couple of months later. How much of the story is true remains a mystery.

At the time Hervé Guibert wrote about Gina's photo exhibit in Paris, it was rumored that there had been a misunderstanding between him and the star. If this is true, and presuming that Gina was aware of the Frenchman's harsh feelings for her, would she have invited him to visit her villa where only a select few were usually welcomed? Or did the writer come to see Lollobrigida before the Paris photo exhibition?

The title of the story is also somewhat puzzling. Gina has never been the shadow of another actress or artist, and dislikes to be imitated as well. Who is imitating whom in the story? Could it possibly be that the antifeminist writer would like to fashion himself after Gina because of her beauty while simultaneously resenting her hold over him? Or is he saying that Gina is imitating herself in her younger days?

The combination of reality and fiction allowed monsieur Guibert to express his precise feelings for the female protagonist. The fact that the author didn't identify Lollobrigida by name saved him a lawsuit from Gina.

\*\*\*

On February 17, 1981, Elizabeth Taylor and Gina Lollobrigida were photographed together during the Luncheon of Stars at the Helmsley Palace Hotel in New York. The purpose of the event was to announce that the Actors' Fund of America would celebrate its centennial with a three-hour ABC-TV show, *Night of 100 Stars*, at Radio City Music Hall in November of that year. Broadway producer Alexander H. Cohen was in charge of the gala at which Princess Grace of Monaco, Joan Collins, Bette Davis, Tony Perkins, Janet Leigh, Elizabeth Taylor, Gregory Peck, Jane Russell, Gina Lollobrigida, Burt Lancaster, Robert De Niro, Lillian Gish, Jane Fonda and dozens of other stars would be present. "It wasn't the *Night of 100 Stars* after all - 218 stars were shining!" observed the queen of TV's *Dynasty*, Joan Collins, in her autobiography, *Past Imperfect*.

For the event at the Helmsley, Gina wore a flowered lavender chiffon dress. Thank heaven this time Liz and Gina didn't repeat the fashion nightmare of the 1961 Moscow Film Festival when the two actresses appeared at the Kremlin reception wearing identical Dior dresses. Actress Ann Miller seemed to be more intrigued by Liz's figure than her gown. "Oh, hasn't she lost weight? It must be forty pounds. I'm envious, I have to tell her." And with that, the star of *Easter Parade* (1948) rushed off.

Following the *Luncheon of Stars*, Gina was the main attraction at the opening of Starbucks, a New York disco, sometime in March. There, Miss Nabila Khashoggi, the teen-aged daughter of Arab billionaire Adnan Khashoggi, was photographed standing by Gina. Still in the same month, la Lollo was jigging again at another disco. This time she was seen at Xenon's during the celebration of St. Patrick's Day. With so much going on in New York, Italians were probably wondering when *La romana* would go Roman again.

Eventually, Gina returned to Italy but soon left for China with a small Italian cultural delegation. The Chinese had recently opened their doors to the Western cinema and Charlie Chaplin films along with *Fanfan la Tulipe* and *The Hunchback of Notre Dame* were being shown in the country. Gina was soon recognized when she walked along Chinese streets.

At the year's end, *Variety* announced that Gina was directing and starring in a short documentary. According to the source, *Qatar Today* was made by the Qatar Ministry of Information and Bocca di Leone of Italy. The short film uses a real-life wedding to give continuity to its version of life in the Gulf state today. In the documentary, Gina questions the bride regarding numerous stages of her life. The film then cuts away to use backgrounds such as the former pearl fishing industry and the Dukan oil fields. With Lollobrigida in the film, the Ministry hoped to reach an international audience.

Between 1972 and 1982 Gina had produced three albums, three documentaries, photographed dozens of important figures, and worked as a fashion photographer in Paris, Rome and New York. During those ten years she had taken a total of 200,000 photographs. Among her many projects, there was also one which consisted of "flowers and animals with super-imposed figures of herself and children portrayed in a private wonderland of harmony and beauty."

# 225–Imperial Gina

Working as a photojournalist had also given Gina the opportunity to demonstrate her adventurous spirit, whether photographing stone age people in the Philippine jungles or descending 24,000 meters to the bottom of a gold mine in South Africa. It was during this South African adventure that one of the cameras in her bag was completely damaged due to humidity.

*\*\*\**

Always eager to expand her artistic calling, Gina accepted an offer to tour several American cities as hostess of the Fabris Museum Collection, drawing large crowds. She opened the show on November 4, 1982 in New York at Ginori on Fifth Avenue. The $250,000 rare and historic collection of Italian porcelain sculptures had been first produced in the late 18th-century by Fiorina Fabris and had survived the Napoleon invasion and the two world wars. Recently discovered in the walled city of Bassano del Grappa, the pieces were now being handled by Gina, the perfect choice to present the valuable Italian antiques to the American public.

When Gina finished touring with the Fabris collection, she returned to her studio for a photograph session with Ursula Andress whom she considered a beautiful woman and easy to photograph. At 45, the Swiss film star still preserved her gracious curves; like Gina, she didn't smoke, avoided alcohol, had a balanced life style and ate tons of salads.

Lollobrigida was very pleased with the photographs and hoped to display some of them in a future exhibition. The fact that an actress-turned-photographer was photographing another actress wasn't as entertaining as when Ursula told *Paris-Match* that she was also an incurable shutterbug. She had got her passion for cameras from her ex-husband John Derek, and like Gina, her favorite model was her four-year-old son, Dimitri.

Photography has become a hobby - a profession in some cases - among the world's most famous V.I.P.'s. *Time* magazine (May 4, 1987) published a mini feature on shutterbugs including a cross-section of notables from Gina Lollobrigida to French chef Paul Bocuse and Vermont Democrat Senator Patrick Leahy. Gina was still working on her fifth album featuring animals and children. The fourth, *Il segreto delle rose* (The Secret of Roses), a collection of her favorite flower, appeared in 1984 through Electa Editors of Milan. Of this exquisite selection of 67 plates featuring roses of all colors and shades, my favorite is *Perle noir* (Black Pearl), a juxtaposition of two dark red roses.

\*\*\*

In the early Eighties, Gina Lollobrigida was still a big name in Europe and America. It's difficult to write about the lady in the past as a successful actress and photographer because she's a living legend. In a survey to identify the most popular women in Italy, the most beautiful, the best actress, and the woman with the most talent and personality, Gina was classified among the first six with Sophia Loren sometimes placed above, sometimes below Lollobrigida.

Three decades had passed since la Bersagliera had visited New York to promote *Bread, Love and Dreams* and the glamour she then portrayed had not left her. When a columnist for the *Sunday Mirror* was assigned to interview Gina in her Roman villa, the writer thought that "if Liz Taylor could look matronly at fifty, la Lollo had to be a shambles at fifty-five." This pre-judgment was proved completely false. When the columnist met the actress she was surprised to see no change at all! "Her face still has the same devastating, sex-kitten quality which hits you between the eyes in films like *Trapeze* and *Buona Sera Mrs. Campbell*. Her waist, which is tightly cinched by a wide jewelled belt, is tiny enough to get two hands around."

Gina's system to avoid aging is based on controlling the birth wrinkles through constant and attentive care never to stress her facial muscles. Gina, should this information be correct, never laughs but smiles, she hardly ever wrinkles her forehead, she avoids tiring her eyelids, and she usually doesn't stretch the circumference of her mouth beyond what is necessary to emit sound and words.

Notwithstanding, Gina's beauty and virtuous character haven't always been acknowledged. Throughout her two careers she has on many occasions been the victim of severe criticism. The array of ill-natured comments and incriminating photographs which many stars are inflicted with have left Gina with a thick skin.

To criticize Gina Lollobrigida has always been a habit among a minority group in Italy. There, her fashion, the jewels she wears, many of her films and photos were many times the focus of malicious comments. While Americans loved her clothes, there were those in her native land who judged her wardrobe out of fashion. But this minority who tried to destroy her never found weapons strong enough for Gina's untouchable personality. The actress has lived her life as she pleases with no desire for revenge on those who had or have an evil eye on her. Many were the times at the very beginning of her film career when she was mistreated by movie moguls who left her vowing to seek revenge the day she became a star in demand, but hate never took root in her heart, and with the passing of time she forgot and forgave those who wronged her.

\*\*\*

In the ever beautiful ski resort area of Crans-sur-Sierre (Switzerland) one finds Gina's paradise, a house she acquired some 27 years ago. In December 1982, after TV appearances in Germany and Hungary, Gina flew to her Swiss nest where, for the first time, she opened its door to the press. Gina, who has always been very jealous of her privacy, allowed the readers of the Italian weekly *Oggi* to see the interior of the residence. Like her Roman villa, the house is tastefully decorated with objects from all over the world and paintings by Gina herself.

La Bersagliera's fast rhythm of life, however, offers her little time to enjoy her refuge on the Swiss mountain where a ski slope was named after her. Gina's career as a photojournalist kept on calling her to distant places until 1984, when she squeezed a brand new career into her already crowded calendar.

Gina's imminent Broadway debut was honored at a cocktail party hosted by Harry Rigby and Terry Kramer in early June 1984 at Le Grande Cornich in the River Hotel facing the Hudson River. Six months previous to this event, the actress had divulged that she'd start her new career with Tennessee Williams' *The Rose Tattoo*. The screenplay had yielded an Academy Award for Anna Magnani in 1955, the first of the few films that she made in Hollywood, and now Gina would be the first Italian actress performing in English on Broadway in the fascinating role of Serafina, a volcanic and coarse Sicilian woman.

When producer John Dillinger first approached her with the script, Gina refused it twice. "I wasn't sure about it then," she told the *L. A. Times*. "I felt it was not right for me," she concluded. Her judgement changed when a friend ran her a tape of the film version and she fell in love with the part. "Anna Magnani was just wonderful," said Gina.

"She deserved the Oscar. That face - it was so powerful." It was then that Gina realized that the role of Serafina - like that of Carla Campbell - fit her like a glove.

For more than 20 years Gina had constantly received offers to perform on the stage, but had refused them all, including a musical, *La donna dell'anno* which was subsequently offered to Raquel Welch. Once, Leonard Bernstein tried to convince Gina to do a Broadway show. Luchino Visconti brought him to her villa and Leonard played his music for her, knowing that she had a trained voice. He failed.

Acting on the stage isn't the same as shooting a movie. If you blow a line while filming a scene it can be taken dozens or hundreds of times again, but not on the stage. Lollobrigida confessed she was terrified of live audiences and that she loved the theater when she was watching a play. The thought of performing several times a week for months augmented her fear. She was so conscious of the responsibility that she was having constant nightmares. In one of them la Lollo was on the stage and she hadn't rehearsed with any of the actors and she didn't know what to do.

Nevertheless, when Gina turned down the part she made it clear that the reason she was doing so wasn't because she doubted her ability to play the difficult part of Serafina, but because she was suffering incurable stage fright. Producer Dillinger didn't take her "no" for an answer. He phoned her in Rome and told her that if she didn't do the play he'd come over and kill her! Gina chose the lesser of the two evils. But by this time she had already fallen in love with the part and accepted it in her heart. Upon her arrival at the River Hotel for her welcome in New York, 23-year-old Christopher Atkins was introduced as one of Gina's co-stars in the play. This attractive man who played opposite Brooke Shields in *The Blue Lagoon* had been cast as Jack, the sailor who is in love with Serafina's 15-year-old daughter, Rosa. (Young Christopher had also starred with Kristy McNichol in *The Pirate Movie* and appeared in the TV series *Dallas* with Linda Gray.)

At that stage of the production, however, nothing had been decided on who would be Lollobrigida's leading man in the role of Alvaro, the man who takes Serafina's husband's place after his death in a truck accident in the first act. (The husband never appears in the play.) In the movie, Burt Lancaster had rendered a fine performance and the question was who would match him opposite the Italian actress. Gina, I heard through the grapevine, was choosing her own leading man and had in mind the Puerto Rican Raul Julia, but he seemed to be reluctant. The play was cancelled for the time being.

New plans were made for Gina's Broadway debut in early 1985. The company would perform in Baltimore and Toronto before opening on Broadway. Gina was still undoubtedly very enthusiastic about the play. The forced postponement didn't discourage her. Preparations for rehearsals were made and Gina could hardly wait for her debut as a stage actress.

Against her will, Gina never got to play Serafina. Problems began to pile up with the death of the producer. Next, one theater was too large, while another was not in good condition. Before the summer of 1985, *The Rose Tattoo* had completely vanished from Gina's agenda. Talking to *Le Figaro*, the actress acknowledged that the project had gone down the drain and that the happening had been a big disappointment for her. Nevertheless, she was ready to get on with life. "I throw bad things away from me and I focus on new activities. I always have my enthusiasm and joy for living," Gina told a reporter.

Gina Lollobrigida doesn't waste time. Before the play died, she had opened her own chain of photo and art boutiques where Ginettes (Ginetas) sell her photos, paintings, drawings and original sculptures. Naturally, the trade name is controlled.

\*\*\*

Sometime in the fall of 1984 the press announced Gina's American television acting debut with a guest role in *Falcon Crest*, the CBS TV soap opera tracing the emotional ups and downs of a California wine-growing family. Starring the veteran Jane Wyman, the series first appeared in 1981 to dethrone *Dallas* and *Dynasty*. Gina's part, that of Francesca Gioberti - Angela Channing's (Wyman) foreboding half sister - had been offered first to Sophia Loren, but there were rumors that the former Mrs. Reagan preferred to work with someone else. Later it was revealed that the reason why signora Ponti didn't get the part was the outrageous amount she had requested for the five episodes in which she'd participate.

A Lorimar Production, *Falcon Crest* was an instant success with the audiences. The fourth season, the one Gina joined in November 1984, also included Sarah Douglas, David Selby, and Lorenzo Lamas (the son of Esther Williams). Celebrities like Mel Ferrer and Lana

Turner had made guest appearances in previous episodes, and there had been murmurs that a feud had erupted between the once Hollywood goddess Lana and Wyman, known by co-stars and crew as "The Iron Lady." Every time a guest star joined the cast, suspense reigned in the studio. So, when it was officially announced that Gina might be the next guest star, the Italian actress fielded a barrage of questions concerning Wyman. Gina saw no reason why she should fear the American star. "I think she's a lovely lady and a beautiful actress. It will be a pleasure to work with her and the entire cast," offered Lollobrigida.

An Earl Hamner creation, *Falcon Crest* was published in 1984 as a novel by Patrick Mann based on Hamner's series. The show, originally christened *The Vintage Years*, tells the story of powerful Angela Channing in California's wine country. The pivotal point in the plot is Angela's desire to drive her nephew Richard Channing off his land. The complicated cunning saga also involves the nephew's wife, Angela's alcoholic daughter, Angela's grandson - played by Lorenzo Lamas - and a long list of fascinating characters whose final decoy is *Falcon Crest*.

Gina, who had spent a lot of time in New York, watched prime time TV dramas often and she loved them all; whenever she had to go out she asked friends to tape the shows for her because she just didn't want to miss them. So when she was asked if she would be interested in doing *Falcon Crest* for a few weeks she jumped at the chance. Gina had decided to return to acting, and American TV, she thought, was a good place to do it. Meanwhile, she'd try to solve production problems involved with *The Rose Tattoo*. Had the Broadway project been realized la Lollo would have had a double brilliant come back to show business.

Working on a TV series was a completely new experience for Gina and she was thrilled with the idea. Soap opera characters, who seemed to be all either good or bad, weak or strong, intrigued the actress, for in real life, she felt, "we are all a mixture of these things, are we not?" Gina's renewed fervor after 12 years behind the cameras was rewarded with good reviews and a Golden Globe nomination.

When Gina joined the cast in November, several outstanding writers had become involved with the show including Stephen Black, Dick Nelson, Kathleen A. Shelley and others. Production was then in the hands of John Perry, who considered Gina's episodes "terrific."

Not everybody in the cast, however, spoke of la Lollo so graciously. British actress Sarah Douglas - who had joined the series to play Pamela Lynch, the show's "supervixen answer to *Dynasty*'s Joan Collins" - told columnists that Lollobrigida behaved like a prima donna during the several weeks they were filming. Miss Douglas had nothing good to say about her Italian colleague. "She's been causing incredible mayhem and havoc on the set. Nobody talks to her anymore. She threw a daily temper tantrum. She wasn't able to remember whole pages of dialogue. The producers wished they'd never hired her."

These accusations were countered by Perry's defense of Lollobrigida: "Gina at all times was totally prepared. She knew her lines. She was well-rehearsed. She came in and did her work without any problems. We are not sorry she was our choice."

A source close to the production suggested that "maybe Gina was too much competition for Sarah professionally and in terms of how beautiful Gina is." Lollobrigida, talking to *Star*, defended herself in the following words: "It just doesn't make sense. I'm amazed." The actress then maintained that if Miss Douglas' allegations were true, "why did they expand my role in *Falcon Crest*? Why did they rewrite my last scene at the last moment so that my character says, 'I will return,' leaving it open for me to come back when I finish my Broadway show?"

As for Sarah's remark about Gina's prima donna-like behavior, Gina retorted that "prima donnas are not professional. They think of themselves first, instead of the show and the people they work with. Not one person in this world can ever say I am not professional."

Had Lollobrigida acted as described by the British actress, she'd probably have been terminated soon and her relationship with Wyman would have catapulted into a true war. Gina's track record was that of a perfectionist; she was never late for work at the studios, and commanded the respect of co-stars and crews in general. While performing in *Falcon Crest* she worked 15 hours a day, was up most nights rehearsing and lost nearly 15 pounds.

In one particular scene where Francesca returns to the Channings' (after suffering a difficult time with them), "she does this incredible, exciting Italian dance to get out the poison and to throw it in their faces." Gina stayed up all night perfecting the dance. When she performed it in front of the camera she asked for reshots until she was entirely satisfied. According to Gina, Sarah probably got snippy because la Lollo wanted the dance to be reshot. Gina, however, wasn't the only one interested in a retake. "The reason we reshot," said Perry, "is that on that day there were some lab problems and some of the film was ruined. And since we had to re-shoot anyway, and were so impressed by Gina's performance, we decided to make her dance longer." Another possible source of Miss Douglas' discontent lay in the plot itself; in the episodes which were broadcast during November, Francesca stole Richard Channing away from his "bitchy" secretary Pamela Lynch.

It was during the filming of the dance scene that Gina learned that her villa had been robbed by armed men, and that two of her friends had been taken as hostages. Thinking about her son who was visiting the Appia Antica, la Lollo burst into tears. Fortunately nobody was hurt. When the cast learned about the happening, people at the studio were hugging and trying to comfort Gina; this demonstration of warmth towards her didn't please the "person who said those things about me, so she told the lie that I made a mess of the show," commented Gina to *Star* magazine.

It wasn't the first time that Sarah Douglas had been involved in a problem with another actress. When a columnist compared her with Joan Collins she stated that the latter was much older. Later when the two ladies met at a Hollywood party Sarah told Joan she had been "terribly misquoted." Collins rebounded with: "I hope for your sake you were, my dear." Like most soap operas, *Falcon Crest* continued with the practice of adding new characters to maintain audience interest. At the time Gina was chosen for the new part, actress Jane Greer, an RKO star of the late Forties, also joined the family. (Actually, 70-year-old Ginger Rogers had been approached first for the new part.) Kim Novak joined the show in December of 1986, and was followed by Patricia Apollonia Kotero, who first stirred audience in the 1984 punk movie *Purple Rain*.

Apart from Miss Douglas and the robbery, the year ended successfully for Gina. She enjoyed a brilliant return to the show business world, and won another lawsuit in November.

Gina's antagonist, for once, wasn't a peeping paparazzo or a nasty columnist, but rather a fashionable New York restaurant where in June of 1980 she had broken off an incisor when she bit into a brown, pebble-like substance while eating a fried shrimp. At the time of the misfortune, the actress was coincidentally accompanied by her dentist, Dr. Marc Den-Huri, who immediately took her to his clinic not too far from Trader Vic's, the restaurant in question.

When Lollobrigida sued she explained that because of the broken tooth she had been forced to delay a trip to Rome where she was expected to take photographs for a fur dealer, causing her to lose money. The star also claimed that her hotel bill was climbing higher and that her suffering should also be taken into consideration.

On November 8, 1984, a Manhattan Supreme Court Justice ruled in her favor. In Judge Louis Kaplan's words, "a restaurant is expected to use ordinary care to remove harmful substances that consumers would not ordinarily anticipate to find when they bit into a fried shrimp." Gina had sued for $10 million; she collected $90,000.

While in the States, signora Lollobrigida also found time to photograph glamorous ladies from rival TV shows like *Dallas* and *Dynasty*. La Lollo camera sought Linda Evans (Crystal in *Dynasty*), Audrey Landers and Priscilla Presley. Gina was well impressed by these actresses 20 or 30 years her junior, and she particularly liked Priscilla. She thought her new subject was "a stunning woman" who didn't trust her beauty since she was nervous having photographs taken of her.

Linda Evans was more at ease. Gina was struck by her magnetic personality and found Linda "truly wonderful to photograph."

When Gina visited Audrey Landers (Afton in *Dallas*), her sister Judy was there and Gina photographed both of them, impressed by their youth.

Towards the end of 1986, American TV was programming new soap operas and "the most eagerly anticipated mini-series of all," according to the *Ladies' Home Journal*, was *Fresno* - a parody of *Falcon Crest* - starring Carol Burnett.

\*\*\*

After her successful adventure with *Falcon Crest*, Gina accepted a small but significant part in *Deceptions*. The four-hour TV mini--series tells the story of identical twins - a bored jet-setter in London and a middle-class New Jersey housewife who exchange identities and enjoy a new life for a week.

Charming *Hart to Hart* protagonist Stefanie Powers plays the double role of the twins - Stephanie Roberts and Sabrina Longworth - opposite Barry Bostwick as the former's professor husband. Co-starring are Brenda Vaccaro as Stephanie's jealous friend, Helen Adams, and Gina Lollobrigida as special guest star in the part of Princess

Alessandra. The cast also includes Jeremy Brett, Sam Wanamaker, James Faulkner, John Woodvine and Fabio Testi.

Producer William Hill and directors Melville Shavelson and Robert Chenault collaborated on *Deceptions*, which was aired on NBC in 1985. The production, based on Judith Michael's novel, was shot in the US, England and Italy.

Tired of housecleaning and peanut butter and jelly sandwiches, unsophisticated Stephanie accepts Sabrina's invitation to spend their birthday together in Venice as guests of gorgeous Princess Alessandra.

The show opens with Stephanie Roberts' funeral services in a London chapel where Lollobrigida, dressed in black, appears for the first time in the story. Her black dress and hat contrasting with a pearl necklace give her a very distinguished look; her presence dominates on the screen.

We then flash back three months prior to Stephanie's death; she is cruising on a yacht in Portofino (Italy) with her good-looking sister's former lover, Carlo (Fabio Testi). When Gina returns to the screen she's with Sabrina at a cocktail party, exquisitely dressed in a beaded long gown; Gina's charm and natural rapport with the camera vividly demonstrate that the Lollobrigida of *Imperial Venus* still moved and looked like a true star 22 years later.

The arrival of the sisters at Princess Alessandra's palace and the birthday party are Gina's best scenes out of the seven in which she appears; in these two events her lines are longer and her performance as a very wealthy and merry widow is first-class. When the twins arrive Lollobrigida is clad in a gorgeous green décolleté gown embroidered with sparkling beads; she wears long beaded necklaces and her soft, shoulder length hair is flattering. For the sisters' birthday party Gina, reminiscent of a fairy godmother, wears a splendid Elizabethan dress; her hair sparkles and glows with pearls and a tiara. Garbed in a variety of costumes, Alessandra's guests coquettishly mask their identities in a replica of a traditional 16th-century Venice Carnival. Wearing identical gowns, perfectly matched coiffures and masks, the two sisters fool those in the salon, who can't tell which one of the two is the real Sabrina.

In the actress' last two appearances (one at Sabrina's art gallery where she takes Stephanie for her sister, and then at a restaurant where she's reunited with the real Sabrina), la Lollo isn't quite as glamorous, but her clothes and carriage still proclaims she's someone special.

# 235--Imperial Gina

\*\*\*

Thirty-five years after Gina began her continuous love affair with France, she was received with great pomp at Théâtre de L'Empire in early March to present part of the 1985 *Cesar Awards*. Gina arrived in Paris via London and had a special gown sent to her from Milan. On that day Kirk Douglas was made "Commander of the French Order of Arts and Literature" by the French Minister of Culture Jack Lang. Gina, who on numerous occasions accepted prestigious French awards herself, received the insignia of "Officer" of the same order. The week after, la Lollo was honored again, for a new copy of *Bread, Love, and Dreams* was being shown in Parisian cinemas and *Bread, Love, and Jealousy* followed immediately.

\*\*\*

Now that la Lollo had made her comeback to show business via American TV and the French had bestowed upon her one of their highest honors, Italy couldn't remain silent. It's curious that Romans were sometimes slow in offering the best to their "Gina nazionale." It was first Christian-Jaque's *Fanfan la Tulipe* that brought her great popularity at home and abroad before Blasetti and Comencini created *Times Gone By* and *Bread, Love, and Dreams* for her. The actress' return to show business as a guest star in American soap operas reconfirmed this fact. When would the Caesars of the Italian entertainment world blow the trumpets for la Bersagliera's comeback?

In mid-August 1985 *Onda Tivu*, the Italian TV guide, featured Gina on its cover standing beside TV personality Pippo Baudo, the "Pippo nazionale." Gina - who hadn't worked in Italian TV since she did *Pinocchio* - had been recruited as the "inviata speciale" (special correspondent) of the *Domenica In*, a Sunday afternoon show where she'd interview world celebrities. The "Pippo nazionale" was to begin a new program, *Fantastico 6*, to be aired on Saturdays and scheduled to start on October 5. Mino Damato, another very popular TV host, was to take Pippo's place together with hostess Elisabetta Gardeni on the new *Domenica In*."

It wasn't foreseen, however, that a small anti-Gina group at the Radio Televisione Italiana (RAI UNO) would protest the addition of Gina Lollobrigida. Names weren't mentioned, but those voting against her at the studio bar on a particular day agreed that the tone of the program would be journalistic and Gina was too much of a glamorous star for it. Mostly, they were afraid that she'd eventually control the program. Before a final decision was reached, Damato, despite his neutrality, said he was "happy to work with a true star." Gina, in her villa, took a "non comment" attitude.

The Roman deities sided with Gina and on the last *Domenica In* hosted by "Pippo nazionale," he walked onto the stage with a gorgeously gowned "Gina nazionale" and introduced her as the special correspondent for the new series to begin early in the fall. Even though she wouldn't appear every Sunday throughout the long afternoon show, her position was secure and the audience would see her on the TV for several weeks together with famous guests as long as her contract lasted.

For Gina it was another victory. The legendary Bersagliera was overjoyed with the new assignment. And who better than Gina for the special correspondent role? She knew half of the world, and working as a photojournalist had indirectly trained her for *Domenica In*. When questioned about his impression of Gina joining the family, Baudo told columnist Danilo Maggi that he felt very, very good indeed about it. But did Italian youth know who Gina Lollobrigida was? They did; but since the program was family oriented the number of youngsters watching it would probably be limited.

La Lollo's first interviewee for the new *Domenica In* was India's Prime Minister Rajiv Gandhi. From there on the list of V.I.P.s on Gina's talk show in the Italian studio or on location included personalities such as Sammy Davis Jr., Burt Reynolds, Gregory Peck, Kirk Douglas and Bo Derek.

No longer known as the Paris of South America, Buenos Aires was proud to receive Gina Lollobrigida, who arrived in town in the first week of November to do a tape with the nation's President, Raúl Alfonsin. When her mission was over in the Land of the Tango, Gina flew to Rio to interview Pelé and Falcão.

Like the silver screen and photography, *Domenica In* was sending the actress around the globe; when she wasn't in Rome she was in distant lands.

Before Gina left for Buenos Aires, however, she had made a tape with Bo Derek at the American film star's Los Angeles ranch. It was during this taping that the small anti-Gina group found opportunity to lay blame on her for something trivial. As Gina was chatting with her guest about love, she said: "the moments I like the best are before and during," a phrase that wasn't well-received by some. The anti-Lollo voices remarked that Gina's opinion wasn't important since she wasn't the one being interviewed. Gina defended her point of view and ultimately there was a tentative reconciliation in a Roman restaurant. The problem continued unresolved. Gina finished her contract in December. The assignment had been for seven shows and she completed all of them.

***

Gina Lollobrigida maintains an air of elegance about her; whether at her photo studio or at a film festival, she never forgets she's a star and dresses as such, preferring classics to trendy fashions. On the 12th of December, 1985, her consistent good taste was publicly recognized with an award for being one of the ten most elegant women of the year bestowed upon her by the Best International Committee of *The Best* magazine founded by Massimo Gargia. Well-known in the crème de la crème of the French and Italian social circles as a party host, signor Gargia is also responsible for the "Best Ten" annual award.

The year's honorees of the 10th gala included American stars and princesses and Gina was the only Italian among the top ten. For the event she wore a gown designed by herself. "Chanel, Valentino, Saint Laurent, Dior - I've bought them all," said the star. "Today is so much joy for me to design myself," she concluded.

For years the actress had refused to wear someone else's creations. She enjoyed creating her own fashion, a pastime she sometimes pursued while watching television. If she was upset, she sewed with even greater fervor. "One time I was so miserable I made a dress covered with pearls." Her philosophy is that people appreciate beauty, and she sees no reason why she should disappoint them.

So, when Gina accepted her Best Award in New York, she was just dazzling. Columnist Linda Blandfor (writing for the *Guardian*) exclaimed: "Here then, ladies and gentlemen, is the look of the moment in New York. Feast your eyes upon Gina Lollobrigida." Then, referring to the actress' most recent photograph that illustrated the page, she wrote: "The photograph is new and truly does not lie: the cleavage, the huge eloquent eyes, the allure, the make-up. Here is the beauty that wiggles so generously on high heels down the corridor of the Pierre Hotel." The description goes on and on with perfectly chosen adjectives that would make any other beauty feel like second best.

Shortly after the night of December 12th, *Oggi* released some superb Gina photographs wearing her own creations - the gowns she elegantly sported in New York. The splendid yellow, light blue and lavender dresses matched the three mink coats dyed by Sergio Soldano. The wardrobe was another of Gina's personal triumphs, and underscored how self-reliant the lady truly is.

\*\*\*

Life is something like a jigsaw puzzle composed of a series of events and people. The attraction of writing about someone's life is the attempt to reconstruct the images that were cut and scattered with the passing of time. La Lollobrigida's is a rich puzzle, so engraved with names, places and events that I sometimes wondered how to begin on a particular corner. Such was the case with the Orson Welles-Gina Lollobrigida episode that was brought to light in February of 1986, some 26 years after the event. The Wellesian chapter in Gina's life dates back to the early period of her career in Rome when she was still attending the Accademia di Belle Arti and appearing as an extra in her first films in 1946.

The actor-director, regarded as an unfulfilled genius, was much impressed by Gina's beauty and saw in her what he imagined to be the spirit of a certain type of woman. When that man of great talent and originality was introduced to Gina she was together with another future Italian star, Paola Mori, who eventually became Welles' third wife. Some 12 years after their encounter, the two legendary figures of the celluloid met again in Rome at the actress' villa when the magician of the screen undertook a short film about the Italian cinema and Gina Lollobrigida.

Towards the end of the Fifties, Welles coming from Rome, stayed at the Ritz in Paris and from there proceeded to New York, leaving in his hotel room three unlabeled cans, each containing a ten-minute reel. The unclaimed items ended up in the lost and found at the Ritz. Five years later, by some mysterious means, those cans were found by Claude Fusée, President of Atlantic Films. But it wasn't until 1986 that curious hands decided to project the film to see what it was all about. Surprise!

# 239--Imperial Gina

Wearing a white shirt, Welles appears on the screen at the beginning of the film announcing that he's leaving in search of Gina Lollobrigida. After promising to find her in the first two reels, he finally meets the actress at her villa in the third. Welles included a little bit of everything in the film: the background tune from Carol Reed's *The Third Man*, photographs of Caruso, la Callas, and la Duse, as well as those of Italian starlets. The short movie also comprised much of Welles himself, a sequence with Paola Mori, paintings by Steinberg evoking Italy, the Roman countryside and Subiaco, an encounter with Rossano Brazzi and another with Vittorio De Sica where he speaks about la Lollobrigida: "She is so Italian!" Then, passing from comic books to a Gina photograph, there is the following comment: "This is not from a comic book." Next we see Welles smoking his cigar in front of the gate of la Lollo's villa. The scene ends with a sponsor's message which indicates that the film was made for TV. (In 1982 Welles revealed that he had made a film about Gina for CBS.) When Welles opens the gate he is welcomed by three German shepherds. He places the cigar in an ashtray resting in the mouth of a wooden dog. An imperial Gina appears coming down the stairs of the house. Her beauty is superb. Welles asks Gina: "Will you die poor?" "I hope not... If I were not ambitious that would be the end," she answers. "The end of what?" he asks. I believe the film finishes with this scene; the producers were unhappy with the project and decided to drop it.

The last time Gina and Welles met was at the *Night of 100 Stars* in 1981, but on that occasion they didn't discuss the project. So many years had passed that they had probably forgotten about it.

When the film was screened at the 43rd Venice International Film Festival in September of 1986, Gina disclosed that when Welles came to see her on that afternoon of 1957 or 1958, the visit lasted for four or five hours and they talked about cinema, Gina's career and her goals. She also said that the interview was rather private and the two agreed that should the film be used in any manner, Welles should obtain her permission first. Events obviously took a different course. Lollobrigida expressed her desire that, aside from its showing at the Venice Film Festival (mostly as a tribute to the genius of the American cinema), the work be shown only at charity events.

The picture was also a surprise for Gina, who had never seen it herself, and had no idea how Welles had intended to portray her. I assume the actress wasn't disappointed with the film; at least her comments to the press didn't reveal so. After all, she considered Welles a "truly extraordinary man."

\*\*\*

When Welles' film was divulged in February of 1986, Gina was in Germany to preside over the 36th Berlin International Film Festival. She was joined by Lindsay Anderson, Otar Iosseliani, August Coppola (brother of Francis Coppola), Mexican actress Rosuara Revueltas, Nobert Kuckelmann and six other judges (with the responsibility of choosing those who deserved the awards). Twenty-five films were competing.

The program opened with Fellini's entertaining *Ginger and Fred* - the most anticipated film of the festival, starring Marcello Mastroianni and Giulietta Masina. On its second night, *Bread, Love and Dreams* was screened as a special feature in honor of la Lollobrigida and it was a repeated success. (The film was awarded the "Silver Bear" in 1954.)

The festival, however, didn't have a happy outcome. When the winning picture - Reinhard Hauff's *Stamnheim* (a film about West German terrorists in the 1970's) - was announced Gina caused a sensation by denouncing it as a political, not an artistic, choice. Nanni Moretti's *La messa è finita* was awarded a "Silver Bear". In the same category were Soviet director Georgi Schengelaja's *Young Composer's Odyssey*, and the Japanese film *Gonzar the Spearman*, by Masahiro Shinoda. American Dean Parisot's production *Tom Goes to the Bar* was awarded a Golden Bear for best short film, with the "Silver Bear" award given to Hungarian Csaba Vraga for his short production *Augusta Feeds*.

Maurice de Hadeln, a festival official, was clearly displeased with Gina's response, but the actress strongly felt that *Stamnhein* (The Trial) had been chosen for purely political reasons. In her opinion, as registered in *Der Spiegel*, the vote had been pre-fabricated and the film had no artistic value. Her efforts to so convince the jury were in vain. Gina was exhausted and even thought of abandoning her leadership, but endured to see the final frustrating six-five vote. Gina's disapproval of the winner was obvious when she presented the "Golden Bear".

When questioned by *Der Spiegel* whether her judgment would have been the same had the terrorist movie been Italian, Gina intelligently answered that a good film, be it German or Italian has no boundaries.

Nearly four months after the Berlin incident, those gathering at the 30th anniversary of the "David di Donatello" award paid tribute to Gina Lollobrigida, Marcello Mastroianni, the veteran Alessandro Blasetti and other celebrities of international show business. Although *Ginger and Fred* had failed in Cannes and Venice (its screening in Berlin wasn't for competition), Mastroianni was awarded the statuette for best actor of the year. Federico Fellini, Ettore Scola and Nanni Moretti didn't appear to receive their gold medals. The same decoration was bestowed upon Mastroianni, Lollobrigida, Mariangela Melato and Monicelli's *Speriamo che sia femmina* (We Hope It's a Female) - it won seven statuettes. Among the recognized foreign films and stars were *Back to the Future*, William Hurt (for *Kiss of the Spider Woman*), Meryl Streep (for *Out of Africa*), and directors Sidney Pollack and Akira Kurosawa (for *Out of Africa* and *Ran*, respectively).

The day following the night of the "David di Donatello", directors Luigi Commencini, Alberto Lattuada, Mario Monicelli and Lina Westmüler, and the stars Vittorio Gassman, Gina Lollobrigida, Marcello Mastroianni and Monica Vitti were received by Italy's President, Francesco Cossiga, who bestowed special honors upon them.

\*\*\*

Precisely 40 years after Gina's first film *Return of the Black Eagle*, she informed the Italian press that she had found the ideal script for her return to the large screen. La Lollo, however, superstitiously refused to disclose too many details about the script. Nevertheless she revealed that the role was that of an older woman recounting the most significant episodes of her younger days and that the story took place in 1925. The part, according to Gina, was completely different from any other character she had played before.

While Gina prepared herself for the new production (no shooting schedule was mentioned), her admirers in Italy were about to see her in a TV commercial that had been recently made in Milan. In her golden era, Gina had always refused to do commercials regardless of how tempting the financial rewards. In those days, requests for her to endorse perfume, soap, beer and other products were frequent, but the answer was always "no." But times have changed and stars often appear in TV ads without losing their prestige. (Sean Connery,

Brenda Vaccaro, Jane Russell, Alain Delon, Fellini, Zeffirelli and many other celebrities have appeared on the "tube" to endorse products.)

La Bersagliera's advertising debut was well remunerated by the sponsor, a kitchen appliance manufacturer, *Moulinex*. The setting is her villa. It's Christmas time and Gina is working with her photography while a chef prepares a delicious light dinner for her using the time-saving *Moulinex*. Could it be a microwave oven? The experience was successful and Gina was seen in four new *Moulinex* commercials.

\*\*\*

Since "there's no business like show business," Gina's return to the environment caused much joy to the paparazzi who stuck to her like parasites. Publishers got into the act by releasing old film stills of the actress; and such was the case with the August 1985 Italian issue of *Playboy*, which published la Lollo photographs in risqué (but not offensive) scenes of *The Dolls*, *That Splendid November*, and *King, Queen, Knave*. The text praised Gina's talent, mentioned her guest appearance in *Deceptions*, and touched on the French decoration she had received in March of that year.

In contrast to Playboy's homage of sorts was a defamatory piece about the actress which appeared in the May 1986 issue of *Novella 2000*, an Italian gossip magazine. As in the old days, the case ended up in court.

The brief article was illustrated with three Gina stills: one from 1947 at the very early stage of her career, another as Lady Godiva on horse in a scene from *Strange Bedfellows*, and the third - the one that caused Gina's anger - depicted a young lady in the nude sitting on a horizontal tree trunk. As soon as *Novella 2000* reached Rome's newspaper stands, the actress immediately asked her lawyers Nobiloni and De Caprio to interfere. Gina declared that the photo was that of a woman "only slightly resembling me." Roman judge Bonaccorsi ordered the magazine to be taken out of circulation.

The incriminatory photograph had supposedly appeared in *Modern Sunbathing and Hygiene Annual*, an American magazine sometime in 1948. *Novella 2000* asserted that when Gina came to see Howard Hughes in the early days of her career, she agreed to pose unclad for the magazine, whose main readers were supporters of sunbathing au naturel. When Hughes (a man whom it's said advocated nudism in private only) saw the fleshy photograph, he went into a state of anger and refused to give Gina a contract.

The whole story is apocryphal. To begin with, Gina didn't go to America until July 1950, while *Novella 2000* has her visit to Hughes dated in 1948. And should the Hollywood czar have denied Gina a contract, why did he try to stop her from working in America for nearly nine years? Gina had signed an option with him and had refused to marry him, inciting Hughes to try every possible means to halt her career in the United States. Moreover, the photo isn't clear. The lady's eyes and part of the nose, lips and neck are heavily shadowed, making it very difficult to identify the model. Besides, when Gina accepted Hughes' invitation to come to Hollywood she had already been discovered and appeared in at least a dozen films and had no need to use her curves as bait to land a part in a movie. One of Gina's unbending convictions was that she shouldn't and wouldn't undress or appear topless in any film no matter how good the part was. Had the photo in question been the real Lollo, Gina would have made a fool of herself and her attorneys by taking the case to court.

June 5 was set for a hearing with the lawyers of both parties present. According to a letter from a friend in Milan (who phoned the editors of *Novella 2000* for me), the hearing had been postponed and a new date hadn't been set yet. Unfortunately, I was unable to unearth further information on the topic.

\*\*\*

Following the defamatory Italian publication, the Belgian international film magazine *Ciné-Revue*, featured Lollobrigida and Ursula Andress on its cover. La Lollo in red from head to toe, and la Andress in a red bathrobe were being photographed by Angelo Frontoni in his Rome studio while Gina focused her camera on the Swiss star. During the session, the Italian Cartier-Bresson explained that she personally handles the make-up and coiffure of her subjects as well as the lighting in the studio when she's working.

In mid-August, Gina shone in a glittering blue dress at a New York party celebrating *Me and My Girl*. And on the 30th she was the focus of attention at the opening night of the 43rd Venice

International Film Festival, attended also by the Italian President of the Senate, Amintore Fanfani, at the Palazzo del Cinema at the Lido.

Gina's presence at the festival, especially requested by its President Gian Luigi Rondi, was reminiscent of her triumphal visits to the Lido at the height of her career. During the three days the star stayed at the Excelsior, she was constantly photographed as she had been 25 years earlier. Venetians were delighted, remarking that the event had again the perfume of its golden years.

*Portrait of Gina*, the Welles film about the Italian cinema and la Lollo, was shown at the Sala Grande on the first day of the festival. Unfortunately, Gina's friend and Welles' third wife, Paola Mori, died in a car accident just a few days before the festival, having told signor Rondi she'd be present to see the anticipated film.

Another Welles work, the unfinished *It's All True* (1942), was also scheduled. Divided into three parts, the film pivoted around a bit of Mexico with *My Friend Benito*. The following two parts were about Brazil: *The Story of the Samba*, which captured the Rio Carnival of 1942 when Welles visited the country and *Four Men on a Raft*. Thanks to the American Film Institute, a 22 minute segment of the uncompleted project was restored and screened for the first time.

The jury for the festival had Alain Robe-Grillet as president, assisted by directors Chantal Ackermann (Belgium), Jörn Donner (Finland), Pál Gabor (Hungary), Alberto Lattuada, Nanni Moretti (Italy), Nelson Pereira dos Santos (Brazil), Eldar Shenghelaja (Russia), Fernando Solanas (Argentine), Bernhard Wicki (Germany), actor-director Peter Ustinov (Great Britain), producer-director Catherine Wyler (USA), movie critic Roman Guber (Spain) and art critic Pontus Hulten (Sweden). Actress Claudia Cardinale refused to appear at the Lido because her film *La storia* (The Story) wasn't being screened for competition.

Exactly a month after her distinguished presence at the Lido, Gina Lollobrigida was seen by an estimated 300 million viewers on *Classic Aid*, broadcast by 29 television stations directly from Geneva. The special gala concert was a co-production of UNHCR (United Nations High Commissioner for Refugees) and the French television TF1, produced by Yves-André Hubert. The charity performance involved 30 world-famous stars of classic music under the baton of the renowned Lorin Maazel, also co-ordinator of the event held at the Grand Casino. Esa-Pekka and Muhai Tang took turns conducting the Philharmonic Orchestra of Monte Carlo. Prince Rainier and Princess

# 245–Imperial Gina

Caroline of Monaco joined the public figures attending the event, at which June Anderson, Yasuko Hayashi, Miguel-Angel Estrella, Frank-Peter Zimmermann and others performed. Peter Ustinov acted as Master of Ceremonies, while Gina Lollobrigida, Catherine Deneuve, Clarissa Mason, Dietlinde Turban and Sally Burton introduced the artists.

Gina's beauty and elegance at 59 were unbelievable! Wearing a pink embroidered gown (probably her own design) and a superb necklace with matching earrings of pearls and diamonds, she crossed the stage radiating the glamour that has never left her. Catherine Deneuve, in a black dress embroidered in silver (set off with original pearl earrings), also made a beautiful figure on stage next to Gina.

Sometime in October of that year Gina was seen at a Roman reception escorted by Massimo Gargia. For those who delight in gossip columns, the press mentioned that Gina had been seen in the company of the gentleman for quite a while, even though the signore had tried to pass unnoticed as much as possible. Despite the media's efforts in matchmaking, however, Gina remains single.

A few weeks after the Roman soirée, Lollobrigida and Ursula Andress were in Barcelona to tape a segment of "Plató vació" for TVE, a local station, to be broadcast on December 9. The glamorous stars arrived incognito.

\*\*\*

A flamenco aficionada, Gina flew from Rome to Madrid in early June 1987 as a special guest to attend the reopening of the chocolate shop San Ginés, the most prestigious and "castiza" in the city. The event was celebrated at the Joy Eslava with an authentic flamenco fiesta with señoras and señoritas wearing the typical "mantón de manila" (large, embroidered silk shawl). Gina went completely Spanish; she wore an exotic pink and white dress made of a wide "mantón."

Throughout the night of "rumbas" and "sevillanas" Gina was the attraction of the event and was photographed with several notables including the Duque of Cádiz. Among other V.I.P.s present at the grand fiesta flamenca were the Princesses of Orleans and Tessa of Bavaria, the Bulgarian Queen and her son Prince Kardan, and a host of well-known faces of Madrid's high society.

On the fourth of July, while Americans celebrated another year of their independence, major Italian newspapers carried lavish articles on Gina's 60th birthday with headlines such as *Gina's Splendid Sixty.* The actress, referring to her age, told the *Corriere della Sera* that she felt "like a good wine which improves with age." The Spanish weekly *Semana* published the most up-to-date photos of the star in her villa; the pictures justify la Bersagliera's comparison of her age with old wine. Gina's birthday also made headlines in leading newsprint from Buenos Aires to Tokyo.

*** 

When Paolo Brogi, writing for *Europeo* (December, 1987), asked Gina what her impression was of today's eroticism in the cinema when compared to her films in the Fifties and Sixties, Gina remarked that these days new actresses show the buttocks first and then the face. When signor Brogi asked the young actress Francesca Dellera who her favorite Italian actress was, she answered, "Sophia Loren."

Was the interviewer willfully trying to generate a feud between the two actresses? Signorina Dellera and Gina were being cast to star in Giuseppe Patroni Griffi's TV remake of Gina's very successful 1954 *La romana.* Dellera was to play Adriana, one of Alberto Moravia's most famous characters, a role that had brought Gina enormous triumph. In Griffi's version of this Luigi Zampa film, Gina was cast as Margherita, Adriana's mother.

Needless to say that Gina was excited to perform a role that somewhat resembled that of Serafina, the central character in *The Rose Tattoo.* Speaking of her new part, Gina told Maria Grazia Fantasia of the *Forum Press* (Rome) that she was "immediately attracted to the character which I [Gina] already felt inside me." Gina, who admires women with determined and combative natures, identified herself with Margherita. Elaborating on the part, Gina described Margherita as "a faded woman, wounded by life, but who still finds the courage and strength to fight in the illusion of giving her daughter the life of comfort and wealth that she had been denied, abandoning every moral rule for the sake of reaching the aim she has set herself."

Concerning the daughter's part, a particular erotic touch of the new Adriana is her appearance in one of the scenes in her birthday suit - a "no-no" in the days of Fifties censorship. Actor Giuseppe Pianviti was to play opposite Dellera as her leading man.

With the news of Gina's participation in the TV remake of *La romana* (the film was shown in three segments), la Lollo achieved one more goal in her long career and concluded the year under the spotlights.

\*\*\*

During her interview with *Europeo* Gina expressed that on several occasions she had been offered handsome sums to write her autobiography. Doing so wasn't a high priority for she regarded the genre a sort of strip-tease, and she didn't feel inclined towards that kind of spectacle. Gina had also been approached throughout the years by unknown faces eager to write about her life and she refused every single one of them, even a biography like this composed entirely out of sincere admiration. "There's a fellow in Kyoto," she pointed out, "who has pursued me for years. Now, sooner or later, he'll finish an incorrect biography." For signora Lollobrigida, a work about her life should stress, above all, that she made herself successful without the help of any one and that her encounter with the cinema had been unforeseen; her dream was to have been a soprano lirico. Have I written anything different? I depended heavily on the actress' interviews to the world press in my determination to correctly portray Gina Lollobrigida as she is. It was my sheer perseverance which had demonstrated how serious I was about seeing my project to fulfillment.

\*\*\*

In the spring of 1988 Gina was hopscotching to Spain, France and Italy for TV talk shows and print interviews. In early March she was invited to appear in the *Angel Casas Show* produced by the Autonomous Catalan Television, Barcelona. Moments before she went in front of the cameras, the veteran actress agreed with a press interview under the condition that no questions concerning her private life be asked. "I think my past, my present and my future as a woman belong exclusively to me."

Among other topics during this brief conference with the Catalan press, Gina talked about her experience with *Falcon Crest* and her recent role in the new version of *La romana*.

After the Spanish talk show, Parisians were delighted to see la Lollo in a TV (TF1) tribute to the Egyptian/Italian chanson singer Dalida on April 8. Among the chief guests reminiscing about her were Omar Sharif, Gilbert Bécaud, Anouck Aimée, Alain Delon, Yves Montand, and Jean-Paul Belmondo. For the occasion, Gina wore gold lamé and "loads of diamonds and sapphires." La Lollo delivered her speech in good French, and in the words of the poet James Kirkup who watched the show, "[she] was undoubtedly the star of the evening, and came on last."

With her 61st birthday around the corner, Gina still looked her gorgeous self in each photograph. Notwithstanding, the most revealing one appeared in *Time* magazine (June 6) with Gina posing by Michael Jackson and Sophia Loren! It's one of only two photographs which I have seen the two stars together. The "ex-gloved One" was in the Eternal City for a rock show at the Flamenco soccer stadium.

\*\*\*

The place, Musée des Arts Décoratifs (Paris); the event, the 13th gala for "The Best" annual award on 19 December, 1988. Held alternatively in the world's most modish capitals - London, Rome, New York, Paris - the award honored again the 10 best dressed men and women of the year.

Massimo Gargia was the man responsible for the event which was co-hosted by Jacques Mouclier, President of the Féderation Française de la Couture, and Robert Bordaz, President of l'Union Centrale des Arts Décoratifs.

As it happened in New York in 1985, Gina Lollobrigida was awarded for being among "The Best," adding another prize to her collection. Robert Wagner, Jill St. John, Rupert Everett, Brigitte Nielsen, and Italian actor Nino Manfredi joined Gina on "The Best" list.

Sometimes escorted by a notable or by her handsome 32-year-old son, Gina continues to make appearances in the V.I.P. world. However, Milko Jr. isn't fond of being photographed at social events, even posing next to his famous mother. Working in a world completely different from Gina's - Milko Jr. is into computers - he probably abhors photography for being too much exposed to it in his childhood.

# 249--Imperial Gina

After four decades of continuous success in her various activities, one can obviously see that it wasn't just la Lollo's looks that kept her popular; she needed brains, too. Still professionally active and full of joie de vivre, Gina also finds time to think of the less privileged. The documentary that she'll make on hospitals in need of help in Cameroon (WC Africa) will contribute to Father Ildebrando's foundation "Pace e Amore." (The Padre's institution, along with the organization presided over by Maria Teresa of Calcutta, collects funds for leper children.) Life for Gina Lollobrigida is a non-stop marathon and nothing makes her happier than being on the track. The many triumphs she achieved in her careers, and the youth that she still radiates are the results of Lollobrigida's three-word motto: "work, love, and fantasy."

At a Hollywood gala for the benefit of AIDS victims, organized by Elizabeth Taylor - courtesy of Angeli/Orion Press.

"Two Italian works of art: Michelangelo's *David* and Gina Lollobrigida." (Ron Galella). Event: Million dollar Extravaganza, The Waldorf-Astoria Hotel (May 4, 1970).

# EPILOGUE

When I stepped into the hall of Gina's house I was received by one of her sisters who informed me that the actress wasn't at home but would soon be back. While we chatted, I was overjoyed to learn that Gina would concede me an interview. At the same time, I was nervous and wondering what I'd say when the Imperial Gina walked into the hall.

Life is indeed composed of "work, love, and fantasy." Alas, my dream was over when the alarm clock brought me back to reality. I have had many other dreams about Gina during the years I spent working on this book. In some of them she was captivating and engaging; in others, she vehemently declined to see me.

In one scene of *Solomon and Sheba*, the Arabian Queen discusses Solomon with her counsellor, Baltor (Harry Andrews). When Sheba refers to the King of Israel as "a dreamer, a man of peace," Baltor counters that Solomon is "a man of ideas, and there is nothing more dangerous than a man with an idea."

During the two August days in 1985 as I stood before Gina's villa, I was a man with an idea, though far from dangerous. I was convinced of what I wanted and nobody possessed the power to make me forsake it. I had undertaken the task of writing a biography of Gina Lollobrigida. The idea became a reality and I hope it pleases the actress, for it's the only way I can repay her for the happiness she has brought into my life through her talents and beauty.

When Gina was in New York in December of 1985 to receive her award as one of the world's ten most elegant women, she remarked to columnist Linda Brandford: "I'm popular all over the world, people like me. It's a good feeling. You see, the people made me a star. I am surprised at all the excitement still about me. I said: 'My God, after all these years, I think I should be forgotten'."

Time, however, has been powerless in its usually unmerciful mission of making people and events fade away, for Gina Lollobrigida is still vivid in the minds of moviegoers and art lovers. On February 2nd, 1989, Gina received the "Donnaroma" prize from the hands of the Italian Minister of the Exterior, Giulio Andreotti. The award, in its second edition, pays tribute to prominent women in diverse activities. The selection of these outstanding women, which included Gina among other notable Roman signore, was realized through a public poll by *Il Messaggero*.

Gina Lollobrigida is still admired by men and envied by women who erroneously attribute her present day Venus-like countenance to plastic surgeons. Today, 18 years after her last big screen performance, *King, Queen, Knave*, Gina is still the center of attraction on the international stage of celebrities. After she was awarded the "Donnaroma" trophy, la Lollo, all dressed up in a gorgeous embroidered red gown, was the most applauded star at the "César Award Gala" at L'Empire Theatre (Paris) in early March.

To close the Spanish TV series *Más estrellas que en el cielo* (More Stars Than in Heaven) in the spring of 1989, host Terenci Moix received Gina Lollobrigida before the cameras in Madrid. For the talk show Gina chose a décolleté silver spangled dress that, like her many other gowns, gave her the glamorous air worthy of a true-class A star.

For photography lovers, Gina told her host that a new photographic essay would soon be published. *Innocence*, a tentative title, has taken her some ten years to finish and features children and animals; the funds will be donated to the poor children of the world.

What does the future hold for Gina? She isn't concerned with it for la Bersagliera only lives the present. Will she ever remarry? At the moment, the actress is still the sole master of her villa on the Appia Antica. Is she in love now? Yes, with photography. Her second career plays a major role in her life and one of these days we may unwittingly pass her, creatively disguised, while photographing people and places. But then again, la Lollo may surprise us with some new talent. Will there be any new lawsuits? Probably, should someone step on her toes.

This unauthorized biography of the actress remains unfinished. There are gaps to be filled and much may be added to the life of la Bersagliera-the living legend. My search for the actress will continue. And after this book reaches the Appia Antica, if the Roman deities are on my side, I may yet have the good fortune of going beyond the green gate without the German shepherds chasing me. At this point, however, I know that Gina doesn't look upon me benevolently; as she has consistently opposed this work, I have (against my will) caused her distress. How ironic that I have hurt someone whom I have really admired for more than 30 years.

Yet, like the actress, I also believe that life consists of "work, love, and fantasy." I have put all the work and love a man in his prime has into this book. Will the fantasy ever come true?

In *That Splendid November* - courtesy Pierluigi/Orion Press).

Lollobrigida as Adriana's mother in Giuseppe Patroni Griffi's 1988 remake of *La romana*. Photo Forum Press (author's collection).

# FILMOGRAPHY

*Aquila nera* (Return of the Black Eagle). DCI, 1946.
Directed by Riccardo Freda.
Cast: Rossano Brazzi, Irasema Dilian, Gino Cervi, Rina
Morelli, Harry Feist, Paolo Stoppa, Inga Gort, Luigi Pavese,
Pietro Haroff. (GINA LOLLOBRIGIDA appears as an extra.)

*Lucia di Lammermoor* (Lucia of Lammermoor). Opera Film, 1946.
Directed by Piero Ballerini.
Cast: Nelly Corradi, Afro Poli, Mario Filippeschi, Aldo
Ferracuti, Italo Tajo, Loretta Di Lelio, Adelio Zagonara.
(GINA LOLLOBRIGIDA has another unbilled part.)

*Il segreto di Don Giovanni* (When Love Calls). Pegoraro, 1947.
Directed by Camillo Mastrocinque.
Cast: Gino Bechi, Silvana Pampanini, Gino Saltamerenda,
Liliana Laine, Aroldo Tieri, Carlo Romano, Mario Siletti,
Checco Durante. (GINA LOLLOBRIGIDA is still an unbilled
extra.)

*Il delitto di Giovanni Episcopo* (Flesh Will Surrender).
Lux Film-Pao, 1947.
Directed by Alberto Lattuada.
Cast: Aldo Fabrizi, Yvonne Sanson, Rolando Lupi, Ave Ninchi,
Jone Norino, Nando Bruno, Alberto Sordi, Francesco De Marco,
Lia Grani, Gino Cavalieri, Gian Luca Cortese, Amedeo Fabrizi,
Maria Gonnelli, Giorgio Moser, Marco Tulli, Folco Lulli,
Galeazzo Benti, Ferrante Alvaro De Torres, Gilberto Severi,
Diego Calcagno, Silvana Mangano, GINA LOLLOBRIGIDA.

*Vendetta nel sole* (A Man About the House). Excelsa Film-London
Film, 1947.
Directed by Leslie Arliss and Giuseppe Amato.
Cast: Dulcie Gray, Margareth Johnston, Kieron Moore, Jone
Solinas, Marisa Fimiani, Fedele Gentili, Guy Middleton, Felix
Aylmer, Reginald Purdeli, Lillian Braithwaite, Fulvia de
Priamo, GINA LOLLOBRIGIDA.

*L'elisir d'amore* (This Wine of Love). Prora Film, 1947.
Directed by Mario Costa.
Cast: Nelly Corradi, Gino Sinimberghi, Tito Gobbi, Italo
Tajo, Loretta Di Lelio, Carmen Forti, Flavia Grande, GINA
LOLLOBRIGIDA, Silvana Mangano.

*Follie per l'opera* (Opera Fans). Scalera-Gesi/Malenotti, 1948.
Directed by Mario Costa.
Cast: Aroldo Tieri, GINA LOLLOBRIGIDA, Constance Dowling,
Carlo Campanini, Franca Marzi, Aldo Silvani, Beniamino
Gigli, Tito Bechi, Tito Schipa, Maria Caniglia, Nives  Poli.

*I pagliacci* (Love of a Clown). Itala Film, 1948.
Directed by Mario Costa.
Cast: GINA LOLLOBRIGIDA (dubbed by Onelia Fineschi), Tito
Gobbi, Afro Poli, Galliano Masini, Filippo Morucci.

*Passaporto per l'Oriente* (A Tale of Five Women). ALCE - Aleanza
Cinematografica Europea, 1949-1951.
Directed by Montgomery Tully, Romolo Marcellini and Geza
von Cziffra, Wolfgang Staudte, Emil E. Reinert.
Cast: Bonar Colleano, Barbara Kelly, GINA LOLLOBRIGIDA,
Marcello Mastroianni, Enzo Stajola, Eva Bartok, Karin
Himbold, Anne Vernon, Raymond Busières, Lana Morris, Lily
Kahn, Danny Green, Carls Jaffe, Mc Donald Kork, Oleth Orr,
Geoffrey Summer, Philip Leaver, Arthur Gomez, Dany
Daubertson, Liliana Tellini, Annette Poivre, Lamberto
Maggiorani, Charles Irwin, Vera Molnar, Graig Ivan.

*Campane a martello* (Children of Chance). Carlo Ponti for Lux
Film, 1949.
Directed by Luigi Zampa
Cast: GINA LOLLOBRIGIDA (dubbed by Andreina Pagnani),
Yvonne Sanson, Eduardo De Filippo, Carlo Romano,
Carla Giustini, Clelia Matania, Agostino Salvietti,
Ernesto Almirante, Gino Saltamerenda,
Salvatore Arcidiacono.

*La sposa non può attendere* (The Bride Can't Wait).
  Lux Film, 1949.
  Directed by Gianni Franciolini.
  Cast: Gino Cervi, GINA LOLLOBRIGIDA (dubbed by Dhia
  Cristiani), Odile Versois, Giacomo Furia, Nando Bruno,
  AveNinchi, Ada Colageli, Giani Baghino, Mario Meniconi,
  Adriano Ambrogi, Cesarina Rossi, Leopoldo Valentini.

*Miss Italy* (Miss Italia). Carlo Ponti for ATA, 1950.
  Directed by Duilio Coletti.
  Cast: GINA LOLLOBRIGIDA (dubbed by Dhia Cristiani),
  Richard Ney, Costance Dowling, Luisa Rossi, Carlo
  Campanini, Luigi Almirante, Umberto Melnati,
  Marisa Vernati, Mario Besesti, Mino Doro,
  Lilia Landi, Carlo Hinterman, Mirella Uberti,
  Antonio Juva, Barbara Leite, Dina Perbellini,
  Odoardo Spadaro, Giuseppe Pierozzi,
  Enrico Luzi, Silvio Bagolini.

*Cuori senza frontiere* (The White Line or Hearts Without
  Boundaries). Carlo Ponti for Lux Film, 1950.
  Directed by Luigi Zampa.
  Cast: GINA LOLLOBRIGIDA (dubbed by Lidia Simoneschi),
  Raf Vallone, Cesco Baseggio, Enzo Staiola,
  Ernesto Almirante, Gino Cavalieri, Fabio Neri,
  Mario Sestan, Antonio Catania, Giordano Cesini,
  Callisto Cosulich, Tullio Zezich, Piero Grego,
  Gianni Cavalieri.

*Vita da cani* (A Dog's Life). ATA, 1950.
  Directed by Steno and Mario Nonicelli.
  Cast: Aldo Fabrizi, GINA LOLLOBRIGIDA, Delia Scala,
  Tamara Lees, Marcello Mastroianni, Nyta Dover,
  Bruno Corelli, Michele Malaspina, Tino Scotti,
  Pina Piovani, Lidia Alfonsi, Pasquale Misiano,
  Eduardo Passarelli, Enzo Maggio, Noemi Zeki, Livia
  Renzin, Anna Pabella, Giuseppe Angelini, Siria
  Vellani, Giorgina Nardini, Vittorina Benvenuti.

*Alina.* Acta Film, 1950.
Directed by Giorgio Pàstina.
Cast: GINA LOLLOBRIGIDA, Amedeo Nazzari, Doris
Dowling, Juan De Landa, Otello Toso, Lauro
Gazzolo, Camillo Pilotto, Nino Cavalieri,
Vittorio André, Oscar Andriani.

*La città si difende* (Four Ways Out). Cines, 1951.
Directed by Pietro Germi.
Cast: GINA LOLLOBRIGIDA, Renato Baldini, Cosetta
Grecco, Fausto Tozzi, Paul Müller, Patrizia Manca,
Enzo Maggio, Emma Baron, Tamara Lees.

*Enrico Caruso, leggenda di una voce* (The Young Caruso).
Maleno Malenotti for Asso Film, 1951.
Directed by Giacomo Gentilomo.
Cast: Ermanno Randi, GINA LOLLOBRIGIDA (dubbed
by Dhia Cristiani), Carletto Sposito, Maria von
Tasnady, Gino Saltamerenda, Maurizio Di Nardo,
Franca Tamantini, Lamberto Picasso, Nerio
Bernardi, Elena Sangro, Ciro Scafa, G. Verna,
G. Rosmino, R. Laurienzo, R. Spiombi, Mario
del Monaco.

*Achtung! Banditi!* (Beware of Bandits!). Cooperativa
Produttori Cinamatografici, 1951.
Directed by Carlo Lizzani.
Cast: GINA LOLLOBRIGIDA, Andrea Checchi, Lamberto
Maggioraani, Vittorio Duse, Giuseppe Taffarel,
Franco Bologna, Maria Laura Rocca, Giuliano Montaldo,
Pietro Tordi, Pietro Bruno Berellini.

*Fanfan la Tulipe* (Fanfan the Tulip). Films Ariane-
Filmsonor-Giuseppe Amato, 1951.
Directed by Christian-Jaque.
Cast: Gérard Philipe, GINA LOLLOBRIGIDA (dubbed by
Adriana Parrella), Noël Roquevert, Olivier Hussenot,
Marcel Herrand, Jean-Marc Tennberg, Jean Parédès,
Nerio Bernardi, Geneviève Page, Sylvie Pelayo,
Georgette Anys.

*Amor non ho... però... però* (Love I Haven't...But...But).
Franco Riganti for Excelsa Film, 1951.
Directed by Giorgio Bianchi.
Cast: Renato Rascel, GINA LOLLOBRIGIDA, Franca Marzi,
Aroldo Tieri, Kiki Urbani, Luigi Pavese, Nyta Dover,
Guglielmo Barnab, Carlo Ninchi, Virgilio Riento,
Adriana Danieli), Galeazzo Benti.

*Altri Tempi* (Times Gone By) - Episode "The Trial of Frine."
Cines, 1952.
Directed by Alessandro Blasetti.
Cast: Vittorio De Sica, GINA LOLLOBRIGIDA, Giovanni
Grasso, Dante Maggio, Vittorio Caprioli, Arturo
Bragaglia, Carlo Mazzarella, Turi Pandolfini.
(Other episodes: Aldo Fabrizi, Enzo Staiola,
Andrea Cecchi, Alba Arnova, Paolo Stoppa, Sergio
Tofano, Amedeo Nazzari, Elisa Cegani, Roldano Lupi,
Enzo Cerusico, Rina Morelli, Barbara Florian,
Vittorio Vaser, Maurizio Di Nardo, Geraldina
Parrinello.

*Les belles de nuit* (Beauties of the Night). Rizzoli
Film and Franco London Film, 1952.
Directed by René Clair.
Cast: Gérard Philipe, Martine Carol, GINA
LOLLOBRIGIDA, Magali Vandeuil, Marilyn Burferd,
Raymond Bussières, Jean Parédès, Paolo Stoppa,
Bernard Lajarrige, Albert Michel, Henri Marchand,
Raymond Cordy, Paul Demange, Pierre Fleta, J.E.
Chauffard, Bernard Dheran, Christian Chantal,
Marcelle Legendre, Monique Darval, Chantal Tirède.

*Moglie per una notte* (Bride for a Night).
Rizzoli-Camerini, 1952.
Directed by Mario Camerini.
Cast: Gino Cervi, GINA LOLLOBRIGIDA, Nadia Gray,
Armando Francioli, Paolo Stoppa, Galeazzo Benti,
Paolo Panelli, Eugenia Tavani, Nietta Zocchi,
Marisa Pintus.

*Le infideli* (The Unfaithfuls). Excelsa Film/Ponti-De
Laurentiis, 1953.
Directed by Steno and Monicelli.
Cast: May Britt, Anna Maria Ferrero, Pierre Cressoy,
GINA LOLLOBRIGIDA, Irene Papas, Marina Vlady, Tina
Lattanzi, Giulio Cal , Charles Fawcett, Carlo Romano,
Margherita Bagni, Milko Skofic, Tania Webber,
Bernardo Tafuri, Paolo Ferrara, Carlo Lamas.

*La provinciale* (The Wayward Wife). Ponti-De Laurentiis, 1953.
Directed by  Mario Soldati.
Cast: GINA LOLLOBRIGIDA, Gabriele Ferzetti, Alda
Mangini, Franco Interlenghi, Renato Baldini, Nanda
Primavera, Marilyn Buferd, Barbara Berg.

*Beat The Devil*. Romulus-Santana and Jack Clayton, 1953.
Directed by John Huston.
Cast: Humphrey Bogart, Jennifer Jones, GINA LOLLOBRIGIDA,
Robert Morley, Peter Lorre, Edward Underdown, Ivor
Barnard, Bernard Lee, Marco Tulli, Mario Perroni,
Alex Pochet, Aldo Silvani, Giulio Donnini, Saro Urzi,
Juan De Landa, Manuel Serano, Mimmo Poli, Rosario
Borelli, Katherine Kath.

*Crossed Swords*. J. Barrett Mahon and Vittorio Vassarotti, 1953.
Directed by Milton Krims and Vittorio Vassarotti.
Cast: Errol Flynn, GINA LOLLOBRIGIDA, Cesare Danova,
Roldano Lupi, Nadia Gray, Paola Mori, Alberto
Rabagliati, Riccardo Rioli, Renato Chiantoni, Piero
Tordi, Silvio Bagolini.

*Pane, amore e fantasia* (Bread Love, and Dreams). Marcello
Girosi, 1953.
Directed by Luigi Comencini.
Cast: Vittorio De Sica, GINA LOLLOBRIGIDA, Roberto Risso,
Marisa Merlini, Tina Pica, Virgilio Riento, Maria Pia
Casilio, Memmo Carotenuto, Vittoria Crispo, Nietta
Zocchi, Gigi Reder, Fausto Guerzoni, Checco Rissone,
Nino Vingelli, Alfredo Rizzo, Attilio Torelli,
Ada Colangeli.

# 261--Imperial Gina

*Le grand jeu* (Flesh and the Woman). Michel Safra for
Speva Film, 1954. Directed by Robert Siodmak.
Cast: GINA LOLLOBRIGIDA, Jean-Claude Pascal, Arletty,
Raymond Pellegrin, Peter Van Eyck, Tammerson, Odette
Laure, Margo Lion, Gérard Buhr, Paul Amiet, Leila Ferida,
Lila Kedrova, Umberto Melnati.

*La romana* (Woman of Rome). Excelsa-Ponti De Laurentiis, 1954.
Directed by Luigi Zampa.
Cast: GINA LOLLOBRIGIDA, Daniel Gélin, Franco Fabrizi,
Raymond Pellegrin, Pina Piovani, Xenia Valderi, Renato
Tontini, Gianni Di Benedetto, Bianca Maria Cerasoli,
Ada Colangeli, Vincenzo Milazzo, Riccardo Ferri,
Riccardo Garrone, Alfredo De Marco, Aldo Vasco.

*Pane, amore e gelosia* (Bread, Love, and Jealousy or Frisky).
Marcello Girosi, 1954.
Directed by Luigi Comencini.
Cast: Vittorio De Sica, GINA LOLLOBRIGIDA, Roberto Risso,
Marisa Merlini, Tina Pica, Virgilio Riento, Maria Pisa
Casilio, Memmo Carotenuto, Vittoria Crispo, Tecla
Scarano, Nino Vingelli, Nico Pepe, Saro Urzi, Fausto
Guerzoni, Checco Rissone, Gigi Reder, Attilio Torelli,
Yvonne Sanson.

*La donna più bella del mondo* (Beautiful but Dangerous).
Maleno Malenotti, 1955.
Directed by Robert Z. Leonard.
Cast: GINA LOLLOBRIGIDA, Vittorio Gassman, Robert Alda,
Anne Vernon, Tamara Lees, Mario Del Monaco, Nanda
Primavera, Nico Pepe, Enzo Biliotti, Gianni Baghino,
Valeria Fabrizi, Gino Sininberghi, Marco Tulli,
Rolf Tasna, Perter Trent, Loris Gizzi, Nicla di Bruno.

*Trapeze.* Hecht-Hill-Lancaster, 1956.
Directed by Carol Reed.
Cast: Burt Lancaster, GINA LOLLOBRIGIDA, Tony Curtis,
Katy Jurado, Thomas Gomez, Minor Watson, Gérard Landry,
Jean-Pierre Kerrien, Sidney James, Gamil Batib,
Pierre Tabard, John Puleo, Les Gimma Boys.

*Notre Dame de Paris* (The Hunchback of Notre Dame). Robert
and Raymond Hakim for Paris Film and Panitalia, 1956.
Directed by Jean Delannoy.
Cast: GINA LOLLOBRIGIDA, Anthony Quinn, Jean Danet,
Alain Cuny, Philippe Clay, Danielle Durmont, Robert
Hirsch, Jean Tissier, Valentine Tessier, Jacques
Hilling, Jacques Dufilho, Robert Blin, Boris Vian,
Marianne Oswald, Pieral, Camille Guerini, Darnia,
Robert Lombard, Albert Remy, Hubert de Lapparent,
Paul Bonifas, Madeleine Barbelec, Albert Michel,
Daniel Emilfork, Georges Douking.

*Anna di Brooklyn* (Fast and Sexy). Milko Skofic for Circeo
Cinematografica, 1958.
Directed by Carlo Lastricati.
Cast: GINA LOLLOBRIGIDA, Vittorio De Sica, Dale
Robertson, Amedeo Nazzari, Peppino De Filippo, Carla
Macelloni, Gabriella Pallotta, Luigi De Filippo, Clelia
Matania, Renzo Cesana, Mario Girotti, Augusta Ciolli.

*La Loi* (Where the Hot Wind Blows). GESSI Cinematografica-
Titanus- Le group des quatres, 1958.
Directed by Jules Dassin.
Cast: GINA LOLLOBRIGIDA, Pierre Brasseur, Marcello
Mastroianni, Melina Mercouri, Yves Montand, Paolo
Stoppa, Teddy Belis, Raf Mattioli, Vittorio Caprioli,
Lydia Alfonsi, Gianrico Tedeschi, Nino Vingelli,
Bruno Carotenuto, Herbert Knippenberg, Joe Dassin,
Marcello Giorda, Anna Arena, Luisa Rivelli, Edda
Soligo, Anna Maria Bottini, Franco Pesce.

*Solomon and Sheba*. Edward Small and Ted Richmond for Theme
Pictures, 1959.
Directed by King Vidor.
Cast: Yul Brynner, GINA LOLLOBRIGIDA, David Farrar,
Marisa Pavan, Joan Crawford, Laurence Naismith, Jose
Nieto, Alejandro Rey, Harry Andrews, Julio Pena,
Finlay Currie, William Devlin, Jean Anderson,
Jack Gwillim.

*Never So Few*. Edmund Grainger for Canterbury/MGM, 1959.
Directed by John Sturges.
Cast: Frank Sinatra, GINA LOLLOBRIGIDA, Peter Lawford,
Steve McQueen, Richard Johnson, Paul Henreid, Brian
Donlevy, Dean Jones, Charles Bronson, Philip Ann,
Robert Bray, Kipp Hamilton, John Hoyt, Whit Bissel,
Richard Lupino, Aki Aleong.

*Go Naked in the World*. Aaron Rosenberg for Arcola/MGM, 1960.
Directed by Ranald Mac Dougall.
Cast: GINA LOLLOBRIGIDA, Anthony Franciosa, Ernest
Borgnine, Luana Patten, Will Kuluwa, Philip Ober, John
Kellogg, Nancy R. Pollock, Yale Wexler, Rodney Bell,
John Gallaudet, Chet Stratton, Maggie Pierce, Bill Smith.

*Come September*. Seven Pictures Corporation, 1961.
Directed by Robert Mulligan.
Cast:  Rock Hudson, GINA LOLLOBRIGIDA, Sandra Dee,
Bobby Darin, Walter Slezak, Brenda De Branzie,
Rossana Rory, Ronald Howard, Joel Gray, Ronnie
Haran, Chris Seiz, Condy Conroy, Joan Freeman,
Nancy Anderson, Claudia Brack, Michael Eden, Anna
Maestri, Stella Vitelleschi, Melinda Vickotic,
Charles Fawcett, John Stacy, Edy Nogara,
MILKO SKOFIC, JR.

*La bellezza di Ippolita* (She Got What She Asked For). Arco Film/
Cineriz/Francinex/Path , 1962.
Directed by Giancarlo Zagni.
Cast: GINA LOLLOBRIGIDA, Enrico Maria Salerno, Milva, Lars
Bloch, Carlo Giuff , Franco Giacobini, Ariel Mannoni,
Angela Portaluri, Franco Balducci, Renato Mambor, Piero
Palermini, Bruno Scipioni.

*Venere Imperiale* (Imperial Venus). Guido Giambartolomei, 1962.
Directed by Jean Delannoy.
Cast: GINA LOLLOBRIGIDA, Stephen Boyd, Raymond Pellegrin,
Gabriele Ferzetti, Micheline Presle, Massimo Girotti,
Lilla Brignone, Giulio Bosetti, Tino Carraro, Evi
Maltagliati, Tina Lattanzi, Laura Rocca, Tom Fellegui.

*Mare matto* (The Wild Sea). Francesco Cristaldi for Lux/Les
   Films Ariane, 1963.
   Directed by Renato Castellani.
   Cast: GINA LOLLOBRIGA, Jean-Paul Belmondo, Tomas Milian,
   Odoardo Spadaro, Adelmo di Fraja, Vincenzo Musolino,
   Piero Morgia, Anita Durante, Rossana Di Rocco, Michele
   Abruzzo, Dominique Boschero.

*Woman of Straw*. United Artists, 1964.
   Directed by Basil Dearden.
   Cast: GINA LOLLOBRIGIDA, Sean Connery, Ralph Richardson,
   Johnny Sekka, Laurence Hardy, Danny Daniels, Alexander
   Knox, Peter Madden, André Morel, Robert Bruge, A.J.
   Brown, Peggy Marshall, Edward Underdown, George Curzon.

*Strange Bedfellows*. Panama/Frank Production, 1964.
   Directed by Melvin Frank.
   Cast: Rock Hudson, GINA LOLLOBRIGIDA, Gig Young, Edward
   Judd, Terry Thomas, Arthur Haynes, Howard St. John,
   David King, Peggy Rea, Joseph Sirola, Nancy Kulp, Lucy
   Landau, Bernard Fox, Edith Atwater, James MacCallion,
   Hadley John Orchard, Frederic Worlock, Alan Cailou,
   Arthur Gould Porter.

*Le bambole* (The Dolls or Four Kinds of Love). Lucari/Documento
   Films, 1964.      Episode *"Monsignor Cupido."*
   Directed by Mauro Bolognini. (The other three episodes
   were Dino Rissi's *"The Phone Call,"* Luigi Comencini's
   *"Treatise of Eugenics,"* and Franco Rossi's *"The Soup."*)
   Cast: GINA LOLLOBRIGIDA, Jean Sorel, Akim Tamiroff,
   Gianni Rizzo, Camillo Milli.

*Io, io, io... e gli altri* (Me, Me, Me... and the Others).
   Luigi Rovere for Cineluxor/Rizzoli Films, 1966.
   Directed by Alessandro Blasetti.
   Cast: Walter Chiari, GINA LOLLOBRIGIDA, Vittorio De Sica,
   Marcello Mastroianni, Silvana Mangano, Nino Manfredi,
   Silva Koscina, Elisa Cegani, Caterina Boratto, Grazia
   Maria Spina, Vittorio Caprioli, Franca Valeri, Mario Pisu,

Paolo Panelli, Lelio Luttazzi, Elio Pandolfi, Mario
Valemarin, Giustino Durano, Mario Scaccia, Andrea Checchi,
Saro Urzi, Umberto D'orsi, Carlo Croccolo, Graziella
Granata, Salvo Randone, Marisa Merlini, Luisa Rivelli,
Gianni Rizzo, Marina Malfatti, Daniela Surina.

*L'amante italiana* (The Sultans). Cineurop, 1966.
Directed by Jean Delannoy.
Cast: GINA LOLLOBRIGIDA, Louis Jourdan, Philippe Noiret,
Corinne Marchand, Muriel Baptiste, Daniel Gélin, Renée
Faure, Claude Gensac, Rosy Varte, Lucia Modugno.

*Hotel Paradiso.* Peter Glenville for MGM, 1966.
Directed by Peter Glenville.
Cast: Alec Guinnes, GINA LOLLOBRIGIDA, Robert Morley,
Peggy Mount, Marie Bell, Akim Tamiroff, Derek Fowles,
Ann Beach, Leonard Rossiter, Douglas Byng, Peter
Glenville, Robertson Hare, Edra Gale, Dario Moreno.

*Le piacevoli notti* (Pleasant Nights). Mario Cecchi Gori for Fair
Film, 1966.
Directed by Armando Crispino and Luciano Lucignani.
Cast of the second story: GINA LOLLOBRIGIDA, Adolfo Celi,
Daniele Vargas, Eros Pagni.
Cast of the other two stories: Vittorio Gassman, Ugo
Tognazzi, Maria Grazia Buccella, Magda Konopka, Gigi
Ballista, Filippo Scelzo, Ida Galli, Luigi Vannucchi,
Dante Posani, Luigi Proietti, Ernesto Colli, Glauco
Onorato.

*Le avventure e gli amori di Miguel Cervantes* (The Young Rebel).
Protor Film-Prisma Film, Procinex, 1966.
Directed by Vincent Sherman.
Cast: Horst Buchholz, GINA LOLLOBRIGIDA, Louis Jourdan,
Jose Ferrer, Francisco Rabal, Fernando Rey, Soledad
Miranda, Lewis Jordan, Antonio Casas, Angel Del Pozo,
Ricardo Balacios, Maurice De Canonge, Jos Jaspe,
Claudine Dalmas, Jos Nieto, Enzo Curcio, Gaudenzio
Di Pietro, Andrès Mejuto.

*La morte ha fatto l'uovo* (Plucked). Summa Cinematografic/Cine
Azimut/Les Films Corona, 1967.
Directed by Giulio Questi.
Cast: GINA LOLLOBRIGIDA, Jean-Louis Trintignant,
Ewa Aulin, Jean Sobieski, Renato Romano, Giulio Donnini,
Vittorio Andr, Biagio Pelligra, Ugo Adinolfi, Cleofe
Del Cile, Conrad Andersen, Lisa Ferrero, Monica Millesi.

*The Private Army of Sgt. O'Farrell*. Naho Production for United
Artists, 1967.
Directed by Frank Tashlin.
Cast: Bob Hope, Phyllis Diller, Jeffrey Hunter, GINA
LOLLOBRIGIDA, Mylène Demongeot, John Myhere, Mako,
Henry Wilcoxon, Dick Sargent, Christopher Dark, Michael
Burns, William Wellmann Jr., Robert Donner, Jack
Grinnage, William Christopher, John Spina.

*Buona Sera Mrs. Campbell*. Conaught Productions/United
Artists, 1968.
Directed by Melvin Frank.
Cast: GINA LOLLOBRIGIDA, Shelley Winters, Phil Silvers,
Peter Lawford, Telly Savalas, Lee Grant, Janet Margolin,
Marian Moses, Philippe Leroy, Noami Stevens, Giovanna
Galletti, Argentina Brunetti.

*Un bellissimo novembre* (That Splendid November). Adelphia
Compagnia Cinematografica/Les Productions Artistes
Associés, 1968.
Directed by Mauro Bolognini.
Cast: GINA LOLLOBRIGIDA, Gabrielle Ferzetti, André
Laurence,  Paolo Turco, Margarita Lozano, Danielle Godet,
Isabella Savona, Corrado Gaipa, Jean Mancorps, Pasquale
Fortunato, Llena Rigan , Grazia Di Marzo, Franco Abbinia,
Maria Di Benedetto, Ettore Ribotta, Vanni Castellani,
Amalia Troiani, Maria Rosa Amato, Giuseppe Naso.

*Stuntman*. Ultra Film/Marianne Productions, 1969.
Directed by Marcello Baldi.
Cast: GINA LOLLOBRIGIDA, Robert Viharo, Marie Dubois,
Paul Muller, Jean-Claude Bercq, Marisa Mell, Giuseppe

Lauricella, Claudio Perone, Aldo De Carellis, Carla
Antonelli, Benito Boggino, Umberto Raho, Marina Lando,
Dennis Hall, Sandro Pellegrini, Giuseppe Liuzzi, Maria
Pia Nardon, Camilla Moser, Virgilio Conti, Mimmo Poli,
Paola Natale, Carla Foscari.

*...E continuavano a fregarsi il milione di dollari* (Bad Man's
River). International Appolo Film-Zurbano Film, 1970.
Directed by Eugenio Martin.
Cast: Lee Van Cleef, GINA LOLLOBRIGIDA, James Mason,
Gianni Garko, Sergio Fantoni, Jess Hahn, Simon Andreu,
Diana Lorys, Aldo Sanbrell, Luis Rivera, Lone Ferk.

*Le avventure di Pinocchio* (Pinocchio). Sanpaolo
Film-Cinepat, 1971.
Directed by Luigi Comencini.
Cast: Andrea Balestri, Nino Manfredi, GINA LOLLOBRIGIDA,
Franco Franchi, Ciccio Ingrassia, Ugo D'Alessio, Lionel
Stander, Vittorio De Sica, Mario Adorf, Enzo Cannavale,
Domenico Santoro, Riccardo Billi, Zoe Incrocci, Pietro
Gentili, Mimmo Olivieri, Carmine Torre, Vera Drudi, Orazio
Orlando, Mario Scaccia, Jacques Herlin, Carlo Bagno,
Giusepope Caffarelli, Furio Meniconi, Galliano Sbarra,
Nerina Montagnani, Caporali, Siria Betti, Mario
Cardarelli, Luigi Leoni, Clara Colosimo, Pino Ferrara,
Roberto Pistoni, Luigi De Ritis, Carlo Colombaioni, Mario
Ercolani, Bruno Bassi, Giovanna Lucci, Willy Semmelrogge.

*Un ospite gradito...per mia moglie* (King, Queen, Knave). David
L. Wolper for Maran Film and Wolper Pictures Ltd., 1972.
Directed by Jerzy Skolimowski.
Cast: GINA LOLLOBRIGIDA, David Niven, John Moulder
Brown, Mario Adorf, Carl-Fox Duering, Christopher
Sandford, Christine Schuberth, Felicitas Peters,
Erica Beer, Elma Karlowa, Morgens von Gadow.

*No encontré rosas para mi madre* (The Lonely Woman). C.P.
Cinematografica/Hidalgo A. Valasco/Les Productions du
Bassau, 1972.
Directed by Francisco Rovira-Beleta.

## Luis Canales--268

Cast: Renaud Verley, Susan Hampshire, Danielle Darrieux, GINA LOLLOBRIGIDA (guest appearance), Giacomo Rossi Stuart, Conchita Valasco, Maribel Martin, Javier Loyola.

# FILMS AVAILABLE ON VIDEO

The following Gina Lollobrigida movies can be found on tape even though not all of them were necessarily released in America. As a matter of fact, some of them were printed in Japan. Also, in the expanding video field with new titles being constantly added to the list, most up-to-date video guides can't keep up with distributors. Therefore, *Where The Hot Winds Blows*, now available on the American market, is listed as unreleased in Leonard's Maltin's 1989 edition of *TV Movies & Video Guide*.

*The White Line* (1950)
*Fanfan la Tulipe* (1951)
*Beauties of the Night* (1952)
*Bread, Love and Dreams* (1953)
*Beat the Devil* (1953)
*Woman of Rome* (1954)
*Trapeze* (1956)
*The Hunchback of Notre Dame* (1957)
*When The Hot Wind Blows* (1958)
*Solomon and Sheba* (1959)
*Never So Few* (1959)
*Imperial Venus* (1962)
*Mare matto* (1963)
*The Young Rebel* (1966)
*That Splendid November* (1968)
*Bad Man's River* (1970)
*King, Queen, Knave* (1972)

# GINA LOLLOBRIGIDA ON TELEVISION

*Il mattatore* (The Entertainer), 1959
*Stasera GINA LOLLOBRIGIDA* (Tonight GINA LOLLOBRIGIDA),
1969
*Le avventure di Pinocchio* (Pinocchio) - 1971
*Canzonissima* (1971)
*Made in Italy* (1981)
*Night of 100 Stars* (1982)
*Falcon Crest* (five episodes), 1984
*Deceptions* (1985)
*Domenica In* (Autumn of 1985)
*La romana* (1988) - a remake broadcast in three installments.

Note: Throughout her career Gina Lollobrigida also appeared in
numerous TV talk shows including *The Dean Martin Show*, *The Sammy
Davis Jr. Show*, *The Engelbert Humperdinck Show*, *The Bob Hope Show*,
*Platò vaciò*, *The Angel Casas Show*, *Màs estrellas que en el cielo* (More
Stars Than in Heaven).

# PHOTOGRAPHIC WORK

*Italia Mia* (1972)
*Manila* (1976)
*The Philippines* (1976)
*Il segreto delle rose* (1984)
*Innocence* (to be completed)

# PHOTOJOURNALISM

*Kissinger Close-up* for *Ladies' Home Journal* (July 1974)
*Les collections a Rome* for French *Vogue* (March 1978)
*Gina Lollobrigida: Notre reporter chez les couturiers* for French *Vogue* (September 1978)

Numerous interviews and/or photo sessions including, among others, Indira Gandhi, Paul Newman, Audrey Hepburn, Ursula Andress, Alberto Moravia, Rajiv Gandhi, Vittorio De Sica, Fidel Castro, Federico Fellini, Raúl Alfonsin, fashion designer Valentino, Domenico Modugno, Eduardo De Filippo, Audrey Landers, Linda Evans and Priscilla Presley.

# PHOTO EXHIBITIONS

Gina Lollobrigida has displayed her photographic work in most of the world's major capitals including: Amsterdam, Tokyo, Copenhagen, New York, Milan, Paris, Berlin, Barcelona, Madrid and Moscow.

# DOCUMENTARIES

*A Portrait of Fidel Castro* (1975)
*The Philippines* (1976)
*Qatar Today* (1982)

# BIBLIOGRAPHY

"Actress Gina Mum on Nuptial Plan." *L. A. Herald-Examiner.* Nov. 1969.

"Actress Sues Producer: Gina Tired of Acting with Donkey, She Says." *L. A. Times.* 3 April. 1955.

"After Quitting TV Seg 6 Times, Gina Is Definitely out." *Variety Daily.* 6 Oct. 1970.

Arce, Hector. *The Secret Life of Tyrone Power.* New York: William Morrow, Inc., 1979.

Arched, Army. "Just for Variety." *Variety Daily.* 23 Aug. 1965.

Armes, Roy. *French Cinema.* London: Secker & Warburg, 1985.

"At Home... with Gina Lollobrigida." *Star.* 15 Jan. 1985.

Bacon, Janes. "Sex Has Gone Far Enough, Says Gina." *Mirror-News.* 10 Oct. 1956.

"Barbelés et chiens défendent Lollo future maman." *Paris-Match.* No. 428 (June 1957): p. 74.

"'Les Belles de Nuit' de René Clair ont gagné la bataille de Venise." *Paris-Match.* No. 184 (September 1952): pp. 14-17.

"Los bellisimos 62 años de Gina Lollobrigida siguen causando admiración." *Semana.* No. 2562 (March 1989): pp. 88-89.

Bender, Marylin. "Gina Lollobrigida Likes Her Fashion to Sparkle." *L. A. Times.* 8 May 1963.

Bergan, Ronald. *The United Artists Story.* New York: Crown Publishers, Inc., 1986.

Bernardi, Luigi. "Torna a suon di musica." *Oggi.* No. 50 (December 1982): pp. 114-119.

----------. "Torno al primo amore." *Oggi.* No. 12 (March 1986): pp. 12-16.

Berruti, Rómulo. "Gina Lollobrigida, entre nosotros." *Clarrin Espectáculos.* 7 Nov. 1985.

Blandford, Linda. "Boom, Boom la Lollo." *Guardian.* 16 Jan. 1986.

Blum, Daniel. *A New Pictorial History of the Talkies.* New York: G. P. Putnam's Sons, 1982.

Bossanti, Sandra. "Italia di ieri: C'era una volta Gina Lollobrigida. La Bersagliera in congedo." *Epoca.* No. 1319. (January 1976): pp. 71-73.

"Boston Not to See Lollo's Latest Via Howard Hughes." *Variety Daily.* 12 Dec. 1956.

"Broadway Goes Italian." *L. A. Herald-Examiner*. 10 Apr. 1973.

Brode, Douglas. *The Films of the Fifties*. Secaucus: The Citadel Press, 1976.

Brogi, Paolo. "La mia vita alla Bersagliera." *Europeo*. No. 49 (December 1987): pp. 118-123.

"Broken Kneecap But Oooo, la Lollo's." *L. A. Times*. 17 Feb. 1969.

Brown, Jay A. *Rating the Movies*. New York: Beekman House, 1982.

Bruno, Giuliana and Nadotti, Maria. *Off Screen: Women and Film in Italy*. London: Routledge, 1988.

Calcagno, Paolo. "Si, ritorno al cinema." *Corriere della Sera*. 6 Mar. 1986.

Carassiti, Cesare. "Dopo le foto gli sberleffi." *Oggi*. No. 50 (December 1986): pp. 111-115.

Caronte, Luigi. *Subiaco nel turismo, nell'arte, nella storia*. Rome: Edizione Lux, 1964.

Carroll, Harrison. "Gina's 7-Year-Old Son Can Throw Her Around." *L. A. Herald-Examiner*. 15 Feb. 1965.

Casserly, John. "Big Storm Seen Headed Here... Gina and Sophia." *L. A. Herald-Examiner*. 4 Apr. 1954.

Cimagalli, Dino. "La 'Lollo' piange in tribunale ricordando la guerra e Subiaco." *Il Messaggero*. 13 May. 1972.

"'Classic Aid' Music in the Service of Refugees." *Refugees*. No. 35. (November 1986): pp. 9-10.

Cohen, Daniel, and Cohen Susan, ed. *Encyclopedia of Movie Stars* New York: Gallery Books, 1985.

----------. *Screen Goddesses*. London: The Hamlyn Publishing Group, 1984.

Collins, Joan. *Past Imperfect*. New York: Simon and Schuster, 1984.

"Contract Tights Get Lollobrigida in Trouble." *L. A. Times*. 20 Jan. 1958.

"Cordiale visita a Gina Lollobrigida." *Il Popolo*. 7 Jan. 1955.

"Crash Lames Actress." *Hollywood Citizen-News*. 27 Feb. 1969.

Cruz, Bernardo de Souza. "Gina Lollobrigida, Madona do Século XX." *O Cruzeiro*. No. 26 (April 1955): pp. 78-80.

"Das Votum war vorfabriziert." *Der Spiegel*. No. 10 (March 1986): pp. 137-138.

Davis, Meltons. "Gina in Focus." *Attenzione*. No. 9 (October 1982): pp. 36-39.

De Bausset, Philippe. "Son Petit Milko Sera Canadien." *Paris-Match*. No. 585 (June 1960): pp. 66-69.

"'Donnaroma' A Gina Lollobrigida." *Il Messagero*. 2 Feb. 1989.

Dugas, David. L. "Gina Not Ready for Character Parts Yet." *L. A. Times*. 9 Dec. 1967.

Eames, John Douglas. *The MGM Story*. New York: Crown Publishers Inc., 1979.

"Entusiastici commenti a Subiaco per i successi di Gina Lollobrigida." *Il Messaggero*. 26 Oct. 1954.

*Las Estrellas*. Madrid: Ediciones Urbion, 1982.

Faldini, Franca and Fofi Goffredo. *Il Cinema Italiano D'Oggi*: 1970-1984. Milan: Arnoldo Mondadori Editore, 1985.

----------. *L'Avventurosa Storia del Cinema Italiano 1935-1959*. Milan: Feltrineli, 1960.

"Film Man Counters Gina's $320,000 Suit." *L. A. Times*. 17 Jun. 1952.

Finler, Joel W. *The Movie Directors Story*. London: Octopus Books Limited, 1985.

Fliegers, Serge. "Gina Will Make Movies in U.S." *L. A. Herald-Examiner*. 24 Jan. 1959.

Fontana, Ivo. "Gina Lollobrigida cumple sesenta años." *Semana*. No. 2472 (July 1987): pp. 67-69.

"Forse Gina Lollobrigida a Subiaco per una 'prima' cinematografica." *Il Messaggero*. 6 Feb. 1962.

"La foto su Novella 2000." *La Stampa*. 7 May. 1986.

Francisco, Charles. *David Niven: Endearing Rascal*. New York: St. Martin's Press, 1986.

Gallavoti, Eugenio. "Cosí Hollywood tentò di mettere a nudo la Lollo." *Oggi*. No. 15 (April 1986): pp. 50-52.

Garcia, Guy D. "People." *Time*. No. 18 (May 1987): pp. 42-43.

Gehman, Richard. "For Lollobrigida: The Love Symbol." *Good House Keeping*. (February, 1961): pp. 198-203.

Gerald, Genevieve. "Les 'poupées terribles' du cinema italien." *Ciné-Monde*. No. 1592 (February 1965): pp. 5-9.

Gero, Eugenio. "Gina Lollobrigida en España." *Hola!* No. 2329. (April 1989): p. 67.

"Gina Admits She's 40, Proud of It." *L. A. Times*. 8 Feb. 1969.

"Gina, Claudia Cardinale Have Vatican Audience." *L. A. Times.*
7 May. 1967.

"Gina dans maternité." *Paris-Match.* No. 480 (June 1958):
pp. 68-75.

"Gina Debuts as Vocalist." *Hollywood Citizen-News.* 16 Aug. 1955.

"Gina Delays Wedding Until Next Spring." *L. A. Herald-Examiner.*
8 Dec. 1969.

"Gina Denies Being Nude in *The Dolls.*" *Hollywood Citizen-News.*
15 May. 1965.

"Gina Gets Divorce in Vienna." *L. A. Times.* 9 Apr. 1968.

"Gina Goes to Qatar." *Variety Daily.* 23 Dec. 1981.

"Gina Injured in Auto Crash." *L. A. Herald-Examiner.*
17 Feb. 1969.

"Gina Lollobrigida, a los 61 años, ha reanudado su carrera de
actriz." *Semana.* No. 2507 (March 1988): p. 39.

"Gina  Lollobrigida a Subiaco su invito dei suoi concittadini."
*Il Giornale D'Italia.* 19 Jan. 1955.

"Gina Lollobrigida è una mamma felice." *Il Messaggero.*
30 Jul. 1957.

"Gina Lollobrigida en Barcelona."  *Hola!* No. 2272 (March 1988):
p. 95.

"Gina Lollobrigida Loses Lead in New Picture." *L. A. Times.* 1959.

"Gina Lollobrigida photographie les collections." *Vogue.*
No. 589 (September 1978): pp. 348-355.

"Gina Lollobrigida Prez of World Film Fest Jury." *Variety Daily.*
23 Jul. 1981.

"Gina Lollobrigida ritorna al cinema." *Il Tempo.* 7 Mar. 1986.

"Gina Lollobrigida Still Searching for Ideal Role." *L. A. Times.*
26 Nov. 1961.

"Gina Lollobrigida vuelve ante las camaras." *Semana.* No. 2499
(January 1988): p. 87.

"Gina  Lollobrigida Walks out on Khrushchev at Moscow Film
Fete." *L. A. Times.* 10 Jul. 1961.

"Gina Pays State $14,200 Tax, Gets Her Jewels Back." *L. A. Times.*
13 Apr. 1965.

"Gina Righteously Spurned Dr. Barnard." *Hollywood Citizen-News.*
12 Mar. 1970.

"Gina se li mangia con gli occhi." *Gente.* No. 39 (September
1986): p. 24.

"Gina Threatens Suit on Book." *Hollywood Citizen-News*. 11 Feb. 1970.

Graham, Sheilah. "Gina Lollobrigida: Happy Since 'Free'." *Hollywood Citizen-News*. 1 Apr. 1969.

Grillet, Thierry. "La ruée ver les morts." *Libération*. 8 Apr. 1988.

Guarino, Grazia. "E scoppiata la guerra per la Lollobrigida a 'Domenica In'." *Eva Express*. 22 Aug. 1985.

Guibert, Hervé. *Le désir d'imitation. Les aventures singulières*. Paris: Les Editions di Minuit, 1982.

----------. "Gina Lollobrigida photographie - voir la vie et le monde deux fois." *Le Monde*. 23 Oct. 1980.

Haber, Joyce. "Gina Lollobrigida - She's Too Complicated for Men." *L. A. Times Calendar*. 29 Aug. 1971.

Haddad-Garcia, George. "La Lollo Shifts Gears." *Hollywood Studio Magazine*. (August 1979): pp. 14-15.

Hafzji, Jimi. "'Live and Let Live.' Says Gina Lollobrigida." *Film World*. No. 3 (March 1975): pp. 41-42.

Halliwell, Leslie. *Halliwell's Film Guide*. London: Collins Publishing Group, 1986.

Hasenclever, Mary. "All This and Talent, Too." *L. A. Herald-Examiner*. 7 Jun. 1953.

Hift, Fred. "Does Lollo Own Lollo, or Does Hughes?" *Variety Daily*. 5 Feb. 1958.

Higham, Charles. *Errol Flynn: The Untold Story*. New York: Dell Publishing Co. Inc., 1980.

----------. *Orson Welles: The Rise and Fall of an American Genius*. New York: St. Martin's Press, 1985.

"Hollywood On the Tiber." *Time*. No. 7 (August 1954): pp. 54-61.

Hopper, Hedda. "What Gina Wants, Gina Gets." *Chicago Sunday Tribune Magazine*. 23 Apr. 1961.

Hotchner, A. E. *Sophia: Living and Loving*. New York: William Morrow and Company, Inc. 1979.

Huston, John. *An Open Book*. New York: Alfred A. Knopf, 1980.

"In the New World a New Life for Gina." *Life*. No. 6 (August 1960): pp. 69-75.

"Incognito: Gina Lollobrigida." *Newsweek*. No. 9 (August 1973): p. 22.

"Italian Beauty Soars Toward Stardom in Hollywood." *L. A. Herald-Examiner*. 1 May. 1953.

"Italy Court Clears Gina of Charges." *L. A. Times*. 8 Apr. 1967.

Jacks, Allen. "No. 1 in Europe, Gina Throws Curves at U.S." *A. L. Times*. 1 Mar. 1953.

Jamain, Monique. "Les premieres confidence de Gina Lollobrigida maman." *Ciné-Revue*. No. 33 (August 1957): pp. 18-19.

Johnson, Robert. "Saga of a Siren." *Saturday Evening Post*. 13 Aug. 1960.

Karney, Robyn, ed. *The Movie Stars Story*. New York: Crescent Books, 1984.

Kobal, John, ed. *Film Star Portraits of the Fifties*. New York: Dover Publications, Inc., 1980.

Leaming, Barbara. *Orson Welles: A Biography*. Middlesex: Penguin Books, 1984.

Lefort, Gérard. "Sur la lagune, un Welles por de vrai." *Libération*. 1 Sept. 1986.

Leigh, Janet. *There Really Was a Hollywood*. New York: Doubleday & Company, Inc., 1984.

"Letters to Doctor 'private' Says Gina." *L. A. Herald-Examiner*. 11 Feb. 1970.

Levy, Alan. Forever, *Sophia: An Intimate Portrait*. New York: Baronet Publishing Company, 1979.

Lewin, David. "Lollo at 40." *Daily Mail*. 29 Jul. 1968.

Liehm, Mira. *Passion and Defiance: Film in Italy from 1942 to the Present*. Berkeley: University of California Press, 1984.

Lloyd, Ann, ed. *Movies of the Fifties*. London: Orbis Publishing Limited, 1982.

----------. *Movies of the Sixties*. London: Orbis Publishing Limited, 1983.

----------. *The Illustrated History of the Cinema*. London: Orbis Book Corporation Ltd. 1986.

----------. *The Illustrated Who's Who of the Cinema*. London: Orbis Publishing Limited, 1983.

"Lollo: 'I'm Going to Have a Baby'." *Daily Mail*. 4 Jan. 1957.

"La Lollo." *Sunday Chronicle*. 30 Jan. 1955.

"Lollo présidente!" *Libération*. 5 Mar. 1986.

Lollobrigida, Gina. "Les collections a Rome." *Vogue*. No. 584. (March 1978): pp. 298-305.

----------. *Il segreto dell Rose*. Milan: Electa Editrice, 1984.

----------. *Italia Mia*. Geneva: Sedifo, 1973.

"Lollobrigida Powders 'Venus'." *Variety Daily*. 22 Jan. 1958.

"Lollobrigida Protests Over Retouched Photo." *L. A. Times*. 28 Mar. 1956.

"Lollobrigida Sues Navarro Productions." *Variety Daily*. 5 Mar. 1978.

"Lollobrigida Trial Adjourns to Oct. 4." *L. A.Times*. 20 Jul. 1966.

"Lollobrigida vs. Howard Hughes." *L. A. Times*. 27 Mar. 1959.

Loynd, Ray. "Gina on Other Side of a Camera." *L. A. Herald-Examiner*. 25 Aug. 1973.

Luban, Milton. "Huston Turn out Amusing Satire." *Hollywood Reporter*. 2 Mar. 1954.

Lydia, Lane. "No Pasta for Gina." *L. A. Times*. 16 Aug. 1959.

MacPherson, Don and Brody, Louise. *Leading Ladies*. London: Conran Octopus Limited, 1986.

Maggi, Danilo. "La Bersagliera? Una carta vincente." *Onda Tivu*. No. 35 (August 1985): pp. 6-7.

Malcom, David. *Sex Symbols*. London: Octopus Books, 1985.

"Mamma Gina and Milko Jr." *Life*. No. 16 (October 1958): pp. 118-120.

Manin, Giuseppina. "La Lollo, prima star al Lido." *Corrieree della Sera.*" 29 Aug. 1986.

Mann, Roderick. "Broadway Beckoned, and Gina Buckles a Bit." *L. A. Times*. 7 Feb. 1984.

----------. "'I'm all Italian - Too Much So to Become a Canadian,' Sighs Gina." *Sunday Express*. 18 Feb. 1962.

Marcus, Millicent. *Italian Film in the Light of Neorealism*. Princeton: Princeton University Press, 1986.

Marinucci, Vinicio. *Tendencies of the Italian Cinema*. Rome: Unitalia Film, 1959.

Marril, Alvin H. *The Films of Anthony Quinn*. Secaucus: Citadel Press, 1975.

Martins, Justino. "Lollo canta pela primeira vez." *Manchete*. No. 176 (September 1955): pp. 33-35.

Mati, Tito. "Quand Gina photographie Ursula..." *Ciné-Revue.*
No. 30 (July 1986): pp. 26-37, 36-37.

Mayer, Sandro. "L'accogliemmo a uova in faccia quando tornò qui."
*Oggi Illustrato.* (May 1971): pp. 54-63.

Meccoli, Domenico. "Prigione dorata in America." *Epoca.* No. 208
(September 1954): pp. 31-37.

Minetti, Maria Giulia. "Ma non tutte trovarono l'America a
Hollywood." *Europeo.* No. 36 (September 1982): pp. 50-52.

"Montreal Finale with Lollobrigida." *Variety Daily.* 29 Aug. 1979.

Morella, Joe and Epstein Z Edward. *Jane Wyman A Biography.*
New York: Dell Publishing Co., 1985.

Morton, Frederic. "The Antic Arts - Gina Lollobrigida." *Holyday
Magazine.* (June 1959): pp. 111-112, 165-166.

Mugiatti, Roberto. "Gina no jôgo da verdade." *Manchete.* No. 774
(February 1967): pp. 30-32; 48-49; 60.

"A Nova Lollo é M.M." *Mundo Ilustrado.* No. 229 (May 1962):
pp. 46-47.

Novas, Himilce. "Gina Lollobrigida: Up front and behind the
camera." *L'Officiel/USA.* (September 1979): pp. 110-112.

"Le 'noveau monde' de Gina Lollobrigida." *Ciné-Revue.* No. 43
(October 1963): pp. 10-11.

Oppenheimer, Peer J. "Gina Lollobrigida: She Likes to Be a
Loner." *Family Weekly.* 27 Sept. 1961.

Packard, Reynolds. "A Suit for Gina, Who Has Many." *Daily News.*
7 Nov. 1955.

Pam, Jerry. "'Bread, Love, and Dreams' Gives Chance to See
Lollobrigida." *Beverly Hills News Life.* 2 Oct. 1954.

Parsons, Louella. "Gina Lollobrigida: She Forecast Her Own
Future." *L. A. Examiner.* 26 Jan. 1958.

----------. "Gina Lollobrigida: A Dream in Any Language."
*L. A. Examiner.* 26 Jun. 1959.

----------. "Gina's Mate, Son Turn Canadians." *L. A. Examiner.*
8 Mar. 1960.

----------. "Glamorous Archaelogy." *L. A. Examiner.*
24 May 1964.

Paul, Frank. "Lollo Fights Howard Hughes." *Sunday Dispatch.*
15 Mar. 1959.

Peary, Danny. *Cult Movies 2.* New York: Dell Publishing Co.
Inc., 1983.

Perona, Piero. "Lollo la civetta." *La Stampa*. 30 Aug. 1986.

Perrotta, Sal. "Gems Seized; Gina Says 'I Feel Naked'." *L. A. Herald-Examiner*. 11 Apr. 1965.

Ponzi, Maurizio. *I Film di Gina Lollobrigida*. Rome: Gremese Editore, 1982.

Ray, Moore. "They Want 'La Lollo' for Bible-Story Film." *Sunday Dispatch*. 31 Oct. 1954.

Ray, Robert B. *A Certain Tendency of the Hollwyood Cinema 1930-1980*. Princeton: Princeton University Press, 1985.

Rhode, Eric. *A History of the Cinema: From Its Origin to 1970*. London: Penguin Books, 1976.

Rochlen, Kendis. "Curvy Gina Thinks Straight." *Mirror-News*. 23 May. 1956.

----------. "No Tizzies, Dusty Feet." *Mirror-News*. 21 May. 1956.

Romano, Nino. "Le secret que Gina Lollobrigida n'avait jamais revelè." *Ciné-Revue*. No. 19 (June 1982): pp. 17-19.

Rondolino, Gianni. *Dizionario del Cinema Italiano*, 1945-1969. Torino: Giulio Einaudi Editore, 1969.

Salvatori, Dario. "Gina Lollobrigida dall' A alla z." *Radio Corriere TV*. No. 11-12 (March 1988): pp. 53-55.

Scaduto, Tony. "'Falcon Crest.' Newcomer Gina Is Upset over Feud with Sultry Co-Star." *Star*. 16 Oct. 1984.

"Scene Only 'seemed' Immoral, Star Says." *L. A. Times*. 16 Jun. 1965.

Scheuer, Philip K. "'Beat the Devil' off Beat Art Comedy." *L. A. Times*. 6 Mar. 1954.

Scott, Vernon. "Male Stars Discussed by Gina Lollobrigida." *Hollywood Citizen-News*. 25 Feb. 1960.

Servat, Henry-Jean. "Au balcon (net) de Gina." *Libération*. 5 Aug. 1985.

----------. "César nous voilá!" *Libération*. 3 Mar. 1985.

----------. "Gina Lollobrigida!: Se Robert de la medaille." *Libération*. 5 Mar. 1985.

"Sexy Signore." *Life*. (September 1951): pp. 62-64.

Shatowsky, Alberto. "Lollo Rainha de Sabá." *Manchete*. No. 394 (November 1959): pp. 60-62.

Shaw, Sam. *Sophia Loren in the Camera Eye*. New York: The Hamlyn Publishing Group Limite, 1980.

Shipman, David. *The Great Movie Stars: The International*

*Years*. New York: Hill and Wang, 1980.

Smith, Jack. "They Shoot Tigers, Don't They, Gina?" *L. A. Herald-Examiner*. 7 Jan. 1970.

"Speaking of Pictures... Lollobrigida Draws Key to Her Closet." *Life*. No. 20 (November 1954): pp. 18-20.

Stampa, Carla. "La Lollobrigida vent'anni dopo." *Epoca*. No. 1079 (May 1971): pp. 99-102.

Starr, Jimmy. "Gina Lives up to Advance Reputation." *Herald Express*. 4 Jun. 1956.

----------. "Lollobrigida and Lancaster Set Tour." *Herald Express*. 9 Apr. 1956.

Stricr, Philip. *Great Movie Actresses*. London: Orbis Publishing Limited, 1984.

"Subiaco esprime il suo aplauso ai concittadini che orano la patria." *Il Popolo*. 2 Nov. 1954.

Swenderson, Marius. "Lollo no Circo." *O Cruzeiro*. No. 31 (May 1956): pp. 83-86.

Taranto, Denis. "E lui il mio capolavoro." *Oggi*. No. 49 (December 1980): pp. 54-57.

Thibaudat, Jean-Pierre. "On a retrouvé le film d'Orson sur Gina." *Libération*. 16 Feb. 1986.

Thody, Henry. "Acting with Gina Lollobrigida." *The Sunday Times*. 17 Jul. 1955.

----------. "I Was a Prisoner in Hollywood." *Sunday Chronicle*. 6 Feb. 1955.

Thomas Bob. "Gina's Italy Film Snafu for Co-Star." *Mirror-News*. 29 Jan. 1958.

----------. "La Lollobrigida Here to Conquer H'Wood." *Mirror-News*. 29 Apr. 1959.

Thompson, Verita. *Bogie and Me*. New York: St. Martin's Press, 1984.

Tinelli, Franco. "La Lollo e Marcos." *La Notte*. 15 Nov. 1986.

Tirri, Néstor. "Gina dice: 'Desconfio de la juventud'." *Clarín Espectáculos*. 7 Jul. 1987.

Towsend, Dorothy. "Gina Lollobrigida Gem-less." *L. A. Times*. 11 Apr. 1965.

"Tragedy in Kremlin: Liz and Gina Appear in Identical Dresses." *Mirror-News*. 15 Jul. 1961.

Tranchant, Marie-Noelle. "Gina Lollobrigida: Comme si c'était hier." *Le Figaro*. 17 Jul. 1985.

Vaccari, Lanfranco. "Il cinema mi rifiuta ma io torno diva in TV e teatro." *Oggi*. No. 7 (February 1985): pp. 54-56.

Vivies, Marie-Helene. "Devant les tours de Notre-Dame en carton Gina la gitane en haillons de haute couture." *Paris-Match*. No. 377 (June 1956): pp. 56-57.

"Voto di compiacimento per Gina Lollobrigida." *Il Messaggero*. 30 Oct. 1954.

Wallace, Irving. *The Intimate Sex Lives of Famous People*. New York: Dell Publishing, 1981.

Waterbury, Ruth. "'Beat the Devil'." *L. A. Herald-Examiner*. 11 Mar. 1954.

----------. "Love, Fame a Luxurious Private Life - and Lots of Money. Put Them All together and They Spell... Gina." *The American Weekly*. 24 Jan. 1956.

Whitcomb, Jon. "Lollobrigida as Sheba." *Cosmopolitan*. (August 1959); 13-16.

Wilkenson, Tichi and Borie, Marcia. *The Hollywood Reporter*. New York: Arlington House, Inc. 1984.

Williams, Dick. "Gina Lollobrigida at Last Reaches Hollywood." *Mirror-News*. 2 Jul. 1959.

----------. "Gina Soon May Do Film in Hollywood." *Mirror-News*. 29 Jan. 1959.

Wilson, Earl. "Gina Most Promising Film Star in Europe." *L. A. Daily News*. 8 Jul. 1953.

----------. "Wedding of Gina 'Off'." *L. A. Herald-Examiner*. 26 Nov. 1969.

Windeler, Robert. *Hollywood Most Enduring Star: Burt Lancaster*. New York: St. Martin's Press, 1984.

Wiseman, Thomas. "'A Battle with Loren? I Don't Understand,' Says Gina." *News Chronicle*. 15 Oct. 1957.

Wlaschin, Ken. *The Illustrated Encyclopedia of the World's Great Movie Stars and Their Films*. London: Salamander Books Limited, 1979.

Zana, Jean-Claude. "Gina Lollobrigida: 'A 45 ans, Ursula est toujours mon plus beau modele'." *Paris-Match*. No. 1807 (January 1984): pp. 137-138.

# INDEX OF NAMES

# INDEX OF FILMS

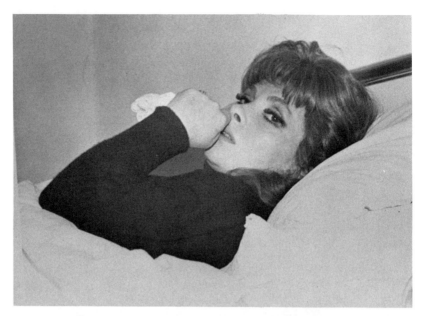

La Lollo hospitalized in Orvieto after she smashed up her Rolls-Royce. (Courtesy *Il Messaggero* - author's collection).

In 1985, Gina received the insignia of Officer of the French Order of Arts and Literature from French Culture Minister Jack Lang (center). On the occasion, actor Kirk Douglas was made commander of the same order. (*Paris-Match* Houvais - author's collection.

With young Paolo Turco in *That Splendid November* (1968). Courtesy Pierluigi/Orion Press.

In *Imperial Venus* (1962).  Courtesy Pierluigi/Orion Press.

Gina Lollobrigida and former Subiaco Mayor, Giuseppe Cicoloni (Gina's right) and members of Subiaco's Town Hall during the actress' visit there on May 24, 1971. (Courtesy of Giuseppe Cicolini).

Gina Lollobrigida introduced her handsome look-alike son Milko Scofic to the Paris social scene foregathered in her honor at the trendy Club '78.